TRIUMPH
SPITFIRE AND GT6

THE COMPLETE STORY

OTHER TITLES IN THE CROWOOD AUTOCLASSICS SERIES

TRIUMPH
SPITFIRE AND GT6

THE COMPLETE STORY

RICHARD DREDGE

THE CROWOOD PRESS

First published in 2014 by
The Crowood Press Ltd
Ramsbury, Marlborough
Wiltshire SN8 2HR

www.crowood.com

British Library Cataloguing-in-Publication Data
A catalogue record for this book is available from the British Library.

ISBN 978 1 84797 703 8

Acknowledgments
Huge thanks are due to a raft of people, without whom this book wouldn't have
been possible. Chief among these is Bernard Robinson of the Triumph Sports Six
Club, who not only helped with period literature for reference and illustration, but
also facilitated the photography of a superb Spitfire Mk2 and GT6 Mk3, the latter
being the multiple-concours winner of Andrew and the late Angela MacGowan.

I'm also grateful to the other owners who allowed me to photograph their cars,
these being Guy and Suzie Singleton (Spitfire 4 and Mk3), Stef and Sylv Graham
(Spitfire 1500), Jo and Jim Wakefield (GT6 Mk1) plus David Aspinall of Anglian
Triumph Services (www.angserv.demon.co.uk), who helped find people and cars –
they were also happy to give their time freely, helping with the text, especially
the chapter on modifying. Thanks are also due to Jane Rowley (Spitfire 4) and
John Bentley (GT6 Mk3), for their help with the front cover image.

Sam Bailey of Bailey Classic Cars (www.baileyclassiccars.com) helped with the
Spitfire MkIV, while Dave Saunders of Triumph Spares of Worcester (www.users.
globalnet.co.uk/~ngo/345222.htm) also helped by supplying various cars for some of
the detail shots. Thanks are also due to Graham Robson for supplying some of the
period illustrations, as well as clarifying some of the detail points in the book.

Typeset by Jean Cussons Typesetting, Diss, Norfolk

Printed and bound in India by Gopsons Papers Ltd.

CONTENTS

TIMELINE

- **1957:** Work starts on Standard-Triumph's new family car, the Herald.

- **1959:** The production Herald makes its début.

- **1960:** Michelotti is commissioned to design a Herald-based two-seater sports car.

**Herald 948
coupé.**

- **1961:** The decision is made to put the Spitfire into series production.

- **1962:** The first-generation Spitfire breaks cover, with an 1147cc engine and four-speed manual gearbox, borrowed from the Herald. The car is also based on a shortened Herald chassis.

- **1965:** The Spitfire MkII goes on sale, still with the 1147cc engine, but with more power and a stronger clutch.

- **1966:** The GT6 débuts at the Earl's Court Motor Show, with a 95bhp 1998cc Vitesse-sourced engine. Overdrive is optional while the bumpers and lighting are carried over from the Spitfire.

GT6 MkI.

- **1967:** The Spitfire MkIII arrives, with a 1296cc engine, a hood that's much easier to use and revised styling.

- **1968:** The Mk2 GT6 arrives with a new dashboard, revised cylinder head and tweaked rear suspension. The straight-six's top end is from the TR5, for better breathing, while the rear suspension adopts rotoflex couplings and wishbones. Styling adjustments include the removal of the louvres in the side of the bonnet, raised bumpers front and rear, and Rostyle wheel trims.

- **1969:** Minor revisions bring better interior padding and an improved steering wheel, and the structure is also strengthened to cope with tougher US crash regulations.

Spitfire 4.

- **1970:** The MkIV Spitfire brings another facelift, plus an all-synchromesh gearbox and more predictable handling, thanks to revised rear suspension. Meanwhile, the Mk3 GT6 goes on sale little changed from its predecessor. The most significant changes centre on a de-seamed shark-nosed bonnet and the rear panels are updated with the family cut-away tail that incorporates less chrome. There are no significant changes under the skin.

- **1971:** Seatbelts are now fitted as standard to the Spitfire.

- **1973:** The Spitfire 1500 makes its entrance, for the US market only. The bigger motor is needed because of all the emissions control equipment that has to be fitted. There's also a wider rear track, to overcome handling issues. Also, a brake servo is now fitted to the GT6, the rear brakes are increased in size and the rear suspension's rotoflex couplings disappear, with the swing-spring rear axle later to be used on the Spitfire being fitted instead. At the same time the instruments are revised, vinyl replaces the brushed nylon seat covers and head restraints plus tinted glass are fitted for the first time. Also, in this year the final GT6 is made.

- **1974:** The Spitfire 1500 goes on sale in the UK.

- **1977:** The interior receives minor fettling for greater comfort.

- **1980:** The final Spitfire is made.

Spitfire 1500.

CHAPTER ONE

INTRODUCTION

If it hadn't been for the Austin Healey Frogeye Sprite, would Triumph ever have embarked on producing its own cheap sports car? Possibly not. Until the arrival of the Frogeye, sports cars were invariably big, costly and produced in relatively small numbers. Even those sports cars which weren't big and costly were invariably rare, usually produced by specialist car companies, which either revived ancient pre-war cars with a new glass fibre bodyshell, or which inserted the mechanicals from some contemporary family car (usually a Ford) and wrapped them up in their own bodywork. However, these cars were often fragile, poorly made, or simply too costly to be truly affordable to the masses. What was needed was a mainstream car maker to introduce something that was fun to drive, cheap and well supported by a large dealer network. When Austin Healey did it with the Sprite, it was only natural that somebody else would try to emulate

the company's success – and that rival was Triumph, with its Spitfire.

Triumph is still one of the world's best-loved marques, yet many years have passed since its demise. The company built cars for just 65 years, starting in 1923, then disappeared into the annals of time with the demise of a badge-engineered Honda, in 1984. Sure, Triumph as a brand existed far longer, as it built push bikes and motorcycles before branching out into cars. But as a car builder it wasn't really around all that long – yet it is still one of the best-supported motoring marques around, thanks to enthusiastic clubs and a raft of great models over the years.

Perhaps one of the greatest reasons for the marque's popularity is the success of the TR range in America. But models such as the Herald, Vitesse, Spitfire and GT6 also played their part, between them providing affordable family

This was as sporty as things got for Triumph in the post-war years. Still, the 1800 and 2000 Roadsters were undeniably stylish.

transport or sporting fun, depending on the model. However, it might not have been that way, after Triumph as a car maker almost disappeared from sight in the 1930s.

It was in 1921 that Triumph purchased the Coventry factory of failed car builder Dawson, with a view to starting up the manufacture of Triumph-branded cars. At that time the company was owned by Siegfried Bettmann, assisted by his general manager Claude Holbrook. Up until this point, Triumph had focused purely on building bikes, with and without motive power attached; buying up the Dawson plant would enable the firm to move up several gears in one go.

By 1923 Triumph had its first car on the market, the 1393cc 4-cylinder 10/20. Designed by Arthur Alderson, who was working for Lea-Francis at the time, the car was costly at £430–£460, the price boosted by the fact that Triumph had to pay Lea-Francis a royalty on each car sold. There then followed a succession of cars that had little to lift them above their rivals, but in 1928 came the breakthrough model, the

Super Seven. Very much in the mould of Austin's rival Seven, Triumph's new baby car was designed by Stanley Edge, who had helped Herbert Austin realize the identically-named car that saved his company from the mire. The Triumph Super Seven didn't enjoy the racing successes of its Austin and MG (Midget) rivals, but that didn't stop it from being highly successful, with more than 17,000 finding owners between 1928 and 1932.

Despite the relative success of the Super Seven, Holbrook decided that he would take Triumph upmarket in the 1930s – a move that would prove disastrous. In 1931 came Triumph's first six-cylinder car, the Scorpion, which sold poorly because of its stodgy handling. Then in 1933, Holbrook decided he would start to buy in Coventry-Climax engines instead of developing his own fresh powerplant, in-house. There followed a line of cars that were designed to take on Riley, Alvis and SS, the most ambitious of which was the 1934 Dolomite, complete with a straight-eight in the nose.

SPITFIRE PROTOTYPES

The first Spitfire prototype, pictured in October 1960.

- There were four Spitfire prototypes built using experimental chassis numbers (with an X-prefix). The first was X659, built by Michelotti in Italy, in October 1960 and based on a modified Herald coupé chassis. This car, which carried the Bomb nickname, was fitted with a 948cc powerplant carrying engine number X854.

- The next prototype was a development car, which carried chassis number X661. Constructed towards the end of 1960, this car was once again based on a modified Herald coupé (this time the whole bodyshell was shortened, rather than just the chassis). The original engine number isn't known, but this car would later be fitted with a production 1147cc engine, carrying number GA 57428.

- It was early in 1962 that the first pre-production Spitfire prototype was built, bearing chassis number X691. Constructed in Coventry, this was the first prototype to be road registered (4305 VC) and it was also the first to feature the final production details with regard to styling. The original engine number isn't recorded, but X691 would later be fitted with an 1147cc unit, carrying number HE18491HE. This car would also go on to be developed into the fastback prototype that would be the precursor to the GT6; it would also be used for mechanical development including the installation of fuel injection.

- The final prototype was X692, which would be the most familiar to Triumph fans of the period. Constructed around the same time as X691, this car would be registered as 412 VC, and not only would it go on to be a well-travelled press car, but it would also be used for endurance testing and rallying. From the outset, the car was fitted with an 1147cc engine, carrying number FC 2 HE. Intriguingly though, the car would be constructed with right-hand drive, and it would then be converted to left-hand drive, only to revert to the original configuration ready for its rallying début in 1964.

In 1937 there was a return to in-house engines for Triumph, each one being designed by Donald Healey. Available with displacements of 1496cc, 1767cc or 1991cc (the last having six cylinders), there was from this point on a rather bewildering array of cars available. Because the 1232cc Coventry-Climax powerplant was still offered in the entry-level cars, there were four engines available across three ranges: Gloria, Vitesse and Dolomite. By 1936 Triumph was posting big losses, and by June 1939 the company was bankrupt.

It wasn't until 1944 that Triumph emerged from the ashes – literally – when Standard's Sir John Black bought the Triumph name and what remained of the factory, after it had been all but destroyed during the War. The site was quickly sold, with Triumph production being integrated with Standard's existing facility at Canley, near Coventry. The first cars

were the 1800 (Razoredge) saloon and Roadster, equipped with 1776cc 4-cylinder engines, with bodywork by Mulliners of Birmingham. Triumph wasn't completely out of the woods yet, but it looked as though the worst was over, with sales picking up and a whole stream of fresh models introduced over the next few years.

The next big step was the introduction of the TRX in 1949, which signalled Triumph's intention to exploit the two-seater sports car market. However, the TRX was too complex, as it featured a power-operated roof, windows and seats, along with pop-up headlamps (this was 1949 remember…). There was no way it could have been built economically, while reliability would be an issue without a doubt. What was needed was something much simpler, that had charm and rugged performance and which could be built and

ALICK DICK

Alick Dick was the managing director of Standard-Triumph during its most interesting period, between 1954 and 1961, when he was replaced by Stanley Markland (who would stay at the company for just two years). Responsible for overseeing the development of the early TRs, Dick also oversaw the launch of the Standard Eight, later Vanguards, plus the Herald.

Alick Sydney Dick was born in Norfolk in 1917, the son of a doctor; by 1934 he was an apprentice at the Standard Motor Company. It was clear from the outset that he had great potential as a manager and by the outbreak of the Second World War he had been promoted to chief buyer for the company's aero-engine factories.

As soon as Standard took over Triumph, Dick was promoted to the position of personal assistant to Sir John Black, who was then managing director of Standard-Triumph. From there his rise through the ranks was swift: by 1947 Dick was assistant managing director and in 1951 he was made deputy managing director. Dick had made more rapid progress than older, longer-serving members of staff around him – but the best was yet to come.

Alick Dick was in charge of Standard-Triumph from 1954 until 1961.

By 1954 there was some dissatisfaction with Black's leadership style: he was seen as dictatorial, and keen to overshadow those around him. It came as no surprise therefore when Dick led a coup to oust Black as managing director of the company – a move that was to initially prove successful for everyone concerned.

However, although sales at first went from strength to strength, the good times didn't last and Standard-Triumph was taken over by Leyland Motors in 1961. Within months, Dick was forced to move on. At first he did very little work-wise, but by 1963 he was managing director of electronics outfit Royston Instruments. By 1968 Dick had left Royston to become a consultant to Volkswagen, based in Coventry. He died in March 1986, aged sixty-nine.

Triumph's first post-war sports cars were the side-screen TRs (top right), which were fast, stylish and reliable, but they were also too costly for many. The main rival to these was the Austin Healey 100 (above); sitting below this was the ultra-cheap Sprite, initially in 'Frogeye' form (right). What Triumph needed was an affordable roadster to take on the Sprite – and the Spitfire was just such a car.

sold at a low price. That car was the TR2, which served as a prelude for perhaps the greatest succession of sports cars ever, from the TR2 to the TR6 – and maybe even the TR7 if we're being charitable…

But we're jumping ahead of ourselves now; we need to step back to the late fifties, when Britain led the world in motoring design and mass production, whether it was mundane family saloons or something rather more exciting. In an age when platform-sharing is the norm if the production costs are to add up, you'll soon see that the concept is far from new. Barely more than a decade after the end of the Second World War, Triumph was already thinking about how it could produce a series of cars all using the same basic platform and the same set of mechanical components.

The car that set the ball rolling was Triumph's Herald, which was unveiled in April 1959. Many questioned the deci-

sion behind introducing a car with such an outdated construction; even at this time, a separate chassis was decidedly passé for a mass-produced car, and thus the new family saloon appeared to be a throwback to the post-war era. However, there was a method in Triumph's apparent madness; it was aiming to introduce a whole family of Heralds, while in theory it would also be possible to engineer something smaller and rather more sporty. Where Austin Healey had its 100, Triumph had its TR2 and TR3 to compete, but something much more affordable was needed to take on the Sprite, as well as MG's Midget. That car would be the Spitfire, while later would come the GT6.

Just like the Herald, the Spitfire was designed by Giovanni Michelotti, who had been drafted in as Triumph's design consultant after the departure of Standard's previous designer, Walter Belgrove. Belgrove had designed the early TRs, which had proved phenomenally successful for Triumph, but he left after a disagreement with some of Triumph's decisions, leaving the company without anybody to pen its key forthcoming models. American designer Carl Otto was commissioned to design the Standard Vanguard III, but it was clear that somebody needed to be found to give Triumph a new design direction.

That person was Michelotti, who was found purely by chance. Indeed, it wasn't even Triumph's Harry Webster who made the discovery; it was one of his business contacts, who happened to disclose in conversation that he knew of a styling house which could design and build prototypes in an astonishingly short space of time. Webster looked into the lead and found that Michelotti could indeed design cars in double-quick time and, through an arrangement with Vignale, those designs could be translated into running prototypes in just a few months.

Alick Dick and Martin Tustin managed the negotiations between Triumph and Michelotti, with the latter being commissioned to design a two-seater TR-based sports car concept, for display at the 1957 Geneva Motor Show. That

HARRY WEBSTER

Mention names, such as Harry Ferguson or Alec Issigonis, and you'll get instant recognition: they were brilliant engineers who moved the motoring game on. But mention the name Harry Webster and the chances are you'll be greeted with a blank expression – despite the fact that he was perhaps as great an engineer as either of the other two.

Although Webster pioneered the use of things such as semi-trailing arm rear suspension, the targa top and through-flow ventilation, he couldn't be credited with being responsible for a true icon of the motoring age, which is why he's frequently overlooked. His CV may have included the Herald, TR4, Spitfire, GT6, 2000, Vitesse and 1300, but none of these have the cachet of something like the Mini (is there anything like the original Mini?). Webster is no doubt destined to remain in the background.

Henry George Webster was born on 27 May 1917 and educated at Welshpool County School. By the age of fifteen in 1939, he'd left school to become an apprentice to the Standard

Harry Webster is one of the great, unsung heroes of Britain's motor industry.

Motor Company; by 1948 he had been promoted to the position of chief chassis engineer. The company had already become Standard-Triumph, which meant that he worked alongside designer Walter Belgrove, who set the TR ball rolling for Triumph, penning what would become the TR2.

Having become director of engineering in 1957, Webster created a talented team that produced a series of new models, despite minimal budgets and ludicrously short development timescales. Nevertheless, innovations were frequent. The 2000 brought real refinement to the middle-class sector, while the TR5 was the first British sports car to have fuel injection as standard equipment.

Webster was director of engineering at Standard-Triumph for more than a decade, but after the formation of British Leyland he was moved to Longbridge to bring order to the faltering engineering operation at Austin-Morris. His six-year term was hampered by a lack of corporate vision and by industrial action. In 1974 he left to become group technical director of Automotive Products in Leamington Spa. He retired in 1982, but became chairman of SKF Steel UK for five years.

At least somebody recognized Webster's talents because he was made a CBE in 1974. He died on 6 February 2007, aged eighty-nine.

GIOVANNI MICHELOTTI

Triumph formed an alliance with Giovanni Michelotti, which would be as strong as the one between Ferrari and Pininfarina – if not quite as long lasting. It came about when Raymond and Neville Flower approached Harry Webster to discuss buying chassis direct from Standard for a sports car they wanted to put into production. They talked about how quickly Michelotti could turn projects round and Webster was intrigued enough to approach the Italian design house himself. The result was a partnership that would last from 1957 right through until 1972, when the Dolomite was introduced. Along the way, Michelotti would style such gems as the TR4, 5 and 6, Stag, 2000/2500, 1300 and of course the Herald, Vitesse, Spitfire and GT6.

Michelotti was born in 1921. With a father who worked in the machine shop at racing car maker Itala, it was inevitable that Giovanni would end up working with cars. Sure enough, aged sixteen, he started working for the coachbuilding firm of Giovanni Farina, where he was little more than a gopher. However, it didn't take long for Michelotti's talents to shine through: it was clear that he was very capable at sketching fresh car designs, and within two years he had already become Farina's chief stylist, following the sudden departure of the previous design head.

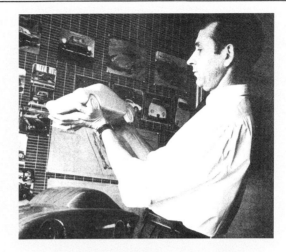

Giovanni Michelotti worked with Triumph for fifteen years, creating some of its most iconic models.

With the Second World War breaking out just as Michelotti assumed his new position, he wouldn't be able to fully immerse himself in his new profession until 1946. This would also be the year in which he got married, before having two children, Edgardo and Daniella. By 1949 Michelotti had left Farina to set up his own design house, initially working from home, then having an office in residential Turin.

With so many coachbuilders in the locale, Michelotti wasn't short of companies to approach in his quest for work, and he was soon kept busy with a string of commissions. He quickly became one of the most prolific car designers around, helping out Ghia, Balbo, Vignale and Bertone; later on he would also be retained by BMW and Hino, as well as Triumph.

The fifties and sixties were to prove enormously good for Michelotti, but things had turned pretty sour by the mid-seventies. Car companies were taking work in-house or using younger, fresher designers. While this initially simply gave Michelotti time to indulge in other pursuits (he loved football and food), by the late seventies things were looking pretty difficult for him financially.

As if major money worries weren't enough, Michelotti was also fighting poor health at the same time. He'd always suffered from sensitive skin, and working with plaster of Paris for his scale models hadn't done him any favours. The result was incurable skin cancer, to which he would succumb in 1980, aged just fifty-nine.

Following his death, Michelotti's company would be run by his son Edgardo, but he was no designer and it didn't take long for the outfit to become little more than a fan club for cars designed by the great man. Still, better that than churn out a series of cars that looked like the Reliant Scimitar SS1, the final Michelotti design to reach production.

Triumph 1300.

**The Spitfire 4 Mk2, launched in 1965, was
barely distinguishable from its predecessor.**

project went so well that it wasn't long before Michelotti was Triumph's retained designer, with his next project being to come up with a replacement for the Standard Eight and Ten. As already explained, their successor would feature a separate chassis, partly so that further derivatives could be produced. Furthermore, developing an all-new car with a unitary construction would take much longer, while exporting Completely Knocked Down (CKD) kits to Australia, India and South Africa would be much easier if the car featured a separate chassis.

When the Herald's construction was decided upon, the initial idea was that there would be various iterations of that car available, such as Saloon, Coupé, Estate and Convertible – which all appeared in due course. However, at this point it hadn't been decided that there would be a two-seater Roadster, although it was suggested by Harry Webster at the time. He was convinced that such a car could not fail, as it would be cheap to develop thanks to the existence of suitable Herald-derived mechanicals, while Triumph had the right image for a cheap sports car, slotting in below its well-established TR models.

However, Webster was making these proposals early in 1960, which was a critical point for Standard-Triumph as things had started to go badly wrong for the company at this time. Although its Herald had been launched reasonably

successfully in 1959, there were too many initial build quality problems. The company's reputation had taken a knock as a result, while sales were below expectations; potential buyers shopped elsewhere, or waited for the issues to be sorted out. As a result, by the spring of 1960 it was clear that something was amiss, with sales well below what had been anticipated. Despite this, the year-end results were healthy, but it wasn't to last. In 1960 UK inflation began to climb sharply, so the Government imposed credit control measures to reduce consumer spending. Predictably, many who were reliant on credit decided they could squeeze another year or two out of their car rather than borrow the money for a new one. Dealers had a particularly hard time. It came as no surprise when, by November 1960, Triumph's balance sheet was dripping with red ink.

At this point, truck builder Leyland Motors made a bid for Standard-Triumph, which it already knew was having a tough time of things. By April of the following year, Standard-Triumph was under new ownership. Leyland initially left the existing management team in place, in a bid to turn things round, but it was clear that they were struggling to get back into the black. As a result, by August 1961 there was a new man at the helm: Stanley Markland.

One of the things that Markland inherited in his new position was a well-established project for a two-seater Herald-based sports car. Harry Webster had proposed such a vehicle in April 1960 and within a few months the project had been given the thumbs up by the Standard-Triumph board. In the meantime, Webster had already asked Giovanni Michelotti to give the exercise some thought, which is why a design study had already been created by October 1960. Codenamed 'Bomb', this first experimental car (with the chassis numbered X659) was shipped to Coventry for Standard-Triumph's board to inspect. Unfortunately, at this point things had started to go badly wrong for Standard-Triumph, so the project was pushed into a corner and quietly forgotten – but not for long.

Once Markland had been installed as managing director, he had to get to grips quickly with everything that the company had been working on. It was in April 1961 that he discovered the Bomb prototype, and he liked what he saw, requesting that Harry Webster should explore further the possibility of putting the car into production. Further analysis of the project suggested that the sums would add up and in July 1961 the green light was given to putting the Bomb into production. At last, Standard-Triumph dealers would have an affordable two-seater sports car to sell.

CHAPTER TWO

SPITFIRE 4 (1962–1965)

The original Bomb prototype's styling was remarkably similar to the final production Spitfire's. However, it's still amazing to think that the nod to Spitfire production was given only in July 1961, yet little more than a year later the wraps were pulled off the showroom-ready vehicle – something which wouldn't have been possible had monocoque construction been adopted for the Herald.

Although it would be more than a year before the Spitfire would be given the thumbs up, the Standard-Triumph board was already thinking about details of the car's construction as early as the spring of 1960. It was at this point that thought started to be given to whether or not the car should feature glass fibre or steel panels. While the former would offer lighter weight, possibly easier crash repairs and perhaps lower tooling and construction costs, the decision was made that steel panelling would be the most reliable way forward.

Although there had been an explosion in glass fibre-bodied cars in the 1950s, notably with Daimler's SP250, it was obvious that few companies had the expertise to build large quantities of plastic panels, while also maintaining quality. It was therefore felt that steel panels was the only way to go: the bodyshells would be stronger and it wouldn't prove so problematic finding a company that could mass-produce the necessary parts.

Although the Bomb project had been put on hold in the latter part of 1960, due to Standard-Triumph's financial woes, some work continued on the viability of putting it into production. As a result, soon after it was agreed that the Spitfire should be built, a company was found which could produce the bodyshells: the Forward Radiator Company.

The Bomb prototype of late 1960 looked very much like the showroom-ready Spitfire, so no major styling changes were needed, but much of the development work was done using a shortened Herald coupé. Bearing chassis number X661, this test mule was painted a dull shade of grey, and initially it was fitted with a 948cc engine. However, once it

became clear that more power would be needed, an experimental 1147cc unit was installed, complete with twin carburettors. With some fine tuning, this would be the engine that would provide motive power for the first two generations of Spitfire.

That first prototype, unveiled to the Standard-Triumph board in October 1960, was fundamentally right, but there were a few key changes required before the car would be production ready. No allowance had been made for wind-up windows, so the height of the door tops had to be increased to make the necessary space available. The dashboard also needed a rethink: Michelotti had incorporated a three-dial binnacle in front of the driver, but this wasn't what Harry Webster had in mind. He preferred to put the gauges in the centre of the dash, thereby reducing costs because the same basic facia could be used for both left- and right-hand drive markets.

The most famous of the Spitfire prototypes, 412 VC would go on to become a press car as well as a development car used for rallying. It would also start out with right-hand drive, before being converted – and then converted back again.

After the original Bomb prototype (X659) and the cut-down Herald coupé (X661) came the first pre-production Spitfires; X691 and X692, registered as 4305 VC and 412 VC respectively. Built in spring 1961, these were used for endurance testing, which they underwent successfully throughout the summer. This was just as well because Standard-Triumph was already committed to unveiling its new sports car at the Earls Court Motor Show in October 1961.

Under the Skin

Although the Spitfire was based on the Herald's chassis, there were several significant changes made which meant the sportster would have to feature hefty sills to increase torsional rigidity as much as possible. Where the Herald's frame featured a strengthening rail on each side, the Spitfire dispensed with these, meaning the bodyshell would have to be that much stiffer. The Spitfire's chassis was also rather shorter than the Herald's. The fact that only two seats needed to be accommodated, instead of four, meant 8.5in (21.5cm) could be chopped out, reducing the wheelbase to 83in (2108mm).

While the chassis was significantly altered compared with the Herald that donated it, the bodyshell was virtually all new. The only components that could be taken from the Triumph parts bin were the windscreen (shared with the TR4) and the inner rear wheelarches, carried over from the Herald 1200. But Standard-Triumph knew it could save cash by using as many Herald mechanical components as possible, which is why the running gear was carried over with the minimum of changes, allowing the company to enjoy considerable economies of scale.

At the front there was double-wishbone suspension, with coil springs, telescopic shock absorbers and an anti-roll bar. There was also the same rack-and-pinion steering that Herald owners had come to love so much, and in the Spitfire this allowed even greater manouevrability than in its bigger brother: the two-seater had a turning circle of just 24ft (7.3m). There was also greater stopping power, as the Herald's drum brakes were substituted for discs – Harry Webster was keen to ensure that his company's products would have the edge over rival Austin-Healey's.

While the front end suspension design worked brilliantly – it was, after all, cutting edge in 1962 – the rear suspension was less impressive. There were drum brakes, which was to be expected, along with swing axles and a transverse leaf spring. This was the design adopted for the Herald, so it was no surprise that the Spitfire also utilized it. However, while the Herald was less likely to be bought by enthusiastic drivers, the Spitfire was snapped up for its dynamic prowess – which was limited by this cheaply-produced suspension layout.

One thing that was not carried over from the early Herald was the 948cc four-cylinder engine. Although the Austin-Healey Frogeye Sprite featured an equally diminu-

Anybody familiar with the Herald's underpinnings will instantly recognize the similarities with the Spitfire rolling chassis. The frame has been shortened, but the rest of the mechanicals have been carried over virtually unchanged.

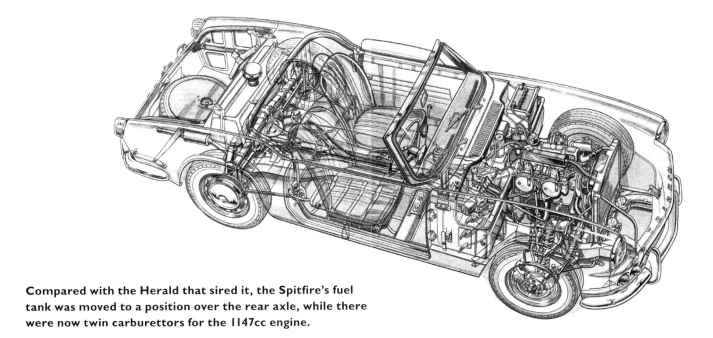

Compared with the Herald that sired it, the Spitfire's fuel tank was moved to a position over the rear axle, while there were now twin carburettors for the 1147cc engine.

tive powerplant, Harry Webster knew that the heavier Spitfire would need more power – and he wanted his new sportster to hit the Frogeye for six anyway. The solution lay in an experimental 1147cc engine that had been developed from the 948cc unit. Fitted with a pair of carburettors, the Spitfire 4 would be endowed with the sort of performance needed to blow the Frogeye into the weeds. The only problem was, by the time the first Spitfires were delivered to their eager owners, the Sprite had received a 1098cc engine, while MG had also introduced its own version of the car, the Midget.

The 1147cc engine that was adopted for the first Spitfires was capable of producing 63bhp at 5,750rpm and 67lb ft of torque at 3,500rpm. This represented a 50 per cent power increase over the Herald 1200, thanks to the fitment of twin HS2 SU carburettors and a slightly wilder camshaft that produced significantly greater valve overlap. To keep the bonnet line as low as possible there was a wider, lower radiator than conventional, with a header tank that sat alongside the rocker cover.

The transmission was carried over pretty much unchanged from the Herald 1200, which meant there was a four-speed manual gearbox with synchromesh on the top three ratios. At launch there was no overdrive option, which kept things simple in terms of rear axle ratios: all cars were fitted with a 4.11:1 diff, just like the Herald.

THE WRAPS COME OFF

On 17 October, 1962, three years after the Triumph Herald was first shown, the world got its first glimpse of Triumph's new budget sportster, the Spitfire, at the Earl's Court Motor Show. There were two examples on display; one was on a turntable behind barriers, where showgoers could look only – the other was alongside, ready to be prodded and poked

When the wraps were taken off Triumph's new baby sports car at the 1962 Earls Court Motor Show, the car went down a storm. There were two cars on hand for showgoers to ogle; this one and a car finished with red paintwork.

The 'VC' registration marks this out as a Coventry-registered factory car. Compare this picture with the shot of the prototype on page 9 and you can see just how few changes were needed to get the car into production.

It came as no surprise when the orders started to flood in thick and fast: at £729 15s 3d the car was more costly than rivals such as the Austin Healey Sprite, but it was also bigger and better equipped. If Triumph had a problem, it was that it couldn't produce the Spitfire fast enough; by the end of the year just 1,289 examples had rolled off the production lines, with a similar figure also being made in January 1963.

At first, all Spitfires were built for the home market only: Triumph wasn't going to run the risk of them going overseas, only for a raft of reliability issues to be raised. So much for confidence in the product! In the event, Triumph's fears proved unfounded, with the cars proving largely trouble-free, allowing exports to begin in earnest. Most of those early exports went to North America, where Triumph already had a loyal following, largely on the back of its well-received TR models.

The first cars sold across the Atlantic were delivered to their eager owners in spring 1963. Aside from the steering wheel being on the left and whitewall tyres being fitted, these cars were the same as those sold in the home market. Triumph had a strong image in the US by this point, so it came as no surprise that the Spitfire was popular, with strong sales from the outset. However, if the car had one failing – and at least that was only picked up by those who bought the car – it was that the rear suspension was not very sophisticated. American dealers had a solution to this though: they could supply a conversion kit which restricted the amount of articulation of the half shafts, ensuring there was less tuck under during hard cornering.

by all and sundry. The former example featured white paint with blue trim plus a black hood, while the latter car was painted red, with black interior trim and roof. They looked fabulous alongside the Herald 1200, TR4 and Vitesse, the last model also making its début that year.

THE NAME'S BOND...

This is the very first Bond four-wheeler built – in 1963.

For some unfathomable reason, not all potential Spitfire buyers wanted an open-topped car; perhaps it was the lack of ease with which the hood of these early cars could be raised and stowed. Whatever it was, it was also possible to buy a Spitfire coupé; well, sort of. It didn't carry Triumph badges however, as it was built by Bond and called simply the GT. In reality the GT was a Herald coupé, as it used that car's chassis, bulkhead and doors, but there was a Spitfire engine fitted along with Bond's own glass fibre bodyshell. The problem as usual was that the Bond's low-volume production meant its cost was on the hefty side; while Triumph charged just £603 for its own Herald coupé (without Spitfire power admittedly), Bond wanted £822 for its GT.

As is common with many cars that survived several generations, the earliest Spitfires also feature the purest design.

CHANGES AFOOT

The first Spitfire 4s had no problem finding buyers, but it quickly became clear that various detail changes were desirable to reduce production costs while also improving usability, durability and refinement. As production progressed, throughout the first year, minor adjustments were made at various times.

While a proposed twin-cam engine swap didn't progress very far – at least in production terms – there were plenty of detail changes that were adopted. Engine bay side valances were added, to prevent the powerplant getting drenched every time the car was driven through a puddle, while the cleanable wire gauze air filters were superseded by disposable paper-element items instead. The radiator header tank was also eradicated, because the cooling system was too efficient, resulting in the engine struggling to get up to temperature in certain conditions.

There were also various modifications made to the interior and exterior trim, such as a one-piece plastic moulding replacing the previous two-piece stainless-steel item for the windscreen surround brightwork – the same move was also made for the Herald, to reduce production costs. There

were also improved door seals along with black floor mats in place of the previous grey items. A shorter piece of brightwork was fitted to the rear wing tops, to provide better clearance for the roof's press studs – the mounting brackets for the rear over-riders were also redesigned to reduce the likelihood of dust getting into the boot.

By the end of the first year, all these changes had been made and things were going well. Customers were queuing up to buy the car and there were no reports of poor reliability – something which had dogged the Herald for the first year after its introduction. That left Harry Webster's team enough time to focus on a steady stream of improvements that were rather more visible than the tinkering they'd had to do so far.

To that end, from October 1963, it was possible to specify overdrive as an extra-cost option, giving the best of both worlds. Without the overdrive switched in (it worked only on third and fourth gears) the car accelerated reasonably briskly because the overall gearing could be kept low. However, when the car was cruising at speed, switching in the overdrive allowed the revs to drop by around 20 per cent – something which helped the engine survive longer, while also protecting the eardrums of the car's occupants.

PAINT AND TRIM OPTIONS

BODY COLOURS	BODY COLOURS	TRIM COLOURS
GUNMETAL	SIGNAL RED	CACTUS
CONIFER	BLACK	MATADOR RED
CACTUS	WHITE	MIDNIGHT BLUE
WEDGWOOD	JONQUIL	BLACK
OLIVE	CHERRY	RED

COMBINATIONS

HERALD 1200 SALOON, COUPÉ, CONVERTIBLE AND ESTATE CAR
HERALD 12/50 SALOON
VITESSE SALOON AND CONVERTIBLE
MONOTONE COLOURS

Body Colour	Trim Colour
Black	Matador Red
White	Matador Red or Black
Wedgwood	Midnight Blue
Cactus	Matador Red
Olive	Cactus
Gunmetal	Midnight Blue
Conifer	Matador Red or Cactus
Jonquil	Black
Signal Red	Black
Cherry	Cactus

N.B.—The Herald and Vitesse Convertibles are available with black or white hoods.

VITESSE SALOON
VITESSE CONVERTIBLE
(Monotone body colours standard. Duotone available at extra cost.)
DUOTONE COLOUR SCHEMES

Upper and Lower Body Colour	Centre Body Colour	Trim Colour
White	Black	Matador Red
Wedgwood	Black	Midnight Blue
Black	Cactus	Matador Red
Cactus	Black	Matador Red
Olive	Cactus	Cactus
Gunmetal	White	Midnight Blue
Conifer	White	Matador Red or Cactus
Jonquil	White	Black
Signal Red	White	Black
Cherry	Cactus	Cactus

N.B.—The Vitesse Convertible is available with black or white hood.

Spitfire 4 paint and trim options.

From launch until May 1963 the following colour combinations were offered:

Paint	Interior trim
Spa White	Black, blue or red
Phantom Grey	Red
Black	Black, blue or red
Powder Blue	Black or blue
Lichfield Green	Black or red
Pale Yellow	Black
Signal Red	Black or red

Between June 1963 and July 1964 there was a new set of combinations available as listed below, then between August and September 1964 Jonquil Yellow was dropped. By October the range was taken back up to six with the introduction of Royal Blue paintwork, which could be ordered with a choice of black or Midnight Blue interior trim.

Paint	Interior Trim
White	Black or red
Black	Red
Conifer Green	Black
Wedgwood Blue	Midnight (dark) blue
Jonquil Yellow	Black
Signal Red	Black

The Triumph Herald was renowned for appealing to women drivers, thanks to its light controls and excellent visibility; the same went for the Spitfire, which was definitely a sports car, but far from a hairy-chested one.

The overdrive offered was Laycock's D-type unit, which was reliable and affordable: it added £57 7s 8d to the £729 15s 3d price of the ex-factory Spitfire. Once the system had reached the options lists, few cars were sold without it – this must also have gained Triumph some extra customers because neither the Austin Healey Sprite nor the MG Midget could be specified with it.

Another option that helped those on long-distance journeys – at least when the weather was inclement – was a factory-fitted hard top. Independent tuner SAH had already been offering one of these since soon after the Spitfire's introduction, but it was rather ugly and the Triumph offering was a far neater solution. Whereas the SAH item was made of GRP, the factory roof was made of steel. So, while Triumph's top was rather heavier, it offered greater refinement once the car was up to speed. Just to show that Triumph was indulging in some joined-up thinking, to make life easier for those who specified the hard top, from December 1963 there was a pair of captive nuts fitted to the Spitfire's rear deck, so the roof could be fixed into place more securely.

The third significant fresh option was a set of sixty-spoke wire wheels, supplied by Dunlop and painted silver. These proved popular, partly because they set the car off rather nicely, but also because they were an inch wider than the standard pressed-steel items. At 4.5in, they provided more grip and better handling than the somewhat puny 3.5in steel items.

With a decent set of optional extras to choose from and proven reliability, plus a higher specification and stronger performance than key rivals, Triumph was on a roll with the Spitfire – so much so that it didn't feel the need to mess with this winning formula until the Mk2 Spitfire arrived in March 1965. However, though badged Mk2, changes from the MkI were hardly ground-breaking, as you'll read in the next chapter.

PRESS REACTION

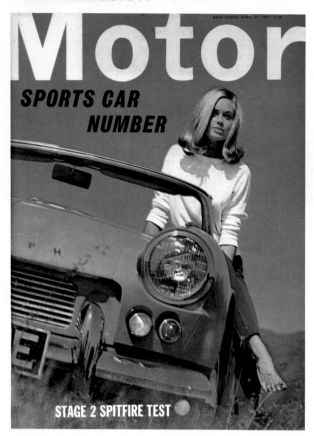

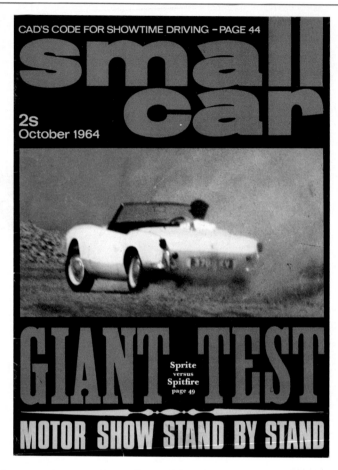

Press reaction for the early Spitfire was almost universally positive.

First to test the new Spitfire was *Motor*, in its 7 November 1962 edition; the headline ran: 'An outstanding new small sports car', leaving the reader in no doubt as to what the testers thought. The magazine was keen on the car's roadholding, styling, packaging, performance and usability. The verdict came: 'A sports car of great merit, the Triumph Spitfire will appeal equally as a comfortable road car and useful competition mount. Its performance in give-and-take conditions makes it an obvious choice for the rally enthusiast although some items of detail obviously call for development'; the underfelt on the car tested, for example, 'was quite wet after a few miles in the rain'.

It would be the following week (16 November) that *Autocar* published its first review of the Spitfire (4299 VC), in which its testers were typically analytical. Noting that: 'the Spitfire is at the upper end of the price scale [of inexpensive two-seater sports cars], yet it has proved on test to be a refined car with a number of advanced features, and to offer appropriately good performance and fuel economy'. Impressed overall by the Spitfire's dynamics, the suspension was criticized for being too firm, but the car was given the thumbs up for its ergonomics, comfort and value; things were helped on the last point by purchase tax changes just as the car was being introduced. It was thanks to these changes that a hefty £90 was knocked off the all-in cost, which represented a useful 12 per cent saving in outlay.

When *Sporting Motorist* got its hands on the Spitfire 4 for its April 1963 edition, it was critical of the amount of headroom available with the roof in place, but apart from that it was almost all good news. The magazine's testers were more favourable towards the comfort levels, boot size, agility and handling, although on the latter point it was noted that confidence levels had to be built as the back end could feel decidedly skittish when the roads got greasy.

In its typical forthright fashion, *Small Car* tested the Spitfire (3606 VC) in its November 1963 edition, comparing it with the Austin Healey Sprite, but not driving the two cars back to back – that wouldn't happen until October 1964. *Car*'s reviewer was keen on the Spitfire's pretty Italian lines, but less sure of it when the roof was put up, noting: 'When the hood goes up it has the effect of putting an apron over a Dior model, but the great hood problem remains unsolved elegance-wise after fifty or more years of experiment.' On this latter point he was incorrect of course; Triumph's own Herald convertible utilized a very neat folding roof mechanism already, and one which would later be adapted to fit the Spitfire.

When *Car* finally drove the Spitfire 4 (3789 KV) against the Austin Healey Sprite for its October 1964 issue, the Triumph scored highly for its sharper looks and driving position, but it was the Sprite which offered the better performance, more predictable handling and higher standard of finish all round.

John Bolster put 412 VC through its paces for *Autosport* in January

1963, writing almost as if he was in Triumph's pay, such was his enthusiasm. He started off by gushing about the car's available performance, cooing about the acceleration and economy, claiming that: 'it has all the performance that the average sports car driver wants'. He was also rather keen about the comfort on offer, stating that: 'the Spitfire is not only a sports car. With its winding windows raised and hood up, it becomes a luxurious coupé'. Perhaps most intriguing was his assertion that: 'The gears are just audible, but the final drive is completely silent'. There can't be many Spitfire owners who have experienced such conditions when driving their car!

However, proving that the world was a very different place in the early sixties, *Car & Driver* agreed with Bolster when it tested the Spitfire. The magazine's opening line was that this was: 'a new small sports car [that] combines silence with lively performance'. The 1147cc engine certainly impressed with its low-down torque that made driving the lightweight sportster a doddle, but the car wasn't so good ergonomically. Still, the light steering, all-independent suspension and strong brakes more than made up for it.

MARKETING THE SPITFIRE 4

New Triumph Spitfire 4
takes the lead among light sports cars

FASTER Top speed 92 mph. Standing ¼ mile 19·5 seconds.

INDEPENDENT SUSPENSION On all four wheels for safer, surer cornering.

STRONGER Tough steel-girder chassis for lifelong strength.

DISC BRAKES On the front wheels. Safer under all conditions.

TIGHTER TURNING 24-ft turning circle for nimble parking.

MORE LUXURY Wind-up windows, king-size cockpit, tailored hood.

With one stride, Triumph take the lead in the light sports car field. In fact, the only thing that keeps the new Spitfire out of the luxury sports car class is its price, £640.19.7 inc. **p.t.**

A member of the Leyland Motors Group

When Triumph launched the Spitfire, the focus was very much on how much fun the car could provide while still offering strength, durability, comfort and practicality.

In later advertising for the Spitfire 4, Triumph played heavily on its motorsport connections, making direct comparisons between the road cars, which its customers could buy and the race cars with which it was competing.

PERIOD MODIFICATIONS

By the time the Spitfire 4 was launched, the Herald had already been on the market for three years. Indeed, in that time the Herald had already moved up from a 948cc engine to an 1147cc unit, while the Vitesse had also reached the market, complete with a 1596cc straight-six. Slotting the latter unit into the Spitfire didn't seem to be something attempted very early in its life, although it would happen later. What was much more popular was the opportunity to fit go-faster bits such as ported cylinder heads, more free-flowing exhausts and suspension modifications to help tame the car's wayward tendencies.

While there was a raft of companies prepared to tune the Spitfire, owners didn't have to talk to anyone other than their friendly Triumph dealer if they wanted some go-faster goodies. That's because from February 1964, Triumph offered three engine upgrade packages to help the Spitfire go faster. The entry-level option was known as the Interim Performance Package, which increased power to 70bhp courtesy of a revised cylinder head that gave a 9.75:1 compression ratio. There was also a downdraught Solex 32 PAIA carburettor and tubular manifold; it certainly looked the part but it's doubtful that many of the £47 packages were sold.

The next rung up the ladder was the stage one kit, priced at £92, which pushed power up to 80bhp thanks to some more serious modifications. Firstly there was an eight-port cylinder head with a 10.5:1 compression ratio, plus a fresh camshaft and revised inlet and exhaust manifolds.

For those who felt that even 80bhp wasn't enough, there was also a stage two kit offered, pushing peak power up to 90bhp thanks to all the stage one tweaks, plus a pair of twin-choke Weber 40DCOE carburettors, twin silencers, a stronger crankshaft, tweaked pistons and con-rods, a diaphragm clutch and revised gear ratios. All this was enough to boost the top speed from 92mph (148km/h) to 107mph (172km/h), while also cutting the 0-60mph time from 15.5sec to just 10.6sec. As such, it represented excellent value – but once again, it appears that few of these kits were ever sold.

Even though it's unlikely that Triumph sold many of its tuning kits, the company felt confident enough in their ability to equip one of its press cars with a stage two set up. Tested by *Autocar*, *Motor* and *Sporting Motorist*, 3139 KV went down a storm with those who reviewed it. Intriguingly, when *Motor* tested the car in April 1964 it was fitted with a full-width radiator grille, which the magazine claimed was part of the stage two conversion. However, when *Autocar* tested the same car in February 1965, it was fitted with a conventional split radiator grille, but when the car reappeared in *Motor* just three months later, once again it featured the single-piece grille – although these were probably archive shots from the first test as the second feature was merely a used car buying guide.

In the first test published, *Motor*'s reviewers were very positive, going so far as to spell out the qualities they expected from a top-notch sports car: speed, accurate steering and good roadholding. They claimed that the stage two Spitfire: 'is outstanding on every count'. The boys also said the car could manage 106mph (170km/h); enough to keep up with the TR4, and that there was unanimity among the panel of reviewers; this was one of the best inexpensive cars they had tried. The problem was, the stage two Spitfire wasn't really that cheap any more because Triumph asked £179 for the engine and transmission adjustments, taking the car up to £820. Also, 3139 KV incorporated various other modifications which Triumph hadn't even got round to pricing when *Motor* tested the car.

By the time *Autocar* tested 3139 KV less than a year later, Triumph had managed to get the abacus working, disclosing that the car as tested would cost the punter a cool £972, thanks to an oil cooler being fitted, along with modified suspension front and rear, wider wheels, a Kenlowe fan and a wood-rim steering wheel. As with *Motor*, *Autocar*'s testers compared the stage two Spitfire's performance with the TR4's, with the former coming out very favourably thanks to its greater economy – it was also a whopping 16sec faster to 80mph (128km/h) from a standing start. Again, the testers were so enthusiastic about the car that they commented: 'Every one of our staff who drove the test car came back looking years younger; as a means of relieving depression, someone even suggested it should be available on the National Health!'

Sporting Motorist also tested 3139 KV, mid-way between *Motor* and *Autocar* (October 1965), also with a standard radiator grille. Although the car went down a storm with *Sporting Motorist*, it was evident that the stage two Spitfire was aimed at the enthusiast driver. Said *Sporting Motorist*: 'A raucous, lusty little beast, it coughs and splutters around town like a consumptive drunk, wearing its racing camshaft on its wing, so to speak. On the open road, this is one of those cars too rarely found which put all the pleasure back into motoring; the engine bursts into life with tremendous vigour and hurls the car along with a shriek which is music to the driver and probably horror to the opposition.'

All of Triumph's tuning kits were available via Sid Hurrell's SAH outfit, which also offered its own go-faster options from autumn 1963. SAH also offered an 8,000rpm rev-counter and an 18-gallon, long-range fuel tank, along with these stage two tuning options:

- Four-port cylinder head kit only, consisting of four-inlet port cylinder head with all essential components, including Weber carburettors, inlet manifolds, exhaust manifold, inlet/exhaust valves, springs, cottors and collars, throttle levers, steady brackets, rods, breather pipe and fuel pipe. £99 1s 6d
- Rocker gear: special heavy-duty valve rocker shaft gear, including pedestals, shaft, arms, recommended for use with above head conversion. £9 5s 5d
- Complete standard stage two kit, including special crankshaft, conrods, pistons, four-port head kit, diaphragm clutch and close-ratio gear kits, special distributor and camshaft, enabling standard engine to be converted into stage two tune. £193 0s 0d
- Complete standard stage two kit as above, but excluding recommended extras such as special pistons, conrods, crankshaft, rocker gear, bearings. £153 10s 0d
- Exchange stage two (standard) engine and gearbox, as a complete built-up assembly against existing standard Spitfire unit, (subject to condition of old units). Exchange price only, including close-ratio gearbox. £222 10s 0d
- Exchange stage two (modified) engine and gearbox: complete exchange engine and gearbox assembly, including all components from options three and five, but including additional SAH equipment and modifications, such as a gas-flowed cylinder head and matched manifolds, oil cooler kit, Lucas sports coil, engine balancing, modifications to block and pistons. £272 10s 0d
- Stage two (modified) engine and gearbox: as above but supplied on an outright purchase basis. £340 0s 0d
- Labour charges for removal/installation of above converted engine and gearbox assembly, including final tuning and road testing. £15 10s 0d

- Close-ratio gear parts (not including any standard parts, gaskets, bearings, that may need replacing, depending on condition of existing gearbox). £23 10s 8d
- Exchange rebuilt close-ratio gearbox only, including all new bearings, thrust washers and other parts as required, but not including fitting charge. £36 19s 0d
- Diaphragm clutch kit, including flywheel, clutch cover and centre plate assembly, release bearings. Can be used with any standard or modified engine. £13 2s 4d

In period, Spitfire tuning invariably involved modifications to the 1147cc engine, but in time the fitment of a six-cylinder engine would become popular instead. In October 1969, four years after the Mk1 had gone out of production, *Hot Car* carried a feature on John Moore, who swapped the 1147cc four-pot in his Spitfire (9494 KX) for a 1596cc six-pot from the early Vitesse. At that stage it wasn't easy to find a 2-litre unit, which is what Moore really wanted, but the 1.6-litre unit provided a healthy dose of extra torque – and just 10bhp over the standard Spitfire unit. It was this reliance on used parts that ensured he didn't have the luxury of being able to fit a GT6 bonnet – which is why he simply cut a hole in the top of the bonnet, pulled up the panelling and filled in the gap with pop-riveted alloy sheeting. Pretty it wasn't, but the car was highly effective once he'd managed to tame the suspension and sort out overheating problems as a result of keeping the original Spitfire radiator.

THE GT6 ARRIVES EARLY

Although Triumph wouldn't build its own fastback Spitfire until 1966 (albeit with six-cylinder power), a sneak preview was offered three years earlier by Paddington-based Fibrepair, which manufactured glass fibre panels for a wide range of cars. It was in November 1963 that the company unveiled its GT conversion, which was a hard top with a little extra – or indeed quite a lot extra.

The idea behind the GT was that it wasn't simply a detachable hard top to shield the car's occupants from the elements – it was actually a conversion, intended to spice up the car's lines while also adding a healthy dose of practicality too. Not only would the car be more comfortable and spacious, but it would also look far sportier, while also being quieter thanks to the extra soundproofing offered by the panelling. Importantly, the GT conversion didn't offer a hatchback in place of the usual boot, although there was now a revised bootlid that better integrated with the revised lines of the car.

Buyers could choose from three levels of trim with the hard top; the cheapest was Standard, finished in flecked white paint and priced at £57 10s. Those with £67 to spend could instead specify the Super edition, which arrived sprayed to match the car's existing colour scheme. An extra fiver (£82) would secure a De-Luxe GT top, complete with headlining and interior light – for those who had already painted their Spitfire a non-standard colour, Fibrepair would spray the roof any colour the customer wanted for an extra £4.

Although most magazines gave the conversion a few column inches, *Sporting Motorist* devoted a whole spread to the car (3476 VB), the verdict being largely positive. While rear visibility was hardly great, noise levels were reduced when the car was cruising at high speed. However, because the test car was also fitted with Fibrepair seats, headroom was at a premium. it was felt to be a decent-value conversion though, and with Triumph offering nothing similar for another three years, it offered plenty of individuality at a time when personalization was most definitely becoming important among the young buyers of sports cars such as the Spitfire.

The Fibrepair Spitfire conversion offered GT6 looks, but without that car's practicality.

SPECIFICATIONS: SPITFIRE 4 Mk1

The Spitfire 4's dash was neatly styled, as it was simply laid out without appearing spartan.

Build dates	Oct 1962 – Dec 1964
Commission numbers	FC 1 – FC 44573
Engine prefix	FC
Gearbox prefix	FC
Differential prefix	FC
Number built	45,753
Basic price	£530
On the road price	£729 15s 3d

Performance

0-30mph	4.8sec
0-50mph	11.3sec
0-60mph	15.5sec
0-80mph	33.0sec
Max speed in first gear	25mph (40km/h)
Max speed in second gear	45mph (72km/h)
Max speed in third gear	70mph (112km/h)
Top speed	92mph (148km/h)
Standing 1/4-mile	19.5sec
Power to weight	81.6bhp/ton
Typical fuel consumption	36mpg (12ltr/100km)

Dimensions, weights and capacities

Length	12ft 1in (3683mm)
Width	4ft 9in (1448mm)
Height (unladen, roof up)	3ft 11.5in (1206mm)
Wheelbase	6ft 11in (2108mm)
Front track	4ft 1in (1245mm)
Rear track	4ft 0in (1219mm)
Ground clearance (laden)	5in (120mm)
Dry weight	1543lb (700kg)
Engine oil	7pt (4.1ltr)
Gearbox oil	1.5pt (0.9ltr)
Overdrive oil	2.375pt (1.4ltr)
Differential oil	1pt (0.6ltr)
Cooling system	9.5pt (5.6ltr)
Fuel tank	8.25gal (37.5ltr)

Engine

Max power	63bhp @ 5,720rpm
Max torque	67lb ft @ 3,500rpm
Max BMEP	144psi @ 3,500rpm
Displacement	1147cc
Bore	69.3mm
Stroke	76.0mm
Compression ratio	9.0:1
Oil pressure	40psi at 2,000rpm
Tappet clearance	0.010in
Fuelling	Twin SU 1.25in HS2 carburettors
Firing order	1-3-4-2
Spark plugs	Lodge CLNY
Spark plug gap	0.025in
Distributor	Delco Remy D200, 7952800
Contact breaker gap	0.020in
Dwell angle	36°
Ignition timing – static	13° BTDC
Centrifugal advance	0° at 800pm 11°/13° at 4,400rpm
Vacuum advance	0 at 2in Hg 9/11° at 9/11inHg
Ignition coil	Lucas HA 125195

Transmission

Clutch	Belleville spring washer
Clutch diameter	6.25in (6.6in from FC 17136)
Clutch output shaft	10 splines
Master cylinder diameter	5/8in

Slave cylinder diameter	3/4in		
Gearbox	3-rail		
Synchromesh	2nd, 3rd and 4th		
Gear ratios	4th = 1.0		
	3rd = 1.39,		
	2nd = 2.16		
	1st = 3.75,		
	R = 3.75		
Optional overdrive	Laycock D-type		
Overdrive ratio	0.802		
Overdrive gear ratios	4th = 0.80		
	3rd = 1.11		
Final drive ratio	4.11:1		

Brakes and steering

Front brakes	9in solid disc
Calliper type	Girling 12.p
Swept area	144 sq in
Rear	7 x 1.25in drum
Swept area	55 sq in
Wheel cylinder diameter	3/4in
Master cylinder diameter	5/8in
Steering	Rack and pinion
Steering wheel diameter	16in (40.64cm)
Turning circle	24ft 2in (7.36m)
Turns between locks	3.75

Suspension, wheels and tyres

Front suspension	Double wishbone
Spring rate	150lb f/in
Camber angle (unladen)	+2° ± 1/2°
Castor angle (unladen)	3° ± 1/20
King pin inclination	6.75° ± 1°
Toe	1/16in-1/8in toe in
Rear suspension	Swing axle
Number of leaves	7
Leaf width	1.75in
Leaf thickness	0.22in
Spring rate	166lb f/in
Toe (unladen)	1/16in-1/8in toe out
Camber angle (unladen)	0.5°
Wheel size (steel)	13 x 3.5 D
Optional wire wheels	13 x 4.5 J
Tyres	Dunlop C41
Tyre size	5.20S x 13
Tyre pressure	Front: 18psi
	Rear: 24psi

Electrics

Earth	Positive
Dynamo	Lucas C40-1
Max current output	22 amps
Starter motor	Lucas M35G
Headlights	50/40w

The rear view of the early Spitfires is especially appealing, with those delicate rear lights and the fitment of quarter bumpers.

PRODUCTION CHANGES (FROM THE COMMISSION NUMBER GIVEN)

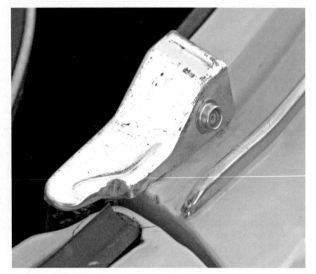

There was no shortage of brightwork on the early Spitfires; the amount would diminish as the model evolved. Twist handles would become pull items, there would be full-width bumpers in place of the early quarter bumpers and an integral folding roof would arrive with the Mk3, obviating the need for these lugs on the rear deck to secure the early offering. Badging would also change radically, while the finishing strip shown below, at the top of the B-pillar, would be moved back within months of the start of Spitfire production, to allow easier erection of the hood.

FC 1876	Frictionless propeller shaft changed to conventional type.
FC 2393	Rubber seal now fitted between dust shield and caliper mounting bracket.
FC 2449	Pistons upgraded to stronger and lighter solid-skirt type.
FC 2604	Metal clips go to plastic for holding on badges.
FC 3200 – FC 5588	A small batch of rear springs gave the incorrect rear wheel camber.

FC 3214 – FC 39528	Front spring spacer (springs arrived at factory 3/8in (10mm) short and spacer was used to correct ride height)
FC 5463	B-post: wing ridge moved back appoximately 1in (2.5cm) from door opening.
FC 5964	Air box area revisions (under bonnet): speedo and tacho cables come out of air box instead of out of the transmission cover, new washer bottle (Tudor) and bracket changed to single-bolt strap type, drain pipe replaced with rubber flap.
FC 8274	A moulded rubber hose replaced the canvas hose between the heater water valve at the bulkhead and the cylinder block.
FC 8779	Door seal changed from double (one fabric, one rubber) to single. Seal colours changed from interior colors to black only.
FC 14196	Rear bumper mounting: upper mounting bracket replaced with bolt and tubular spacer. Lower mounting bracket now attaches to frame underneath instead of through the body.
FC 15089	Grey rubber floor mats and shift gaiter are changed to black rubber.
FC 15576	New vertical link and tie rod lever redesigned to accept the new disc brakes.
FC 16570	Long-stem rear view mirror changed to short-stem, rigid version.
FC 17136	6.25in (15.87cm) coil spring clutch changed to 6.5in (16.5cm).
FC 18814	B-post cap enlarged to fill area left by shortened trim.
FC 20029	Redesigned wiper motor and wiper blades are now fitted.
FC 20061	Flywheel bolts and tab washers are replaced with self-locking bolts.
FC 20753	Millboard engine valances are now fitted.
FC 21927	Gear shift bushing (at base) changed to reduce metal-to-metal contact.
FC 26303	Temperature sender changed.
FC 28017	The exhaust mounting is modified.
FC 30192	Connecting rod material changed from 40 to 45-ton steel. Tab washers (beneath the big end bolts) removed and self-locking bolts used.
FC 37878	Front trunnion seals redesigned.
FC 39925	Header cooling tank removed due to overcooling.
FC 40531	Wire gauze air filters changed to exposed paper filters.
August 1963	Differential drain plug deleted

OPTIONS

Dealer-Fit Options		Special Order (factory-fitted) options	
Badge bar	£3	Adjustable dampers (set of four)	£25
Bonnet lock kit	£1 15s	Brake master cylinder extension	–
Boot rack	–	Carpet set (smoke grey/black mottle)	–
Chrome plated rocker cover	–	Competition rear spring	–
Cigarette lighter	–	Door trim with carpet kick pad	–
Continental touring kit	–	Ignition coil (cold start)	–
Engine bay valance kit	–	Interim performance package	£47
Fog lamp kit	–	Kenlowe fan	£12 9s 6d
Heater kit	£15 2s 6d	Laminated windscreen	£8 11s 10d
Hub cap removal tool	–	Leather seats (red, blue, black)	–
Reversing light	£3 3s 9d	Modified front springs (pair)	£6
Rubber bumper kit (front)	£3	Modified rear spring	£6 10s
Rubber bumper kit (rear)	£4 4s	Overdrive (from 1964)	£58 7s 6d
Seat belts (2 point)	–	Oil cooler	£13 5s
Spot lamp kit	–	Stage I performance package	£92
Sun visors	–	Stage II performance package	£179
Touch-up paints (spray and pencil)	–	Starter Solenoid	–
Tow bar kit (Witter)	£5 10s	Steering Column Lock	–
Wing mirrors (Magnetex D-type)	£1 7s 6d	Sump plate	–
Wheel trim	£0 17s 6d	Tail light fuse	–
Whitewall tyres	£6 17s 6d	Tonneau cover and fittings (black or white)	£12 7s 6d
Wire wheels (from 1964)	–	Wood-rim steering wheel	£7 10s
		Wide-rimmed wheels (each)	£4 5s

SPITFIRE 4 Mk2 (1965–1967)

The Spitfire 4 had proved a success for Triumph but, even by the 1960s, built-in obsolescence was the name of the game in a bid to shift more metal. Although the early Spitfire was well received, and generally well resolved, the sixties was a fast-moving era in consumerism. With fresh car designs being released onto the market each year, there was plenty of scope for improvement – as would be proved over the next decade or so as the Spitfire evolved. However, while there would be some relatively radical changes to the two-seater sportster as the 1960s turned into the 1970s, the first set of tweaks was relatively minor.

Indeed, the arrival of the Spitfire Mk2 went by almost unnoticed by some, as the unveiling, which took place at the March 1965 Geneva Motor Show, was alongside the more glamorous TR4A. Triumph's TR models had long been the focus of attention for a mainstream motoring press hun-

gry for performance and image – both of which the Spitfire could offer, but not in the quantities offered by the TR4A.

The move from Spitfire 4 Mk1 to Mk2 entailed little more than a few minor adjustments to refine the formula laid down by the first edition of 1962. As far as the mechanicals were concerned, engine changes were slight but effective: the result was an extra 4bhp out of the 1147cc four-pot. The slightly higher power output was achieved by revising the camshaft profile; spicing things up marginally (there was extra lift and overlap) meant there was now 67bhp on tap at 6,000rpm. There was no difference in the peak torque generated (it was still 67lb ft), but whereas it had previously been available from 3,500rpm, it was not now accessible until 250rpm higher up the rev range.

The extra horses were liberated through fitting a tubular four-branch exhaust manifold (which would be unique to the

You'd be hard-pressed to tell the difference between the Spitfire 4 Mk1 and its Mk2 successor from this angle; the grille is the main giveaway. Note the factory hard top also fitted to this car, owned by the Triumph Sports Six Club.

The Mk2's interior was the focus of quite a few improvements over the Mk1, such as the fitment of carpets in place of rubber mats, trim along the top of each door and more substantially padded seats.

now installed. To finish off the under-bonnet changes, there was now a single air filter box for the two carburettors, whereas previously each carb had its own filter.

The revised Spitfire also brought with it a new clutch (now a Borg & Beck diaphragm spring set-up), while an overdrive could still be specified at extra cost. The rest of the changes focused on making the car easier and more comfortable to live with, although there were one or two minor cosmetic tweaks: the radiator grille now featured horizontal slats in place of the previous lattice effect, while there was a 'Mk2' script on the boot lid, alongside that denoting 'Spitfire 4'.

Perhaps of more interest to the Spitfire buyer was a more luxurious interior, achieved very simply by fitting trim where previously there had been painted surfaces. In response to criticisms about the down-market cabin of the first Spitfires, Triumph now fitted black leather cloth to the top of each door, along with sections of the dashboard that were also previously painted. The rubber mats originally found on the Mk1's floor were also dispensed with: there were now carpets instead.

It wasn't just about cosmetics though: the seats were more comfortable than before, thanks to extra padding. The frames didn't change but there was some revised stitching to make things look more upmarket.

Aside from a £24 increase to take the Spitfire Mk2's list price up to £666, this was the extent of the significant changes; revised suspension would have been desirable if contemporary press reports were to be believed, but the reality was that few owners pushed their cars hard enough to encounter major handling issues. Those who felt so inclined could always splash out on some modifications from somebody such as SAH, which offered a handling package as part of its line-up, covered in 'period modifications' in chapter two.

While the changes made for the Mk2 were all welcome, there was one upgrade that didn't make it, which was a shift to Coventry Climax overhead-cam FWE power. This was something that Triumph briefly considered in 1964. Jack Brabham was already offering such a conversion for the Triumph Herald, so he was asked to perform the same trick on Spitfire chassis number two, registered 3607 VC. The engine suited the car well and was easy to accommodate, but there were doubts about how long the engine was likely to remain available, while its fitment would have increased the cost of a Spitfire by more than buyers would have been willing to pay. Also, developing the 1147cc engine would prove to be cheaper, while also producing better results. Exit the Coventry-Climax Spitfire.

Mk2), complete with twin downpipes for better breathing. It was the same design of exhaust that Triumph had offered as a factory tuning upgrade on the Mk1 Spitfire; take a look at the 'period modifications' section in the Mk1 chapter and you'll see that this is the same package that the factory offered as the Interim upgrade.

It wasn't just about generating extra power though: there was also a revised inlet manifold, with water heating so that warm up times could be reduced. However, an engine-driven cooling fan was still fitted. An attempt was also made to address complaints from Mk1 owners about fumes entering the cabin: a closed-circuit crankcase breathing system was

SAH

Although there were many companies that were happy to tune Triumphs, most worked on a wide variety of marques rather than concentrating solely on the Canley brand. Perhaps the most focused on Triumph was SAH, which took its name from the initials of founder Sid Hurrell.

By the time the Spitfire reached the showrooms, SAH was already established as the place to go for a hotter Triumph, as the company had started trading – almost by accident – around six years previously. In 1954, Hurrell had bought himself a TR2, which he campaigned throughout the season. He maintained the car himself, and it proved so competitive that other TR drivers asked him to tune their cars for greater power. It became obvious that there was a market for tuned TRs, so Hurrell bought a lock-up garage in Leighton Buzzard, with a hired mechanic helping out. Things progressed so quickly that it didn't take long for the company to occupy four lock-up garages, before moving to purpose-built premises in 1962, still in Leighton Buzzard.

It was pretty much guaranteed that SAH would become the preferred Triumph tuner, thanks to an arrangement he had with the factory in the early days. When Triumph needed an eight-port cylinder head developed, it was Hurrell who was asked to come up with the goods. However, Triumph later produced its own eight-port head in-house, which is why SAH then remained on friendly terms with the factory rather than working closely with it.

Although SAH has a reputation for focusing solely on Triumph, the company actually specialized in Saabs too, after Hurrell had campaigned a Lotus Elite in Sweden. While there he'd encountered a Saab Sport, and he was so impressed by the car's durability that he didn't take long to snap one up, taking it back home to England with him. Having set up a successful Saab dealership in Leighton Buzzard, Hurrell even entered a Saab Sport in the Le Mans 24-Hour race.

By 1959 Hurrell had already established himself as the premier Triumph tuner, largely because of the cars' inherent reliability. His own aftermarket parts were well-known for their durability and effectiveness, which is why by the end of the 1960s Hurrell could claim that his equipment was available in every market in which Triumphs were sold. By 1970, there were over 1,500 items

SAH was the biggest of the Triumph tuners, but also worked on Saabs too.

listed in the SAH catalogue, including tuning parts, glass fibre panels, replacement wheels and seats. Just about everything was produced in-house; even the catalogues for everything were printed by SAH at its Leighton Buzzard headquarters.

Although SAH could supply pretty much anything to upgrade a Spitfire or GT6 (or indeed any Triumph apart from the Stag), the company could also set up a car on its own rolling road. Even the camshaft designs were produced by SAH's own engineers, although it was Piper Cams which produced the end result. Intriguingly, while stronger acceleration and engine efficiency were key to what SAH was trying to achieve, the company was always wary about providing equipment for more go if the buyer didn't also specify suitable equipment for better stopping power and handling ability.

MARKETING THE SPITFIRE 4 Mk2

NEW TRIUMPH SPITFIRE MKII

The new Triumph Spitfire Mk II cornering at speed.

Triumph dispensed with the motorsport references when advertising the Mk2 – because by the time this revised model hit the showrooms, Triumph's Le Mans project had been killed off.

What could be more fun than the Triumph Spitfire?
(The new Triumph Spitfire Mk II)

THE sleek little Spit has always given its pilot more fun £ for £ and lb for lb than anything else on wheels. Now comes the Triumph Spitfire Mk II which is faster, safer and more comfortable than ever.

What we've done for the power. Many basic improvements. We designed a new camshaft (higher lift). We gave the exhaust system a new four-branch manifold, and redesigned the distributor. Then there's a sealed cooling system and a water-heated manifold for faster warm-up. The engine now delivers 67 bhp at 6,000 revs and returns a 0-50 time of 10 seconds.

Now for the comfort. We've come up with a new kind of seat. It's more deeply padded, and reshaped to hug you when you're hustling through the curves. Then there's moulded carpet from door to door and the supplest upholstery on any car (at any price) — two-way-stretch Ambla. Finally, we added safety padding covers for grab handles and door-waist rails.

So now when the Spitfire Mk II is purring in the upper nineties you'll be purring too.

In addition to all this, beautiful Michelotti coachwork on an ultra-tough girder chassis: a tiny 24-foot turning circle; a monsoon-proof top; disc brakes up front and a wind-screen that detaches if you want to be a racer. Your Standard-Triumph dealer can arrange a test drive in a Mk II Spitfire. When are you going to see him?

Ex-works price, inc. p.t.
Spitfire Mk II £666.2.11
Hardtop model £699.19.7
STANDARD TRIUMPH
A member of the Leyland Motor Corporation

Tough enough for Le Mans. Smart enough for les girls.

The Triumph Spitfire Mk. II or how to go one better than a Spitfire

Let's start with some cold hard facts. In the 1965 Le Mans 24-hour race only 14 cars out of 51 starters survived. Two of those cars were works Triumph Spitfires, winning first and second places in their particular class.

This is tribute enough to the Spitfire's toughness and reliability. What follows is a tribute to its speed and its comfort. The Spitfire Mk. II has a top speed of over 95 mph. It will accelerate from 0 - 50 mph in 10 seconds. It will cover a standing ½-mile in only 19.0 seconds.

Inside, the cockpit, once and for all, ends the fallacy that sports cars have to be cramped and draughty. The two bucket seats are set low and well back from the facia. (There's room to stretch your legs). The floor is carpeted. The facia and the doors are padded. The hood closes limpet-tight. (Rain and draughts never intrude on your motoring pleasure).

What we can't tell you in black and white you can learn in a real life test drive. Any Triumph dealer will be pleased to arrange it. It gives him an excuse for being in a Spitfire. p.s. Don't forget to ask him about the hardtop version.

THE FACTS AND FIGURES
The vital statistics: Length, 12 ft. 1 ins. Width, 4 ft. 9 ins. Height (with hood), 3 ft. 11½ ins. A turning circle of 24 ft.
The instruments: Speedometer, tachometer, temperature gauge, fuel gauge, warning lights for main headlamp beam, oil pressure, ignition, and direction indicators.
The suspension: All-round independent suspension.
The fun: Take that trial drive we were talking about (there are no strings attached).

Disc brakes, all-round independent suspension, a 24-foot turning circle, 57 bhp, read on.

New: more urge for the Triumph Spitfire Mk. II

Come-hither comfort—door-to-door carpet, redesigned bucket seats and padding galore!

and that's not all. The Spitfire 4 quickly made a name for itself as a sweet-tempered car with the hidden thrust that's needed to win big league rallies. This didn't surprise us. We'd built in independent suspension on all four wheels, a steel-girder chassis. And we'd added little luxuries like wind-up windows and outside door handles.

When we came to design the Spitfire Mk II we decided to push on further along the same lines: increase power and comfort proportionately.

What we've done for the power. Many basic improvements. We designed a new camshaft (higher lift). We gave the exhaust system a new four-branch manifold, and redesigned the distributor. Then there's a sealed cooling system and a water-heated manifold for faster warm-up. The engine now delivers 67 bhp at 6,000 revs and returns an 0-50 time of 10 seconds.

Now for the comfort. We've come up with a new kind of seat. It's more deeply padded, and reshaped to hug you when you're hustling through the curves. Then there's moulded carpet from door to door and the supplest upholstery on any car (at any price) — two-way-stretch Ambla. Finally, we added safety padding covers for grab handles and door-waist rails.

So now when the Spitfire Mk II is purring in the upper nineties you'll be purring too.

Instead of referencing motorsport, Triumph instead focused on the freedom and fun offered by its budget sportster. However, it also took every opportunity to point out the various improvements that had been incorporated in the transition from MkI to Mk2.

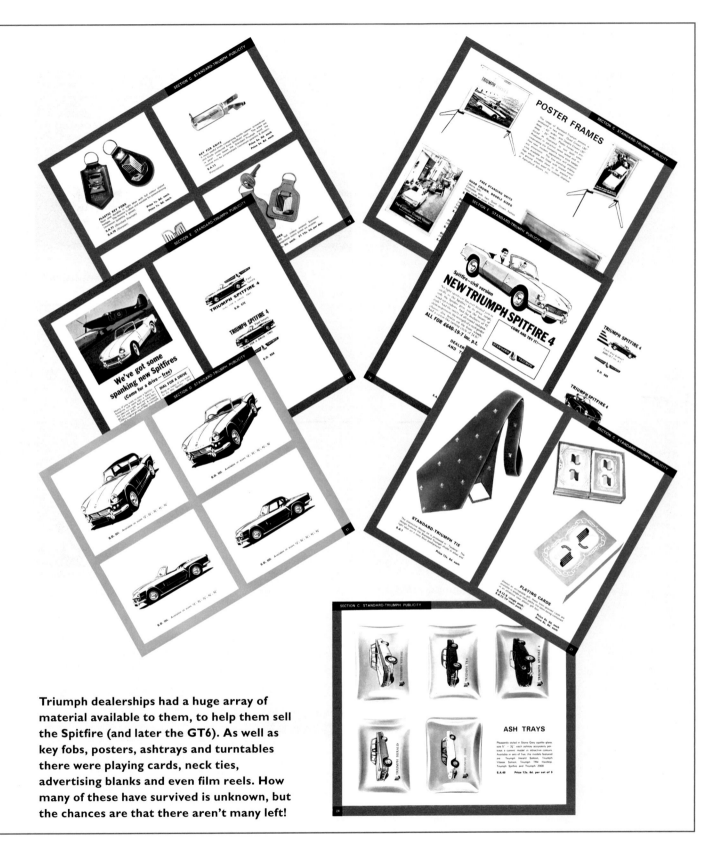

Triumph dealerships had a huge array of material available to them, to help them sell the Spitfire (and later the GT6). As well as key fobs, posters, ashtrays and turntables there were playing cards, neck ties, advertising blanks and even film reels. How many of these have survived is unknown, but the chances are that there aren't many left!

PAINT AND TRIM OPTIONS

Even though the Spitfire Mk2 survived for longer than the Mk1 edition, its colour and trim options were more straightforward. Apart from cars built after October 1965, which weren't offered with black paintwork, the options throughout Mk2 production were:

Paint	Interior trim
White	Black or red
Black	Red
Conifer Green	Black
Wedgwood Blue	Midnight blue
Royal Blue	Black or Midnight Blue
Signal Red	Black

The Spitfire 4 Mk2's bonnet was carried over unchanged from the Mk1, along with the brightwork, badging and lighting.

Ringing in the Changes

As with the Mk1, there were numerous tweaks made to the Mk2 during its two years of production; none were especially significant as all the major tweaks were saved for the Mk3 that would arrive in March 1967. Soon after the Mk2 was introduced it received a redesigned engine block, which was bored out for the camshaft to run in bearings – the first time this had been so. The cylinder head casting was also revised, to provide better cooling of the exhaust ports while, from October 1965, there were fresh con-rods fitted, shared with the 1296cc engine first seen in Triumph's 1300 front-wheel drive saloon.

October 1965 proved to be a turning point for the Mk2, as this is when most of the changes were incorporated, for a mid-life facelift before the Mk3 arrived just over a year later. Most Triumph owners are familiar with their car's automatic rust-proofing system (an engine that leaks lubricant with no effective cure seemingly possible), but Triumph did make an attempt to clean things up with a revised crankshaft rear oil seal and new sump drain plug. These changes, along with revised dampers, were part of the 1966 model year revisions. So too was a fresh wheel design, not that the change was especially noticeable because they were the same as the old but with smaller slots in the rim.

OPTIONS

Dealer-fit Options

Bonnet lock kit	£1 15s 0d
Boot rack plus ski attachment	£11 11s 0d
Brake servo kit (Girling Power Stop)	£13 0s 0d
Chrome-plated tail pipe finisher	12s 0d
Cigarette lighter (push-in)	10s 8d + pur tax
Cigarette lighter (pull-out)	£1 10s 0d + pur tax
Competition brake pads (Ferodo DS11)	£3 3s 6d
Competition ignition coil (Lucas HA12)	£2 5s 0d
Competition front springs	£3 15s 0d
Competition rear springs	£6 12s 0d
Continental touring kit	£10 5s 0d
Dunlop SP41 145/5.5-13 radial tyres	£9 16s 8d
Electric defroster	£1 15s 0d
Fire Extinguisher	£1 19s 6d
Fog lamp kit	From £3 19s 6d
Fuel filter	3s 9d
Hard-top	£33 16s 8d
Hard-top to soft-top conversion kit	£18 10s 0d
Hard-top rear window anti-mist panel	18s 6d
Heater kit	£13 5s 1d
Hood sealer; black or clear	12s 0d
Hub cap medallion	11s 5d
Hub cap removal tool	
Mud flap kit (front only)	£1 7s 6d
Oil cooler kit	£12 5s 0d
Radio: Smith Radiomobile	
Rear hub bearing and sealing kit	
Rev counter-8000 rpm	£6 5s 0d

Reversing light kit	£3 10s 0d
Seat belts (two-point, each)	£4 4s 0d
Seat belts (three-point, each)	£4 14s 6d
Seat covers (Karobes)	
Sill Protector	12s 0d
Spot lamp kit	From £3 19s 6d
Steel wide wheel (each)	£4 5s 0d
Sump plate	£2 12s 0d
Sun visors (pair)	£1 4s 7d
Touch-in paint	5s 6d
Tow bar kit (Witter)	From £5 10s 0d
Trunnion sealing kit	
Underseal 'Carseal'	
Wheel trim	17s 6d
Whitewall tyres (5.20x13)	£6 2s 11d
Wing mirrors	From 19s 6d
Wire Wheels	£36 17s 6d
Wood-rimmed steering wheel	From £7 10s 0d

Special order options

Brake master cylinder extension	
Hard-top	£33 11s 0d
Ignition coil (cold start)	
Laminated windscreen	£7 13s 7d
Leather seats-red, blue or black	
Overdrive	£58 7s 8d
Steering Column lock	
Starter solenoid-cold start	
Tail light fuse	
Tonneau cover and fixings (black/white)	£11 4s 4d

There were several other adjustments made to the interior and exterior trim, few of which would have been noticed by the typical owner. There was now carpet at the base of each door trim, while there were fresh door handles that now featured a push button: they'd previously been pull handles, similar to the early MGB's. Also, the earlier design had incorporated a key slot, but the new ones featured a separate slot below; perfect for scratching that paintwork. To finish things off, there was now a key slot on both sides of the car; only the driver's side had previously been fitted with one.

Of course all these adjustments were incredibly minor, but Triumph had some bigger tricks up its sleeve – which would become apparent when the Spitfire Mk3 was unveiled.

The factory-fitted hard top was made of steel and looked superb. It was also effective at improving high-speed cruising refinement.

MALTESE PRODUCTION

Although it's assumed that all Spitfires were exported from Triumph's Canley factory, this isn't so. In 1962 a company called Car Assembly started building Heralds in Malta, and it wasn't long before Vitesses and Spitfires followed. Constructed from CKD (Completely Knocked Down) kits, just twenty-five cars per month initially rolled off the production lines, although this doubled in 1964.

The cars were largely built by hand, which is why they were usually made to a higher standard than anything that came out of Canley; shutlines were invariably tighter while the paint finish was generally of a much higher standard. Even better, because of their hand-built nature, the customer could choose from a much wider range of exterior colours (including metallics) than if choosing from Triumph's own palette.

PRESS REACTION

Because the Spitfire Mk2 was so similar to the Mk1 edition, not everybody was too bothered about putting the revised car through its paces. For example, *Motor* didn't subject the car to a full test (or indeed one at all, it would seem), despite having run a Mk1 edition as a long-term test car over 12,000 miles.

Even *Autocar* was in no rush to get one over on its arch-rival *Motor*, as it didn't test the revised Spitfire until August 1966 – just a few months before it was replaced by the Mk3 edition. Still, the magazine's testers clearly thought it was worth the wait as they were extremely enthusiastic about the car's dynamics, but less so about the usability. The magazine claimed: 'As soon as it starts up, one is aware that this is a taut, crisply tuned, little sports engine… That extra 4bhp, all at high revs, has made the car noticeably livelier than before… The engine tuning has not made the car less easy to drive in traffic; it still bumbles along happily at 25mph (40km/h) in direct top, or at about 35mph (56km/h) in overdrive.'

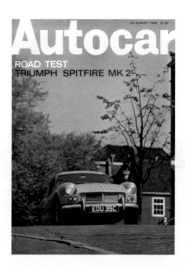

The availability of optional overdrive was a welcome addition, but *Autocar* didn't feel the gear ratios, carried over from the Herald, were ideally suited to the Spitfire's more sporting nature – there was a yawning chasm between second and third that it really didn't need. More welcome was the much-improved interior trim, although the fitment of the same hood arrangement as before wasn't so well received, even if it was effective once erected.

The Spitfire Mk2 was also put through its paces by *Sporting Motorist*, for its April 1965 issue. As the car was introduced alongside the TR4A at the 1965 Geneva Motor Show, *Sporting Motorist*'s testers were able to drive both cars back to back across Europe – with the Spitfire not as far behind as you might think. Commenting on EDU 39 C, *Sporting Motorist*, proclaimed that: 'There is no doubt that the latest alterations have made a good car into an excellent one.'

Turn the page and watch the Triumph Spitfire Mk 2 'hairpin'!

The testers from *Car* magazine were on the same trip. To launch the Spitfire Mk2, Standard Triumph assembled a few road testers from various publications, and asked them to drive from Berkeley Square to the Geneva Motor Show. Just like *Sporting Motorist*, *Car* made reference to the fact that the fitment of wire wheels made the car feel more sure-footed – despite the fact that both magazines photographed Spitfires wearing the standard pressed steel wheels! In *Car*'s case it was EDU 38 C, about which it was noted that: 'The new seats at last put the Spitfire in the same class as the Austin Healey Sprite from a comfort point of view, and since its driving position is a great deal better, despite heavily offset pedals, it should start to draw ahead on showroom-floor appeal.'

The boys from *Road & Track* didn't get onto the same Swiss junket as the Brits, but that didn't stop the magazine's testers from being generally very enthusiastic about the Spitfire Mk2. It was acknowledged that the changes were pretty slight in the grand scheme of things, but the seats were reckoned to be an improvement, the brakes were still excellent and the handling very good too. The lack of an all-synchro gearbox was the main downside, but with the list price unchanged at $2249, the car represented superb value overall.

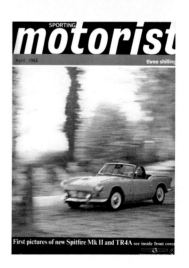

First pictures of new Spitfire Mk II and TR4A see inside front cover

Most magazines were in no rush to test the revised Spitfire, but when they did, they invariably still loved it.

PERIOD MODIFICATIONS

Because there were few changes between the Mk1 and Mk2 editions of the Spitfire 4, the tuning packages offered for the former were invariably also offered for the latter. However, there was one that didn't apply to the original car, which would be offered from 1971 by British Leyland Special Tuning. This enabled Mk2 owners to upgrade the rear suspension of their car to MkIV specification; this is covered more fully in the next chapter, as the conversion was also available for the Mk3.

Aside from the tuning options, all sorts of companies got their act together as the Spitfire became an established part of the affordable sports car scene. One was Belgian outfit Apal, better known for its coachbuilt cars. In January 1966 Apal unveiled a new hard top for the Spitfire. Very much like SAH's own fastback-style hard top, but with a separate boot rather than a hatchback, the Apal roof integrated rather well with the Spitfire's lines.

An alternative was a similar one from the Lancashire-based GT Tops Company. A very neat design offered in white only, this dispensed with the factory boot lid as there was now a fresh lid incorporated into the new roof.

Although the wraparound rear window gave the game away, this roof more than most offered a preview of what Triumph would later produce in-house, in the shape of the early GT6. Supplied with all seals, an extended filler neck and nylon flock or foam rubber interior trim, the top cost £42 10s – or £63 if specified with the optional Weathershields sun roof.

Another conversion that was available, which completely transformed the appearance of the Spitfire was a new nose, available from Kent-based Lenham. With its faired-in headlamps and smiling grille, the fresh front brought a completely new look to the Spitfire, for all of £28; for another £55, Lenham would also supply a hard top to complete the effect.

SPITFIRE 4 Mk2 SPECIFICATIONS

Build dates	Dec 1964 – Jan 1967
Commission numbers	FC50001 – FC88904
Engine prefix	FC50001
Gearbox prefix	FC
Differential prefix	FC
Number built	37,409
Basic price	£550
On the road price	£677 15s 2d

Performance

0-60mph	14sec
Max speed in first gear	28mph (45km/h)
Max speed in second gear	48mph (77km/h)
Max speed in third gear	73mph (117km/h)
Top speed	94mph (151km/h)
Standing 1/4 mile	19sec

Power to weight ratio	86.8bhp/ton
Typical fuel consumption	34mpg (12ltr/100km)

Dimensions, weights and capacities

Length	12ft 1in (3683mm)
Width	4ft 9in (1448mm)
Height (unladen, roof up)	3ft 11.5in (1206mm)
Wheelbase	6ft 11in (2108mm)
Front track	4ft 1in (1245mm)
Rear track	4ft 0in (1219mm)
Ground clearance (laden)	5in (120mm)
Dry weight	1543lb (700kg)
Engine oil	7 pt (4.1ltr)
Gearbox oil	1.5pt (0.9ltr)
Overdrive oil	2.375 pt (1.4ltr)
Differential oil	1pt (0.6ltr)

Changes under the bonnet were more significant, as there was a revised camshaft, revised inlet and exhaust manifolds, plus a redesigned air filter box, which between them liberated an extra four horses.

Cooling system	9.5pt (5.6ltr)	Overdrive gear ratios	4th = 0.80
Fuel tank	8.25gal (37.5ltr)		3rd = 1.11
		Final drive ratio	4.11:1

Engine

Max power	67bhp @ 6,000rpm
Max torque	67lb ft @ 3,760rpm
Displacement	1147cc
Bore	69.3mm
Stroke	76.0mm
Compression Ratio	9.0:1
Oil pressure	50psi at 2,000rpm
Tappet clearance	0.010in
Fuelling	Twin SU 1.25in HS2
carburettors	
Firing order	1-3-4-2
Spark plugs	Lodge CLNY
	(Champion L87Y
	from FC 64762)
Spark plug gap	0.025in
Distributor	Delco Remy 0200, 7953166
Contact breaker gap	0.020in
Dwell angle	36°
Ignition timing – static	13° BTDC
Centrifugal advance	0° at 800rpm
	9°/11 ° at 3,200rpm
	11.25°/13.5° at 4,600rpm
Vacuum advance	0° at 5inHg
	11°/13° at 12inHg
Ignition coil	Lucas HA 125195

Transmission

Clutch	Diaphragm
Clutch diameter	6.5in (16.5cm)
Clutch output shaft	10 splines
Master cylinder diameter	5/8in
Slave cylinder diameter	7/8in
Gearbox	3-rail
Synchromesh	2nd, 3rd and 4th
Gear ratios	4th = 1.0
	3rd = 1.39,
	2nd = 2.16
	1st = 3.75
	R = 3.75
Optional overdrive	Laycock D-type
Overdrive ratio	0.802

Brakes and steering

Front brakes	9in solid disc
Caliper type	Girling 12.p
Swept area	144sq in
Rear	7 x 1.25in drum
Swept area	55sq in
Wheel cylinder diameter	3/4in
Master cylinder diameter	5/8in
Steering	Rack and pinion
Steering wheel diameter	16in (40.64cm)
Turning circle	24ft 2in (7.36m)
Turns between locks	3.75

Suspension, wheels and tyres

Front suspension	Double wishbone
Spring rate	150lbf/in
Camber angle (unladen)	+2° ± 1/2°
Castor angle (unladen)	3° ± 1/20
King pin inclination	6.75° ± 1°
Toe	1/16in-1/8in toe in
Rear suspension	Swing axle
Number of leaves	7
Leaf width	1.75in
Leaf thickness	0.22in
Spring rate	166lbf/in
Toe (unladen)	1/16in-1/8in toe out
Camber angle (unladen)	0.5°
Wheel size	Steel 13 x 3.5 D
Optional wire wheels	13 x 4.5 J
Tyres	Dunlop C41
	(Dunlop SP41 optional)
Tyre size	5.20S x 13 (145 SR13 optional)
Tyre pressure	Front: 18psi
	Rear: 24psi

Electrics

Earth	Positive (negative from 1964)
Dynamo	Lucas C40-1
Max current output	22 amps
Starter motor	Lucas M35G
Headlights	50/40w

The lighting was carried over from the initial incarnation of the Spitfire 4, but there was an extra badge on the tail to denote the newer model.

SPITFIRE Mk2 PRODUCTION CHANGES

From commission number:

FC 50125	Narrower width main bearings.
FC 50624	Narrower width big end bearings.
FC 55198	Battery clamp redesigned.
FC 56031	Wheels slightly revised, with thinner slots.
FC 56578	New push-button door handle with integral lock; now one for the passenger side too. Plus a carpet kick pad added to the interior door panel, while the door catch changed to the anti-burst variety.
FC 60350	Revised cylinder head, for better cooling.
FC 61023	Camshaft bearings now fitted.
FC 61199	Steering column universal joint redesigned.
FC 61708	Rear shock absorbers changed.
FC 62166	Rear trunnion seals redesigned.
FC 62845	Brass coolant drain tap added to the side of the engine block, replacing the brass plug previously fitted.
FC 63500	Door check seal now held in place by clips instead of screws.
FC 64762	Factory-fitted spark plugs changed from Lodge CLNY to Champion L87Y.
FC 66200	Anti-rattle nylon button/rubber stopper added to the steering column.
FC 68072	Temperature sender unit added to the water pump.
FC 69120	Crankshaft rear oil seal revised.
FC 71117	Con rods now have interference fit gudgeon pins instead of floating gudgeon pins.
FC 79642	Crankshaft rear oil seal changed to a silicon rubber seal in place of aluminum.
FC 82247	Engine oil drain plug changed from a threaded plug to a taper-threaded plug, while the oil strainer moved from the sump to the pump.

Also, from around FC 88650, in January 1967, a rain gutter was added to the side of the windscreen.

CHAPTER FOUR

SPITFIRE Mk3 (1967–1970)

When the Mk3 made its début in 1967, it was almost offered with the slant-four that was fitted to the Dolomite and TR7 in the 1970s. Triumph had started working on this engine project way back in 1963, with the unusual design being settled upon to allow a lower bonnet line. One of these 1709cc powerplants was fitted to a Spitfire in 1966, and with 80bhp on tap the car was capable of 98mph (157km/h). However, the 1296cc engine was virtually as powerful and ready for production, while the slant-four needed much more development. It was no surprise therefore when the project was shelved indefinitely and the Mk3 Spitfire made its début with a conventional 1296cc engine.

Unveiled at the March 1967 Geneva Motor Show, the Spitfire Mk3 finally dispensed with the '4' in its name, with the new car incorporating a range of tweaks which were partly the result of fresh North American regulations. Significant sheet metal changes were few and far between, but aesthetically, the key difference was the raising of the front bumper so it now crossed the nose in front of the grille instead of below it. This meant the chrome-plated steel blade was now a full 9in (22.8cm) higher than before, while there were also new rubber-faced over-riders.

The sidelights and indicators were now combined units below the front bumper rather than separate circular items above it, and there were similar changes at the back. Although the tail lights didn't change, the indicators were raised and enlarged, and on the inside of each indicator there was now a circular reversing light.

Less obvious at the front, thanks to that dominant bumper, was a wider grille, which was now the same as the GT6 Mk1's, albeit with a different finish. The change of mark brought with it badging revisions too: the Triumph shield on

One of the most frequently photographed Mk3s in period, from this angle JDU 24D looks reasonably pretty, despite the raised bumper.

MARKETING

Triumph introduce the new Spitfire Mark 3
The big news is under the bonnet!

Triumph's focus in marketing the Spitfire Mk3 was its greater usability as well as its larger engine, compared with its predecessors. However, throughout the campaigns there was always an element of pushing just what great value the Spitfire offered – in isolation as well as when pitched against its rivals.

Up front there's a sleek new look

The Triumph Spitfire Mark 3 inherits the same beautiful Michelotti coachwork as its predecessors. But subtle re-styling has given the Spit a sleek new front. This 'face lift' isn't just a styling gimmick. The new front bumper location gives even better protection. And you'll notice that the overriders now have insets of solid rubber. Also new: a very handsome, very neat, very efficient foldaway hood. And integral side lights and front indicator flashers.

Top-down, toe-down, ton-up.

If this car looks like you can't afford it

look again

(under $2400)

Sports cars probably got their name because only big sports cars could afford them.
Then the Triumph Spitfire came along.
The Spitfire is a real sports car with a long track record to prove it. But it just doesn't cost like sports cars are supposed to.
That goes for the new '69 Spitfire Mk3. It still comes with an engine that can take you to 60 in 13 seconds.
It still has four forward speeds, three of them synchromeshed.
It still has rack-and-pinion steering and four wheel independent suspension.
And it still costs under $2400*.
That includes new features like contour seats with integral head restraints, leather-covered steering wheel, non-glare instrument panel, and pencil stripe sidewalls.
(And of course, all the '69 Federal safety standards.)
So remember when you're looking over the new Spitfire Mk3 at your Triumph dealer that it's the little things about it that make it so great.
Like the price.

Triumph Spitfire Mk3

the bonnet was dispensed with and the boot badges were adjusted to suit. There was still the Spitfire script, but gone was the '4' after it, to be replaced by a separate 'Mk3' mazak casting just below.

The Spitfire Mk3's cabin was also fettled compared with its predecessor, although none of the amendments were especially far-reaching. The instruments were still in the centre of the fascia, although the speedometer now read to 120mph instead of 110mph, no doubt to make life easier for any tuning company which managed to significantly increase the Spitfire's top speed. The 16in (40.64cm) steering wheel was also swapped to a 15in (38.10cm) wire-spoked item that looked much like the one fitted to the TR4A, but the Spitfire's featured a plastic rim whereas the TR's had a leather finish. There was also a move to a negative earth electrical system; an increasing number of aftermarket accessories were becoming available for these cars, and the industry trend was to move away from positive earth electrics.

While all these cosmetic affectations were welcome, of more consequence to those who tested the car – and most certainly to those who bought it – was the fitment of the 1296cc engine in place of the previous 1147cc unit. Although the larger engine was a development of the smaller one, it wasn't a straightforward boring exercise. Simply increasing the combustion chamber diameter would have produced a bit more power and torque, but Triumph could do better than that because it had already developed a significantly more advanced version of this powerplant for its front-wheel drive 1300, launched in 1965.

This more head-on shot shows that the raised bumper didn't work aesthetically from every angle – it's not a disaster, but after the much prettier early cars, it's clear the Mk3 was something of a compromise stylistically.

PRESS REACTION

Autocar was first to report on the Spitfire Mk3, and while it appeared to have got its hands on one of the cars for its 9 March 1967 edition, the magazine wouldn't carry a full review of the car until May of the following year. Even then, the report was brief as a more comprehensive account was promised to follow – not that it did. Still, at least the review was favourable; the car's lines were still admired, its engine still eager and the steering still light and direct.

It was left to *Motor* to offer a truly comprehensive account of the revised Spitfire, and once again the magazine was positive about it, although the writers had to concede that the specification made a big difference: the test car was laden down with extras that made it rather more appealing. Even without these though, the engine's tractability, smoothness and economy were admired, along with the ride and handling.

When *Hot Car* pitched the Mk3 Spitfire (RDU 657H) against Austin Healey's MkIV Sprite in July 1970, it was the latter that came out on top, largely because it felt the Triumph appealed to those with a bit more money. Or as the magazine put it: 'The Spitfire is the car for someone who wants good (but not so sporting) performance with two seats, comfort and sophistication. There's a lot more luggage space and the optional overdrive makes it an ideal tourer.'

Car magazine performed the same test, comparing the Spitfire with the Sprite as it had already done back in October 1964 with the arrival of the first-generation Spitfire. Whereas the Sprite had won the first comparison, it was the Spitfire that took first place in the rematch, after more than 2,000 miles of trans-Europe driving. This time round the Triumph was praised for its agility, grip and refinement, largely thanks to the fitment of Dunlop SP41 tyres in place of the C41s originally specified.

Also noteworthy were the cosseting ride, sharp steering and greater engine flexibility. Indeed, *Car* was so impressed with the Spitfire that it remarked: 'The Spitfire has moved so far ahead in looks and comfort that we would now rate it a natural first choice… On the open road, the Healey offers marginally more fun provided you don't venture abroad, whereas the Triumph (we are told) rates higher in the crumpet stakes and makes a better holiday express at £45 more.'

When *Car & Driver* reviewed the Spitfire Mk3 in September 1967, it was priced at $2,279 – a mere $30 more than its predecessor had cost, and the same list price as the MkI.

Considering the Mk3 was a significant step forward over its predecessors, and the Mk2 was already perceived as being good value, it came as no surprise that this new arrival went down very well with *Car & Driver*'s test team.

The proper roof was a big step forward, and so was the improved mechanical specification ... if not the driving position, the team stating: 'The thrifty will love the Triumph's ability to wring miles out of a gallon even when driven fast. But only an oriental mystic in the bed-of-nails tradition will enjoy the things the car does to one's legs.' Still, at least the fun served up by the car went down a storm: 'The best reason for buying a Spitfire is that the thing is a ball to drive. Everyone starts out with a Spitfire, or something similar, and we don't know anyone who looks back on the experience with anything other than great fondness.' Amen to that.

Now substantially revised, the Spitfire Mk3 proved just as much a hit with road testers as its predecessors.

The Mk3's styling works best with certain colours; this dark blue example looks good with its contrasting chrome. It also sports a very popular twin-box exhaust system, which looks good and sounds even better.

The 1300 employed a development of the 1147cc engine used in the works racing Spitfires. When Triumph's engineers had been creating the eight-port head for the competition Spitfires, they had been hamstrung by the positioning of the cylinder head retaining studs. These studs were located in just the wrong place for optimum inlet port efficiency. As the engine was developed for Triumph's road cars, it made sense to redesign the head and block, which involved a reduction in the number of retaining studs from eleven to ten.

With the bore increasing from 69.3mm to 73.7mm, Triumph took the opportunity to redesign the combustion chambers in the cylinder head, fitting larger inlet and exhaust valves at the same time. Because the valves were also now further apart, the pushrods had to be moved. So, while they were at it, Triumph's engineers took the opportunity to dispense with the separate tubes that had been a feature of earlier engines. The pushrods were now located directly in the head casting, making the manufacturing process simpler, faster and cheaper.

There were other changes too, such as a move to a closed-circuit crankcase breathing system, which sucked crankcase fumes into the inlet manifold to help reduce the likelihood of the air filters getting clogged up. The system relied on a

circular emission control valve attached to the inlet manifold, which was now a water-heated four-port unit sitting on a cast-iron exhaust manifold. Earlier Spitfires had featured a tubular exhaust manifold, but this new one was more efficient, helped by the fact that the rest of the system featured a greater diameter of $1\frac{5}{8}$ inches for better breathing.

Whereas the Spitfire Mk2 could offer 67bhp and 67lb ft of torque, the Mk3's figures grew to a more useful 75bhp

OPTIONS

Dealer-fit options

Bonnet lock	£1 15s 0d	Spot lamp	From £13 9s 0d
Boot rack (removable)		Steering wheel glove-brown leather	£1 4s 6d
Brake servo (Girling Powerstop)	£13 0s 0d	Steering wheel glove-simulated leather	9s 11d
Cigarette lighter (push-in)	10s 8d + p/tax	Sun visors	
Cigarette lighter (pull-out)	£1 10s 0d + p/tax	Touch-in paints	5s 0d
Competition front springs		Tow bar kit	From £5 10s 0d
Competition rear springs		Tow rope and luggage rack strap	£1 9s 6d
Continental touring kit	£10 5s 0d	Wheelbrace	
Door buffer with reflector		Wheel trim	
Electric defroster	£1 15s 0d	Wing mirrors	From 19s 6d
Emergency windscreen		Wing mirror extension for towing	
Exhaust tail pipe finisher		Wire wheels	£36 17s 6d
Fog lamp	From £13 9s 0d	Wooden gear lever knob	
Fuel filter		Wood-rimmed steering wheel	From £7 10s 0d
Hard-top			
Hard-top to soft-top conversion kit	£18 10s 0d	**Factory-fitted options**	
Hard-top rear window anti-mist panel		Alternator conversion kit	
Headlamp converter for continental driving		Dunlop Gold Seal SP41 145x13 radial tyres	£9 16s 8d
Hub cap medallion		Engine valance kit (from FD 16351 only)	
Hub cap removal tool		Front upper ball joint with grease nipple	
Instrument mounting panel-single gauge		Heater kit	£13 10s 5d
Instrument mounting panel-double gauge		Laminated windscreen	£8 12s 1d
Mud flap kit	£1 7s 6d	Leather seats	
Oil cooler kit		Overdrive	£58 7s 8d
Rubber floor mat		Skid plate	
Safety warning triangle	£1 17s 6d	Steering column lock	
Seat belts (two-point, each)	£4 4s 0d	Sun visors	£1 4s 7d
Seat belts (three-point, each)	£4 14s 6d	Tonneau cover and fittings	£11 4s 4d
Sill protectors		Track rod end with grease nipple	
Spark plug spanner		Whitewall tyres (5.20x13)	£6 2s 11d

and 75lb ft – a useful 12 per cent increase. To cope with the extra go, beefed-up front brakes were now fitted in the form of Girling 14LF items, which offered an increase in swept area from 144sq in to 150sq in. The front coil springs were also stiffened to help reduce roll, while the clutch was strengthened to help improve reliability under pressure.

Increased usability was high on the priority list for Triumph's engineers, especially where the folding roof was concerned. The first two editions of the Spitfire featured a hood that was awkward to erect and just as awkward to stow away again; the Mk3 brought with it (at last) a proper folding roof that didn't require a black belt in origami on the part of the car's owner. Based on the same design as the Herald's, the roof could be raised or stowed in a matter of seconds, once the over-centre catches that mated to the header rail were either engaged or released. This roof re-design necessitated a change of header rail at the same time, while the profile of the raised roof was altered, although this wasn't immediately obvious.

PERIOD MODIFICATIONS

By the time the third-generation Spitfire was introduced, there was still a focus on upgrading carburation, but there was also a fresh fuelling option available through SAH: fuel injection. At the Olympia International Racing Car Show, in January 1967, SAH unveiled its Tecalemit Jackson fuel injection system, fitted to a 1998cc six-cylinder engine. Naturally it was a mechanical set-up rather than electronic, but it was still a system which offered an efficiency that could never be achieved using old-fashioned carburettors, boosting power output by 8-10bhp without any appreciable fuel consumption penalty. Available only on cars fitted with a four-inlet port cylinder head, SAH offered a fuel injection kit for £65, with the promise of over 100bhp from the 1296cc unit.

Of course there were other outfits offering tuned Spitfires, with British Leyland Special Tuning being one. By 1970 its efforts at building and selling hotter Spitfires were becoming more widely publicized, even if those efforts were decidedly underwhelming – largely because the team was overstretched preparing 1800s and big Triumph saloons for competition. However, there was officially a Special Tuning Spitfire option, which consisted of a pair of 1.5in (3.8cm) SUs, firmer front springs and competition-spec dampers all round. Hardly far-reaching maybe, but it spiced up the performance to a small degree while also attempting to increase the understeer a bit.

Within a year, Special Tuning had latched onto the fact that there was money to be made from tweaking road cars as well as competition machines, and with the arrival of the Spitfire MkIV at the end of 1970, a useful opportunity presented itself. The MkIV featured a much better rear suspension design, so Special Tuning began offering this later design to owners of earlier cars, in a bid to stop so many of them exiting the road backwards on tight corners.

When *Motor* put an 11,000-mile Mk3 through its paces (26 June 1971), there was no doubt that the conversion was worthwhile. There was more power and torque with little in the way of a fuel consumption penalty; higher up the speed range there was virtually no penalty at all. The magazine also commented: 'The suspension improvements were quite remarkable; if you don't like your handling at the moment, they are almost essential for sheer peace of mind.'

The parts offered for the conversion (with part numbers) were:

- Twin 1.5in (3.8cm) SUs (99 500201A) – £27.89
- Exhaust manifold (99 5000088) – £15.00
- Adjustable front dampers (99 500012) – £13.80
- Suspension kit (CAJJ 4056) (rear spring, dampers, front anti-roll bar) – £25.50
- Headlamp cowls (99 500101) – £1.25

As well as these go-faster parts, there were also various hard tops available for the Spitfire Mk3. For this facelifted car there was a restyled range offered by Lenham, three of which were removable roofs, while there was also a fixed fastback conversion available. Anyone who opted for the latter had to remove the car's rear bulkhead and reposition the fuel tank, and in return there was two plus two seating available – but with so much work involved it would surely have made more sense for the owner to simply buy a GT6 instead (albeit having to forego the occasional rear seats in the process).

Mk3 owners who wanted less hassle could instead opt for one of the removable roofs, the cheapest of which was £35. That was the self-assembly stage one; the stage two offering at £48 came fully built while the stage three was £55. This range topper came assembled and fitted, plus colour matched to whichever car it was to be fitted.

Ashley's hard top increased practicality thanks to a bigger boot, while a replacement glass fibre nose looked sleeker and improved performance thanks to its lighter weight.

The Mk3 Evolves

The Spitfire Mk3 was given a facelift in October 1969, but in the previous two years it had been the subject of a series of detail changes. Most of these were no more than tweaks here and there – sometimes to reduce production costs rather than improve the product – but many of them were also welcomed by Triumph's customers.

The soft top's retaining catches were changed from over-centre to levers, while a vinyl hood stowage cover became standard equipment for when the roof was down. The hood itself had its lining changed from beige to black (with identical modifications made to the frame too), while the lining of the optional hard top also received a colour change from white to beige and then again to black.

Other changes along the way included the adoption of a 13lb cooling system in place of the previous 7lb one, which necessitated the fitment of a new design of radiator and coolant hoses. The fly-off handbrake was also swapped for a conventional design, while the washers and wipers were redesigned so they were both more effective.

However, it was the October 1969 facelift that would prove to be a turning point for the Spitfire Mk3. After years of outselling the MG Midget and Austin Healey Sprite, the positions reversed in 1969; so improvements were needed for the Triumph to regain the top slot. In reality the changes wrought by Triumph's engineers and designers were hardly what you could call far-reaching, but they had the desired effect so were clearly sufficient.

Keen to show that this was a phase two edition of the Mk3, Triumph started a new numbering sequence for the revised car, the first example carrying chassis number FD75000. Externally, the facelift manifested itself most clearly in the matt black surround for the windscreen frame along with

The move from Spitfire 4 Mk2 to Mk3 saw only slight changes to the cabin; there was now a 120mph speedo (previously 110mph) while the steering wheel measured 15in (38.10cm) across (previously 16in (40.64cm)).

PAINT AND TRIM OPTIONS

From the arrival of the Spitfire Mk3 in February 1967 until August 1968, the same colour schemes were offered as for the GT6 Mk1:

Paint	Interior trim
White	Black or red
Royal Blue	Black or Midnight Blue
Wedgwood Blue	Midnight Blue
Conifer Green	Black
Signal Red	Black

In September 1968, Triumph increased the number of paint colours as well as the range of hues available for the interior trim. The new range comprised of:

White	Black, tan or Matador Red
Royal Blue	Black or Shadow Blue
Wedgwood Blue	Black or Shadow Blue
Valencia Blue	Black or tan
Conifer Green	Black or Matador Red
Signal Red	Black or tan
Damson Red	Black or tan
Jasmine Yellow	Black or tan

Spitfire Mk3s, built between September 1969 and April 1970, were offered with a revised set of interior and exterior colours, as listed below. Then, from May to December 1970, the final Spitfire Mk3s were offered with

the same colour options with the exception of Saffron Yellow in place of Jasmine Yellow, still with black or tan interior trim:

White	Black, tan or Matador Red
Royal Blue	Black or Shadow Blue
Wedgwood Blue	Black or Shadow Blue
Valencia Blue	Black or tan
Laurel Green	Black or Matador Red
Signal Red	Black or tan
Damson Red	Black or tan
Sienna Brown	Black or tan
Jasmine Yellow	Black or tan

a single reversing lamp, which now sat in a revamped surround. The grille was also painted matt black, while the badging was redesigned to fit in with the new Triumph style.

There were minor changes for the cabin too, the most significant being the adoption of a new GT6-style steering wheel, with flat spokes. There was also a zip-out rear window for the soft top and, furthermore, the wheels were now 4.5in wide as standard.

Across the Pond…

While Spitfire developments for the European market were all to be welcomed, Triumph had been forced to introduce a series of changes for North American-market Spitfires – changes that weren't necessarily all good news. Most of the revisions were introduced so the car could continue to comply with legislation, but ultimately they were bad news because they drained all the fun and sportiness from the Spitfire – which didn't really leave it with very much.

It was in 1968 that the new regulations came into force, with 1969 model year cars expected to comply with a raft of new rules. There were two key areas that the regulations aimed to address: safety and emissions. New safety rules were introduced in response to Ralph Nader's 'Unsafe at any

Speed' crusade, in which he vilified car makers for building mobile death traps.

The result was a series of measures such as revised interiors and better lighting: the first to protect occupants in a crash and the second to reduce the likelihood of a collision. Triumph's response to this was to redesign the dashboard, placing the instruments directly ahead of the driver. There were also fixed headrests to reduce the chances of whiplash, while the centre console was fitted with extra knee padding to cushion limbs in the event of an impact.

Triumph also had to comply with the Clean Air Act, which was ratified in 1967, forcing all cars made after 1968 to address this subject. While the safety improvements did nothing to diminish the Spitfire's appeal, the emissions laws pretty much strangled the car altogether, albeit by degrees.

The first stage in cleaning up the Spitfire Mk3 entailed fitting an emission control valve on the inlet manifold, which required a reduction in the compression ratio from 9.0:1 to just 8.5:1 to prevent misfiring. This on its own reduced power from 75bhp to just 68bhp, but things were to get worse. For the 1970 model year, Triumph swapped the twin SU carburettor set-up for a single Stromberg, but thanks to the restoration of a 9.0:1 compression ratio the power and torque figures weren't reduced any further. However, a single carburettor was never going to give the flexibility or response of a twin-carb system, although at least the Spitfire was still capable of cruising at over 90mph (144km/h) – not that it would have had anything in reserve at such velocities.

To distract buyers from the now somewhat lame performance, Triumph introduced a few cosmetic adjustments as a consolation. There was a trio of fresh paint and trim colours and refreshed wheel trims – or for those who were flush with cash, there was also the option of a set of spoked alloy wheels, complete with whitewall tyres. Nice…

PRODUCTION CHANGES

From commission number:

FD 2789	Perfect circle scraper piston rings fitted, to reduce oil consumption.
FD 7301	Running lights under the front bumper changed to an all-in-one unit from a lamp on an aluminium plinth.
FD 11732	The optional wire wheels have hexagonal knock offs instead of the previous winged items.
FD 13980	The hood catch changed to a lever arrangement, instead of the previous clamp-style catches, and a hole introduced to the chrome windscreen cap to accept the lever.
FD 16351	Engine valances become optional again (they were standard on Mk2s).
FD 16482	Handbrake changed from the fly-off type to the conventional ratchet variety.
FD 21967	Larger diameter cooling fins added to the dynamo.
FD 24043	The efficiency of the anti-burst door catches is improved.
FD 29587	The hood's cloth underside and frame are now black instead of beige.
FD 30784	The windscreen wipers are moved further apart.
FD 48653	A new radiator and cap, running at 13psi (up from 7) requires stronger hoses, waterpump seal, and a different temperature sender unit.
FD 75000	The aluminium grille painted black, zip-out rear window, wider 13 x 4.5in wheels fitted, windscreen frame painted black, the rear treatment simplified with a reversing light moved to above the number plate, and Triumph letters on the bonnet replaced by a Spitfire name plate. Also, the Spitfire script replaced with a Triumph plate on the rear, the rocker cover painted silver instead of gold, the airbox from black to silver, and US cars receive a round Spitfire emblem on the bonnet.
FD 80521	The aluminium grille replaced with a black plastic item.
FD 81056	The tail light lenses redesigned, so the flat area at the bottom is taller.
FD 89096	The rear brake cylinder diameter reduced from 3/4in to 5/8in.
Oct 1968	There is a new intake manifold, with a metal plate that holds the carburettor return springs.

SPECIFICATIONS

All Spitfire Mk3s came from the factory with pressed-steel wheels as standard, although wire items were optional. Most owners opted for the standard wheels, but alloys have become very popular in recent years.

Spitfire Mk3 specifications

Build dates	Jan 1967 – Dec 1970
Commission numbers	FD 1 – FD 92803
Engine prefix	FD
Gearbox prefix	FD
Differential prefix	FC
Number built	65,320
Basic price	£582
On the road price	£751 10s 3d

Performance

0-30mph	4.3sec
0-50mph	10.1sec
0-60mph	14.5sec
0-80mph	30.7sec
Max speed in first gear	27mph (43km/h)
Max speed in second gear	47mph (75km/h)
Max speed in third gear	73mph (117km/h)
Top speed	95mph (152km/h)
Standing 1/4-mile	18.5sec
Power to weight	95.5bhp/ton
Typical fuel consumption	31mpg (10ltr/100km)

Dimensions, weights and capacities

Length	12ft 3in (3734mm)
Width	4ft 9in (1448mm)
Height (unladen, roof up)	3ft 11.5in (1206mm)
Wheelbase	6ft 11in (2108mm)
Front track	4ft 1in (1245mm)
Rear track	4ft 0in (1219mm)
Ground clearance (laden)	5in (120mm)
Dry Weight	1570lb (712kg)
Engine oil	8pt (4.7ltr)
Gearbox oil	1.5pt (0.9ltr)
Overdrive oil	2.375pt (1.4ltr)
Differential oil	1pt (0.6ltr)
Cooling system	8pt (4.7ltr)
Fuel tank	8.25gal (37.5ltr)

Engine

Maximum power	75bhp @ 6,000rpm
Maximum torque	75lb ft @ 4,000rpm
Displacement	1296cc
Bore	73.7mm
Stroke	76.0mm
Compression ratio	9.0:1
Oil pressure	50psi at 2,000rpm
Tappet clearance	0.010in
Fuelling	Twin SU 1.25in HS2 carburettors
Firing order	1-3-4-2
Spark plugs	Champion N-9Y
Spark plug gap	0.025in
Distributor	Delco Remy 0200, 7953460
Contact breaker gap	0.015in
Dwell angle	40°/42°
Ignition timing (static)	6° BTDC
Centrifugal advance	0° at 600rpm
	15°/19° at 2,200rpm
	26 1/2° at 5,000rpm
Vacuum advance	0° at 5inHg
	7 1/2°/15° at 12inHg
Ignition coil	Lucas HA 12

Transmission

Clutch	Diaphragm
Clutch diameter	6.5in (16.5cm)
Clutch output shaft	10 splines
Master cylinder diam.	5/8in

Gone was the 1147cc engine; there was now a noticeably more muscular 1296cc unit fitted.

Slave cylinder diam.	7/8in
Gearbox	3-rail
Synchromesh	2nd, 3rd and 4th
Gear ratios	4th = 1.0
	3rd = 1.39
	2nd = 2.16,
	1st = 3.75
	R = 3.75
Optional overdrive	Laycock D-type
Overdrive ratio	0.802
Overdrive gear ratios	4th = 0.80
	3rd = 1.11
Final drive ratio	4.11:1

Brakes and steering

Front	9in solid disc
Caliper type	Girling 14.LF MK3
Swept area	150sq in
Rear	7 x 1.25in drum
Swept area	55sq in
Wheel cylinder diam	3/4in, (5/8in from FC 89096)
Master cylinder diam	5/8in
Steering	Rack and pinion
Turning circle	24ft 2in (7.36m)
Turns between locks	3.75

Suspension, wheels and tyres

Front suspension	Double wishbone
Spring rate	150lbf/in

Camber angle (unladen)	+3° ± 1°
Castor angle (unladen)	3.5° ± 1°
King pin inclination	5.75° ± 1°
Toe	1/16in – 1/8in toe in
Rear suspension	Swing axle
Number of leaves	7
Leaf width	1.75in
Leaf thickness	0.22in
Spring rate	166lbf/in
Toe (unladen)	1/16in-1/8in toe out
Camber angle (unladen)	0.5°
Wheel size (steel)	13 x 3.5 D, (13 x 4.5 from FD 75000)
Optional wire wheels	13 x 4.5 J
Tyre	Dunlop C41, (Dunlop SP41/ SP68 radials optional)
Tyre size	5.20S x 13 (145 SR13 with optional radial tyres)
Tyre pressure	Front: 18psi, 21psi with optional radial tyres)
	Rear: 24psi, (26psi with optional radial tyres)

Electrics

Earth	Negative
Dynamo	Lucas C40-1
Max current output	22 amps
Starter motor	Lucas M35G
Headlights	60/45w

By the time the Mk3 had arrived, Triumph had given up on the Spitfire 4 tag; from now on it was simply the Spitfire.

CHAPTER FIVE

SPITFIRE MkIV (1970–1974)

Although the Spitfire still had a decade to run when the MkIV edition was unveiled in 1971, this would prove to be the last major cosmetic change for the car. However, this was no mere tweak of an old formula; Triumph wrought a raft of changes to the Spitfire that would see the exterior design completely overhauled along with the interior, while the mechanicals were also given a thorough reworking too.

With the Spitfire already almost ten years old, the car was starting to look dated inside and out, while the dynamics also left something to be desired. The swing-axle rear suspension simply wasn't good enough any more to compete with more modern and dynamically capable sports cars, so a root-and-branch rethink of the baby sportster was required.

By the time the MkIV was introduced, the rotoflex-equipped GT6 was already on sale; fitting the same design of rear suspension to the Spitfire would provide the ideal solution. The problem was that, for an economy sports car, the rotoflex set-up was too expensive to be adopted, so a cheaper solution was needed. The answer was a design labelled as the swing-spring system, which was a somewhat ingenious fix.

Earlier Spitfires were notorious for their wheels tucking under during hard cornering, caused by the excessive stiffness of the transverse leaf spring. Reducing the stiffness would simply have led to loose handling at speed, made worse with a heavy load in the car. The answer was to largely split the leaf spring in two and reduce the number of leaves from six to five. The top leaf was still a full-width item, bolted to the top of the differential as before. But now the remaining leaves were cut in half and located either side of the mounting on the top of the axle, resulting in similar levels of stiffness to before, when countering vertical loads. However, when cornering, the leaves could shift slightly, reducing their stiffness and virtually eliminating the wheels tucking under.

The most radical overhaul yet of Michelotti's original lines, the Spitfire MkIV featured a cleaner nose and a more modern tail. The factory hard top was also much more square than before – and consequently less charming.

The MkIV wasn't just a pretty face: Triumph's engineers also overhauled the rear suspension to incorporate a swing spring, to ensure the rear wheels didn't tuck under during hard cornering.

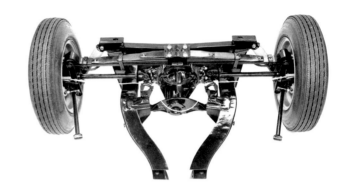

To go with this package, Triumph's engineers also fitted an uprated anti-roll bar at each end of the car: the dynamics were transformed in the process.

Although it was the suspension that needed the greatest attention, Triumph also took the opportunity to standardize some of the components fitted to the 1296cc engine. The unit itself was largely untouched, except for the

WHAT MIGHT HAVE BEEN

Intriguingly, the Spitfire MkIV could have featured an entirely different front-end design, with pop-up headlamps for a much more modern look. As early as 1965 Michelotti came up with a proposal for a six-cylinder Spitfire, called the Fury. It looked sensational, but it would have meant binning the flip-up bonnet, which was a much-loved feature of the Spitfire. There were also doubts about the potential reliability of pop-up headlamps, plus they would have added to the production costs of Triumph's cheap roadster. It was also assumed that US regulations would outlaw pop-up headlamps in the near future, rendering all of Triumph's development work and costs obsolete – so for the MkIV it was essentially a repeat of what had gone before.

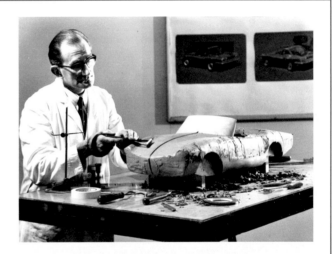

Spitfire MkIV clay model in 1969.

Triumph wouldn't adopt pop-up headlights until the TR7 of 1975 – but this Spitfire prototype of a decade earlier used the same technology, to great effect. It wasn't to be though.

adoption of the con-rods and larger big-end bearings already seen in Triumph's six-cylinder engines, while there was now an alternator instead of the dynamo previously fitted. The crankcase breathing system was also tweaked and a cable-operated accelerator linkage adopted. That was the extent of the changes to the four-cylinder unit – it wouldn't be until the next Spitfire incarnation that more significant changes would be made.

On the face of it, these minor adjustments had led to a significant drop in power for the 1296cc engine in the transition from Mk3 to MkIV. Whereas the earlier Spitfire packed a claimed 75bhp, its replacement could muster all of 63bhp: quite a drop on the face of it. However, things were not all they seemed, as the arrival of the MkIV also saw the adoption of the German DIN system for measuring power outputs. While the Mk3's peak power had been measured without ancillaries fitted, the MkIV's output took them into account.

Despite the power not being reduced for the MkIV, the car was still slower than its predecessor, partly because it featured more standard equipment (raising the kerb weight in the process) while the gearing was also raised, for more relaxed cruising. This higher overall gearing was achieved by

The MkIV was the first Spitfire to feature a fixed windscreen; Triumph also raised the height of the header rail by 2in (5.08cm) during the process. This car was also marked out by the lip spoiler that would be introduced late in the life of the model.

upping the final drive ratio from 4.11:1 to 3.89:1, which also proved to be an aid to high-speed economy. However, Triumph also took the opportunity (at last) to fit synchromesh to first gear – the first time a Spitfire had been so equipped.

It wasn't simply a question of fitting synchromesh though: there was now a new gearbox installed, based closely on the one developed for Triumph's Toledo. Very similar to the one fitted to the GT6 and Vitesse, this fresh transmission also packed a taller first ratio, with 3.5:1 gearing instead of the previous 3.75:1. The result was a reduction in alacrity from the lights, but at last it was possible to get into first gear while on the move – and at the top end things were definitely a step forward, thanks to reduced fuel consumption and noise levels.

A New Look

While the mechanical changes amounted to little more than tinkering, the Spitfire Mk3's exterior design was given a complete overhaul in the metamorphosis to MkIV. As well as a much cleaner front end, there was a redesigned rear too, with lots of other detail changes in between.

The arrival of the Stag in 1970 allowed Michelotti to embark on an overhaul of the Spitfire to turn it into a small-scale version of Triumph's new grand tourer. This was most apparent at the rear, with the new Stag-alike lines, featuring a chrome trim surround, much larger lights (now with integral reversing lamps), flush-fitting boot lid and cut-off wing line. Although the front wings were now de-seamed, there was still a clear seam along the rear wings, but it was now capped with a matt black finishing strip in place of the previous chrome item. The number plate lights were placed in the bumper instead of above the plate and, thanks to the revised wings and boot lid there was fractionally more luggage space than before.

The nose was also given some serious attention, with the flip-up bonnet retained, but without the seams along the top of each front wing. The headlamp surrounds were now painted instead of chrome-plated, and the radiator grille became a more discreet black plastic item. There was also a slimmer bumper fitted, which wrapped more fully around the contours of the nose, and underneath it there were now black plastic under-riders to shrug off parking knocks. Because the front wings were shared with the GT6, the MkIV's wheel arches received the same flaring that was necessary for the GT6's wider wheels and tyres to be accommodated.

OPTIONS

Dealer-fit options

Aerial and speaker installation	
Bolt-on wire wheels (13 x 4.5) up to FH 60000	£47.50
Bonnet lock kit	£2.58
Brake servo kit	£15.00
Cigarette lighter (push down type)	£0.55
Cigarette lighter (pull out type)	£1.31
Continental touring kit	
De-icer aerosol	£0.26
Fire extinguisher	£1.25
Grease gun	£0.50
Hard-top kit (in primer)	From £36.56
Headlamp conversion mask	
Hood stowage cover	
Lamps (spot and fog): round pre-focus	£3.60
Lamps (spot and fog): round quartz halogen	£4.90
Luggage rack	£5.50
Mud flaps	From £1.28
Oil cooler	
Rubber floor mats	From £0.53
Seat covers	From £4.73
Skid plate	
Soft-top conversion kit	From £18.50
Touch-up paints (1/4-pint tin)	From £0.29
Tow bar attachment	From £5.00
Warning triangle	£1.98
Windscreen anti-mist panels	From £0.63
Wing mirrors	From £1.25
Wooden gear knob	£0.88
Wooden steering wheel	From £7.50

Factory-fitted options

Dunlop SP 145-SR13 radial tyres (up to FH 38271 only)	£10.00
Competition DS11 brake pads	
Front upper ball joint with grease nipple	
Grease nipple for rear bearing housing and front vertical link	
Head rests (after FH 60000 only)	
Laminated windscreen	£8.75
Leather seats (up to FH 50000 only)	
Overdrive	£68.75
Tonneau cover (standard from 1974)	£11.41
Toughened (Zebra-Zoned) windscreen	£8.75
Whitewall tyres	£6.25
Wire wheels	£47.50

	Ex-Works Price £ s. d.	Purchase Tax £ s. d.	Ex-Works Total Price £ s. d.
Triumph GT6 Mk.3			
Expanded Vinyl Trim	970 0 0 £970·00	298 13 7 £298·68	1268 13 7 £1268·68
Optional Extras:			
Overdrive	55 0 0 £55·00	16 16 1 £16·80	71 16 1 £71·80
Occasional Rear Seat	15 0 0 £15·00	4 11 8 £4·58	19 11 8 £19·58
Wire Wheels	38 0 0 £38·00	11 12 3 £11·61	49 12 3 £49·61
Triumph Spitfire Mk.4			
Expanded Vinyl Trim Soft Top Model	753 0 0 £753·00	232 7 6 £232·37	985 7 6 £985·37
(Hard Top available at extra cost as 'Stanpart' Accessory)			
Hard Top Model	782 0 0 £782·00	241 4 9 £241·24	1023 4 9 £1023·24
(Soft Top available at extra cost as 'Stanpart' Accessory)			
Optional Extras:			
Tonneau Cover	9 2 6 £9·13	2 15 9 £2·79	11 18 3 £11·92
Overdrive	55 0 0 £55·00	16 16 1 £16·80	71 16 1 £71·80
High Impact Inter-Layer Laminated Windscreen	7 0 0 £7·00	2 2 9 £2·14	9 2 9 £9·14
Wire Wheels	38 0 0 £38·00	11 12 3 £11·61	49 12 3 £49·61
5·20 × 13 Whitewall Tyres	5 0 0 £5·00	1 10 7 £1·53	6 10 7 £6·53
Dunlop S.P. Tyres	8 0 0 £8·00	2 8 11 £2·45	10 8 11 £10·45
Triumph Stag			
Expanded Vinyl Trim Soft Top Model	1650 0 0 £1650·00	506 9 2 £506·46	2156 9 2 £2156·46
Hard Top Model	1685 0 0 £1685·00	517 3 1 £517·15	2202 3 1 £2202·15
Hard and Soft Top Model	1725 0 0 £1725·00	529 7 6 £529·37	2254 7 6 £2254·37
Optional Extras:			
Overdrive	55 0 0 £55·00	16 16 1 £16·80	71 16 1 £71·80
Borg-Warner Transmission	80 0 0 £80·00	24 8 11 £24·45	104 8 11 £104·45

All prices of extras shown are for Factory-fitted equipment only

CONDITIONS OF SALE

The Standard-Triumph Group reserves the right to vary the ex-works price of all products manufactured by it at any time, and all goods are invoiced from the factory at the ex-works price current on the day of delivery.

The Manufacturer further reserves the right on the sale of any vehicle to make before delivery without notice alterations and departures from the specification, design and equipment detailed in its various publications. The technical data and other information contained in this publication have been obtained from authoritative sources and while intended to give a fair description of the vehicle and its capabilities, its accuracy is not guaranteed, nor does the Manufacturer accept any liability for errors or omissions.

Genuine STANPART spares and accessories are available throughout the world. In the U.K. alone there are over 1500 STANPART stockists.

'STANPART' AND 'UNIPART' ACCESSORIES

All accessories recommended by Standard-Triumph Sales are individually tested for their quality and reliability by our Engineering team. This ensures that they are manufactured to the same high quality, compatible with the car of your choice. The following is a brief selection — a more detailed brochure is available and can be obtained through your local Standard-Triumph dealer.

Description	Price each s. d.	£
Always Safety First — Seat Belts — To suit all Models		
Anti-mist Panels — 4 sizes .. .. from	12 6	0·63
Badge Bars — All Models except Sports .. from	3 10 0	3·50
Bonnet Lock Kit — Herald Range, Spitfire & GT6	2 11 6	2·58
Brake Kits — Powerstop — Herald, Vitesse, GT6, TR5, Spitfire & 1300	15 0 0	15·00
Cigarette Lighter — Push down type	* 11 0	0·55
Pull-out type	1 6 3	1·31
De-icer — Aerosol	5 3	0·26
Fire Extinguisher — Aerosol	1 5 0	1·25
Gear Lever Knob — Wooden	17 6	0·88
Grease Gun — Aerosol	10 0	0·50
Hard Top Conversions — In primer .. from	36 11 3	36·56
Heated Backlight — Herald, Vitesse, GT6 1, 1300 & 2000 .. .. from	11 8 0	11·40
Lamps — Spot and Fog:		
Prefocus — Round	3 12 0	3·60
Quartz Halogen — Round	4 18 0	4·90
Rectangular	5 7 0	5·35
Reverse Lamp Kits .. .. from	2 5 0	2·25
Inspection Lamp - Magnetic	1 5 0	1·25
Parking Lamp	10 6	0·53
Luggage Racks — Roof and Boot fitting	5 10 0	5·50
Mats, Rubber, Front & Rear .. .. from *	10 6	0·53
Mirrors, Wing — Selection .. .. from	1 5 0	1·25
Mudflaps — Front & Rear except TR5 & TR6	1 5 6	1·28
Petrol Locking Caps — Herald Range, 1300 & 2000 .. .. from	1 6 6	1·33
Radiator Blinds — Herald & 13/60, 1300 & 2000 Mk.I .. .. from	4 7 6	4·38
Safety Warning Triangle	1 19 6	1·98
Seat Covers — Stretch Nylon .. .. from	4 14 6	4·73
Soft Top — Conversions .. .. from	18 10 0	18·50
Steering Wheels — Wood Rim .. .. from	7 10 0	7·50
Towing Equipment .. .. .. from	5 0 0	5·00
Touch up paint — ¼pt tins — All colours .. from	5 10	0·29

Car Radios : Complete selection by Radiomobile — consult your distributor and ask for TRIUMPH Radiomobile. * Plus Purchase Tax.

Please refer to your distributor or dealer for details of fitting charges for these items.

Ref: 126/1/71/100M

TRIUMPH   65/3

PRICE LIST

HOME MARKET 11th JANUARY 1971

PAINT AND TRIM OPTIONS

Throughout 1971, the Spitfire MkIV's colour options were much the same as for those of the outgoing Mk3. However, Sapphire Blue was offered in place of Royal Blue for the paintwork, while there was also now an extra interior colour offered: Silver Grey.

Paint	Interior trim
White	Black, tan, Shadow Blue or Matador Red
Sapphire Blue	Silver Grey or Shadow Blue
Wedgwood Blue	Black or Shadow Blue
Valencia Blue	Black or tan
Laurel Green	Black, tan or Matador Red
Signal Red	Black or tan
Damson Red	Black, tan or Silver Grey
Sienna Brown	Black or tan
Saffron Yellow	Black or tan

Once again the colour options were overhauled between January and August 1972. Matador Red interior trim was no longer available, while the exterior colours were given a thorough shake up.

White	Black, tan or Shadow Blue
Sapphire Blue	Black, Silver Grey or Shadow Blue
Emerald Green	Black or Silver Grey
Damson Red	Black, tan or Silver Grey
Pimento Red	Black
Sienna Brown	Tan
Saffron Yellow	Black

There was yet another overhaul of the colour options for the period running between September 1972 and January 1973. Buyers could choose between:

White	Black, Chestnut or Shadow Blue
Sapphire Blue	Black or Shadow Blue
French Blue	Black
Emerald Green	Black
Mallard Green	Black or tan
Carmine Red	Black or tan
Pimento Red	Black or Chestnut
Sienna Brown	Black or tan

For the last eighteen months of production (February 1973 until September 1974) there was an increase in the number of combinations offered, with all those on the previous chart still being available. New to the range was Magenta with black trim, or Mimosa Yellow with black or Chestnut trim.

Triumph also made a raft of other detail changes, including fresh badging throughout and redesigned road wheels. Whereas earlier editions of the Spitfire had been differentiated by Arabic script, for the fourth incarnation of the model there was a move to Roman numerals, presumably to separate this model from the original Spitfire 4. Meanwhile, a rectangular Mazak badge was placed on the leading edge of the bonnet and similar emblems were located on the trailing edge of each rear wing. There were fresh wheels too: GT6-style items were fitted, with black plastic centre caps.

The doors also now featured flush-fitting handles and window glass that was squared off at the top trailing edge. To accommodate this it was necessary to redesign the hard top as well as the fabric roof, the former now being much squarer to reflect the more angular boot design. There were also opening rear quarter-lights incorporated in the hard top: they'd never been available before, and they were very useful for improving the cabin's ventilation.

Until this point, the Spitfire's windscreen had been removable: this had always been a car aimed at motorsport enthusiasts who wanted to compete on a budget. By the time the MkIV arrived though, the Spitfire had grown up and it had become aimed at those who wanted to drive something sporty on a day-to-day basis. To that end the windscreen became a fixed part of the scuttle and the header rail was also raised by 2in (5.08cm), in a bid to improve cabin headroom.

The interior was spruced up in a variety of other ways too: it had been allowed to date quite badly and a thorough overhaul was desperately needed. Gone was the central binnacle containing the instrumentation, to be replaced by gauges in front of the driver. This was effectively the same

Although the 1296cc engine was carried over from the Mk3, the MkIV's unit was revised significantly. It was also mated to a gearbox with revised ratios, while the back axle gearing was also adjusted to give more relaxed cruising.

as the late US-spec Mk3 Spitfire dash, which also featured flush switchgear to comply with US regulations. The dash top was now covered with black leather-cloth, while the door trims were redesigned to accommodate flush-fitting door handles.

Also carried over from the final Federal Mk3 was a new seat design, but without the head restraints which were standard on US-market cars. What was fitted to all Spitfires however, was a heater and a set of seat belts, along with a pair of sun visors: earlier Spitfires hadn't featured these as standard. Overdrive was still an extra-cost option though: when specified, it was now activated using a gear knob-mounted sliding switch, instead of via the column-mounted stalk of earlier cars.

Developing the MkIV

Triumph had made a great job of updating the Spitfire in the transition from Mk3 to MkIV, but there was naturally room for improvement. The first changes made were more about cutting production costs though, as Triumph elected to fit the Toledo's cylinder head, in a bid to standardize parts. With its bigger valves, revised porting and slightly milder camshaft, emissions were reduced in the process, but so

too was performance – the peak power output was cut from 63bhp (at 6,000rpm) to 61bhp at 5,500rpm, while the maximum available torque also went down by 2lb ft (from 70lb ft to 68lb ft).

These changes came in from FH 25000, and at about the same time Triumph also began to fit a bright plastic trim around the windscreen in place of the stainless steel item previously used. A few months later there was another change, this time to 155-section tyres in place of the 145-section previously fitted. However, it would be at FH 50000 that such a raft of changes would be introduced that Triumph were justified in announcing a facelift for the Spitfire.

Most of the changes focused on the interior, which received a wood-trim dash in place of the previous black vinyl affair. The instruments were also updated with clearer faces, while the steering wheel was reduced in diameter by half an inch: it now measured 14.5in (36.83cm) across. There was also a new boss, incorporating the horn push, which was surrounded by fake stitching – the logo in the centre was also switched from the previous Triumph shield to the Triumph name.

Apart from the adoption of reclining seats (which were also available with detachable head rests), that was the extent of the interior changes. However, there were several other useful upgrades introduced at the same time,

The Triumph Spitfire Mk. 4. Every compact inch a sports car in the Great British tradition. A car that echoes your go-ahead personality; that is not only fun to drive, great to be seen in, and so good to look at, but immensely practical and reliable.

This is a design that has been honed and perfected over the years to offer you a unique style of open sportscar motoring. So put the fun back into your travels, and enjoy the real pleasures and sensations of open air motoring in the Spitfire.

Lowering the hood when the sun shines is a quick, single-handed job. Then take off for the country, just for the sheer fun of it.

With a touring fuel consumption of 38.2 m.p.g. (*Motor Road Test*), you can enjoy *both* sports car performance and outstanding economy. The four-speed, all synchro gearbox is a delight to use. The gear lever is exactly where you would expect to find it, just a handspan from the steering wheel, encouraging fast and positive changes. Available as an optional extra is an overdrive unit functioning on top and third gears, and operated by a simple flick-switch let into the top of the gear knob. It enables you to make the most of the Spitfire's performance whilst enjoying the additional benefits of even greater fuel economy and more relaxed cruising.

A lively performer in any company, that's the Spitfire.

In the sun or in the wet, the Spit never runs out of fun

Predictably, Triumph continued to emphasize the Spitfire's ability to escape real life; let's face it, that's what marketing is all about! However, it also made capital of the redesigned rear suspension, and how it transformed the car's dynamic abilities.

PRESS REACTION

Motor's review of the MkIV (7 August 1971) was a real mixed bag, but seemed to be broadly in favour of Triumph's revised sportster. Early in the piece the tester commented: 'It is now one of the most attractive sports cars about, with nothing to reveal its age', then saying how unrefined the engine was, while the performance also wasn't great. The magazine also said: 'The gear change is rather awkward… Rather dead steering detracts from the car's sporting appeal though by absolute standards it's not too bad… Much more disappointing is the number of rattles and shakes which emphasize the late 1950s origin of the chassis design'. Despite all this, the verdict ran thus: 'If you are in the market for an attractive economical open two-seater, the latest version is probably better value than ever.'

In its August 1971 issue, *Hot Car*'s reception to the MkIV Spitfire was anything but hot – at least in terms of performance. Its review of TRW 854J focused initially on the lack of urge available, yet it went on to say: 'It's really the best Spitfire yet, despite the lack of performance.' Such an unexpected verdict was due to the tidier styling and greater usability thanks to a better hood design, improved rear suspension and redesigned dashboard.

In its June 1971 edition, *Car* tested the Spitfire MkIV against MG's Midget, with the Triumph coming out on top by quite a margin. Not only did it score for its handling, space, performance and road holding, the only area in which it was marked down was its ride. Okay, so neither model was at the cutting edge of sports car development, but *Car*'s testers were happy to sum up with: 'The much more modern Spitfire should be good for a few more years yet – especially with the boost of a 1500 engine.'

And still the praise was forthcoming, although some road testers were less enthusiastic than before.

one of which was to replace the D-Type overdrive with the stronger J-Type unit. This brought with it a slight increase in gearing, helping to reduce engine revs at high speed, thus cutting fuel consumption – although any gains were marginal.

The rear track was also increased by 2in (5.08cm), helping to improve stability when cornering, while a redesigned fuel tank was fitted from FH 50000. However, this wasn't really a step forward as the old tank could carry 8.25gal (37.50ltr) while the new one could accommodate just 7.25gal (32.95ltr), thus reducing the Spitfire's range significantly. Still, this mid-term facelift was generally very well received, which was just as well because apart from the introduction of a front lip spoiler from FH 60000, this was the only development the MkIV would get – until the arrival of the 1500.

To go with the fresh new lines there was also a completely new style of factory-supplied hard top.

CHANGES OVER Mk3 (FROM THE COMMISSION NUMBER GIVEN)

FH 25501	Vacuum advance tube changed from metal to black plastic
FH 28430	7.25gal (32.95ltr) fuel tank replaces 8.25gal (37.5ltr)
FH 30795	'ECC' label fixed to the right-hand A-post (Non-US cars only)
FH 38271	155 x 13 SR radial tyres fitted
FH 40001	US cars get smaller plastic reservoirs on brake master cylinder
FH 50000	US cars (with US-style commission numbers from FM1, starting in February 1973), get a 1500cc engine, reclining seats, flame retardant interior trim, coarse-grain vinyl, a wood-grain dash, chrome bezels on the instruments, green-tinted lights illuminating the speedometer and tachometer, while the windscreen wiper knob logo is revised. Also, there is now a TR6-style steering wheel containing the Triumph letters, improved rear suspension, a night dimming brake lamp relay (to reduce the intensity of the brake lights at night or when the side lights are on) and a front spoiler is fitted as standard. Fuel and vacuum lines re-routed to the rear of the engine, the left-hand engine valance no longer attached to the suspension turret, drive shafts lengthened by 1in (2.5cm) (along with the handbrake cable and brake hoses), while brake hoses now attached to the rear cylinders via a metal pipe (previously directly connected), radius arms lengthened, their mounting brackets changed, and the front anti-roll bar diameter increased to 7/8in
FH 51203	Badge on the optional wire wheels changed to the British Leyland logo rather than the name 'Spitfire' around the circumference
FH 53956	Fuel line between the pump and carburettor now attached to the bell housing
FH 53211	Timing pointer changed to a graduated timing plate
FH 60000	Front of the chassis redesigned to meet front impact regulations, the black rubber seal around the tail lights changed to a cheaper sponge rubber seal, while the plastic pipe between the carburettor and fuel pump is changed to a metal item. Meanwhile, the interior light switch in the door now metal rather than plastic, optional overdrive changed to stronger the J-type unit (it was previously a D-type) and the overdrive now activated via a switch on the gear knob – previously on steering column
FH 60977	Upgraded Lucas 16 ACR alternator fitted, and the ignition wires now exit the distributor at 90°
FH 62271	Pair of rubber bumpers (water drainage) are added to the corners of the boot lid to help prevent rust
FH 63214	Extra support bracket added to prevent exhaust downpipe and/or exhaust gasket failure

PERIOD MODIFICATIONS

Naturally you could still tune your MkIV to improve the handling or liberate some extra horses, but by the time this fourth incarnation of the Spitfire hit the roads, there was a noticeable vogue for aftermarket hard tops. Numerous outfits offered such products, such as Ashley, One Skid, Perks & Dolman plus Omnibob.

However, two of the most popular suppliers were Lenham along with Williams & Pritchard. In the case of the former there was a £49 option complete with moulded-in leathercloth effect or, for those who were feeling more flush, for £66 there was the more luxurious Torado, with its lift-out roof panel. Meanwhile, Williams & Pritchard offered a fastback-styled hard top, at £79. This increased boot space and made the car look more individual, but it looked like the tacked-on top that it was; this wasn't something that gave your Spitfire the grace of a GT6.

For those seriously lacking in the taste department, there was even the option to fit windows in the roof for an extra £8: go the whole hog and it was possible to blow another three quid on tinted glass all round, which would have looked particularly odd with the rest of the car featuring standard clear glass only.

SAH continued to increase its tuning options, with a new suspension set-up introduced in summer 1971 which was suitable for any Spitfire built so far – including the MkIV. What SAH did was to copy the Vitesse 2-litre Mk2's rotoflex rear suspension design and offer a kit of parts to convert any Herald, Spitfire, Vitesse or GT6 to the same specification. Spitfire buyers could fork out £68 for the kit and fit it themselves, or SAH would do all the work including setting everything up for an extra £30. When *Hot Car* converted its own Vitesse to the new set-up, the results were impressive and came highly recommended, but it's doubtful that many of these kits were ever supplied.

Another MkIV upgrade that proved surprisingly unpopular, even after the car had been available for several years, was a Dolomite 1850 engine transplant. Despite the engine and transmission more or less slotting straight in, few attempted the swap. However, *Hot Car* covered the work involved in its August 1975 edition, when reader Harry Boswell performed the operation on SBM 551J. With these mechanicals, the Spitfire offered decent economy, more relaxed cruising and much better refinement than the standard Spitfire – but despite the conversion being performed in April 1973, little more than two years later the car was being sold on.

An alternative to seeking extra power was to reduce your Spitfire's weight, which is where DJ Sportscars came in. Recognizing that these cars could rot for England – or were frequently crashed by inexperienced owners – the company offered a range of glass fibre panels to reduce weight, repair costs and the chances of further corrosion. For £32.50 you could fit a GT6-style bonnet, complete with power bulge, while a fresh boot lid was just £4.95 and replacement rear wings were all of £3.50 apiece. What all this did for body shell rigidity isn't recorded of course…

Smooth and swift —that's what Dolomite power does for Harry's Spitfire. It's an easy swop

TRANSPLANT SPECIAL

The main well of the sump just clears the cross-member. A one-off exhaust system was made up incorporating an SAH Spitfire silencer

The forward-most portion of the sump had to be dressed back ever so slightly to clear the steering rack, which is mounted as standard

Engine mountings retain the Spitfire chassis brackets and rubbers. Fabricated engine-bracket bolts to the standard holes in the block

To clear the chassis rail the oil filter casing had to be shortened and HB Viva filter element used. The accessibility is pretty good

To clear the back end of the engine the bulkhead had to be dressed back at one point and the tunnel cover 'bulged' with glass-fibre

The Dolomite manifold would have fitted but downpipe was in the wrong place, so Harry made up his own with the downpipe at centre

Courier van radiator corrected cooling problems. Dispensing with engine-driven fan for electric meant a shorter fan-belt, from 100E

The gearlever is a little further back than standard. The speedometer and tacho are both out of the Dolomite and fit unobtrusively

SPITFIRE DOLLY MIXTURE

'Your driving is above average, but you should have used the horn down the twisty lanes and I didn't like the way you crossed your hands on the wheel at that last bend'. No folks, its not an action replay of my driving test, but the aftermath of a test drive in Harry Boswell's Spitfire.

I'm pretty used to driving, and passing judgement on various readers cars, but I'm not so used to having my own driving judged by said reader. But then I wasn't about to get shirty about it since Harry used to be a driving test examiner before entering his present occupation as a TV engineer.

If there is one thing that driving test examiners and TV engineers must have in common, it certain finicky attention when H...

four weeks in Harry's garage, with an engine and gearbox swiped from a crashed Dolomite saloon. On the face of it, fitting an 1850cc slant-four engine in place of the little Spitfire 1300 unit would seem to be a pretty major undertaking, but in practice it doesn't work out like that, and most of the mods involved are of a detail nature.

What helps is that the Dolomite gearbox is externally identical to the Spitfire unit, and also the Dolly engine is used in the same basic bodyshell as the Toledo, of which, of course, the engine is the same basic unit as the Spitfire's.

What this all adds up to is clearance problems ...... minor. On the ...... bulkhead ...

was GT6 with a spacer.

The mods involved are pretty well covered in the pix above. When all was said and done, the overall weight of the car was just 16 lbs more than standard, thanks largely to the alloy head of the Dolomite engine.

Since it was converted in April 1973 the car has been mainly used for local running about by Harry's pretty Chinese wife (who like Harry, is also somewhat of a driving expert). A...... sumption ha...... perfe......

MINILITE NEW SPORTS WHEEL

Fit the new Minilite alloy Sports Wheel – then step back and watch the crowds gather! There's so much more to Minilites than sheer good looks. The exclusive new design has taken 4 years to perfect and incorporates all the unique experience that Minilite have gained from circuit racing and rally wheels.

If your car is one of those listed it will take the new Minilite 13" X 5" wheel.

They're only £34·80 for a set of four, complete with wheelnuts or bolts, bright hubcaps and self-adhesive balance weights.

MINILITE light, strong and safe for only £8·70

To fit these cars ...

B.L.M.C.
Marina
Midget
Sprite
B.M.W
1600
2002
CHRYSLER ROOTES
Avenger
180
Plymouth Cricket
Sunbeam Alpine
Sunbeam Tiger
DATSUN
1300
1600 SS
100A Cherry
160 180 Bluebird
FIAT
124 124 S
125 128
850 Coupe Spyder
FORD
Capri
Corsair
Cortina Mk. 2 and 3
Escort
Pinto
LOTUS
Elan (4 Stud)
Europa
Lotus 7

OPEL
1900 GT
1600 Manta
1900 Manta
Olympia
Rallye Kadett
Rallye Manta
Rekord 'C'
SIMCA
1000 Special
1204 Special
1100 Standard
TOYOTA
Celica
Corona Mk. II
Corolla
1200 SL
1600 S
TRIUMPH
2000
G T 6
Herald 13/60
2·5 P I
Spitfire
Toledo
Vitesse
VAUXHALL
Firenza
Victor
Viva

Please send me _____ set(s) of MINILITE SPORTS WHEELS to Fit my car. Make ...

NAME
ADDRESS

SPITFIRE MkIV SPECIFICATIONS

Build dates	Nov 1970 – Jan 1974
Commission numbers	FH 3 – FH 64,995
Engine prefix	FH
Gearbox prefix	FH
Differential prefix	FH
Number built	70,021
Basic price	£814
On the road price	£1,019.38

Performance

0-30mph	4.8sec
0-50mph	11.0sec
0-60 mph	12.5sec, (14.5sec from 1972)
0-80mph	33.3sec
Max speed in first gear	31mph (49km/h)
Max speed in second gear	50mph (80km/h)
Max speed in third gear	78mph (125km/h)
Max speed in overdrive third	90mph (144km/h)
Max speed in fourth gear	90mph (144km/h)
Max speed in overdrive fourth	87mph (140km/h)
Top speed	90mph (144.km/h)
Standing 1/4-mile	19sec
Power to weight	76.9bhp/ton, (74.5 bhp/ton from 1972)
Typical fuel consumption	32mpg (11ltr/100km)

Dimensions, weights and capacities

Length	12ft 5in (3785mm)
Width	4ft 10.5in (1486mm)
Height (unladen)	3ft 8.5in (1206mm)
Wheelbase	6ft 11in (2108mm)
Front track	4ft 1in (1245mm)
Rear track	4ft 0in (1219mm) [4ft 2in (1270mm) from 1973]

Although the badging said Spitfire IV, this model was still marketed as the Spitfire MkIV – which (confusingly) was quite distinct from the Spitfire 4. It also marked a move to the use of Roman numerals.

Ground clearance (laden)	5in (120mm)
Dry weight	1638lb (743kg)
Engine oil	8pt (4.7ltr)
Gearbox oil	1.5pt (0.9ltr)
Overdrive oil	2.5pt (1.5ltr)
Differential oil	1pt (0.6ltr)
Cooling system	8pt (4.7ltr)
Fuel tank	8.25gal (37.5ltr) [7.25gal (33ltr) from FH 28430]

Engine

Maximum power	63bhp @ 6,000rpm (61bhp @ 5,500rpm from 1972)
Maximum torque	70lb ft @ 3,500rpm (68lb ft @ 2,900rpm from 1972)
Displacement	1296cc
Bore	73.7mm
Stroke	76.0mm
Compression ratio	9.0:1
Oil pressure	50psi at 2,000rpm
Tappet clearance	0.010in
Fuelling	Twin SU 1.25in HS2E carburettors
Firing order	1-3-4-2
Spark plugs	Champion N-9Y
Spark plug gap	0.025in
Distributor	Delco Remy D204 -7953460, (7992128 from 1972)
Contact breaker gap	0.016in
Dwell angle	38°/40°
Ignition timing – static	6° BTDC, (8° BTDC from 1972)
Centrifugal advance	0° at 800rpm 15°/19° at 2,200rpm, (11°/15° at 2,500rpm from 1972) 26 1/2° at 5,000rpm, (20° at 5,000rpm from 1972)
Vacuum advance	0° at 5in Hg, (0° at 3in Hg from 1972) 7 1/2/15° at 12in Hg, (12° at 20in Hg from 1972)
Ignition coil	Lucas 16.C6, (Lucas 15.C6 from 1974)

Transmission

Clutch	Diaphragm

Clutch diam.	6.5in (16.5cm)	**Suspension, wheels and tyres**	
Clutch output shaft	10 splines	Front suspension	Double wishbone
Master cylinder diameter	5/8in	Spring rate	150lbf/in
Slave cylinder diameter	7/8in	Camber angle (unladen)	+3° ± 1°
Gearbox	3-rail	Castor angle (unladen)	4° ± 1°
Synchromesh	All gears	King pin inclination	5.75° ± 1°
Gear ratios	4th = 1.0	Toe	1/16in–1/8in toe in
	3rd = 1.39	Rear suspension	Swing spring
	2nd = 2.16	Number of leaves	5
	1st = 3.5	Leaf width	1.75in
	R = 3.99	Leaf thickness	0.38in (0.25in bottom two leaves)
Optional overdrive	Laycock D-type, (Laycock J-type from 1974)	Spring rate	110lbf/in
Overdrive ratio	0.802, (0.797 from 1974)	Toe (unladen)	1/32in–3/32in toe out
Overdrive gear ratios	4th = 0.80 (0.79 from 1974), 3rd = 1.11 (1.1 from 1974)	Camber angle (unladen)	−1° ± 1°
		Wheel size (steel)	13 x 4.5 J
Final drive ratio	3.89:1	Optional wire wheels	13 x 4.5 J
		Tyres	Dunlop C41, (SP68/G800 from FH 38271)
Brakes and steering			
Front brakes	9in solid disc	Tyre size	5.20S x 13, (155SR x 13 from FH 38271)
Calliper type	Girling 14.LF		
Swept area	150 sq in	Tyre pressure	Front: 21psi
Rear brakes	7 x 1.25in drum	Rear: 26psi	
Swept area	55 sq in		
Wheel cylinder diameter	5/8in	**Electrics**	
Master cylinder diameter	5/8in	Earth	Negative
		Alternator	Lucas 15ACR, (Lucas 16ACR from 1974)
Steering			
Type	Rack and pinion	Max current output	28 amps, (34 amps from 1974)
Turning circle	24ft 2in (7.36m)	Starter motor	Lucas M35J
Turns between locks	3.75	Headlights	60/45w

The transition from Mk3 to MkIV represented the most far-reaching set of design changes the Spitfire would see in its five-iteration lifespan.

CHAPTER SIX

SPITFIRE 1500 (1974–1980)

The world was a topsy turvy place in the 1970s, and nowhere was this more evident than in the British motor industry. However, the fact that the Spitfire 1500 enjoyed two débuts, two years apart on either side of the Atlantic, was not really British Leyland's fault. Confused? I'll explain…

While all early editions of the Spitfire MkIV were fitted with Triumph's 1296cc engine, emissions control equipment on Federal versions of the car took its toll on power, and hence performance, in an alarming fashion. British Leyland's solution was to introduce in late 1972 (for North American cars only) the 1493cc powerplant, which had been introduced in the front-wheel drive 1500 saloon in 1970. A stroked version of the 1296cc engine, this larger engine could muster all of 57bhp in smog-controlled US form. That might not sound much, but it represented a 20 per cent power boost over the final US 1296cc Spitfires, which offered a frankly pathetic 48bhp.

Although these 1493cc US Spitfires had always been badged and sold as Spitfire 1500s, they were in effect nothing more than MkIV editions with a larger engine. It wasn't until the arrival of the 'real' Spitfire 1500 in December 1974 that a whole host of much-needed improvements were incorporated into what would prove to be the final incarnation of Triumph's most affordable two-seater.

Under the skin there were further changes, the most significant of which was the adoption of the 1493cc engine for all Spitfires from now on. However, being a stroked version of the unit fitted to the Spitfire Mk3 and MkIV, it didn't look much different under that large flip-up bonnet. Indeed, apart from a fresh exhaust manifold that fed a pair of downpipes, it wasn't immediately apparent that any such transformation had taken place.

However, you only had to get behind the wheel and it was clear that something had happened under the bonnet,

Bearing in mind that the last of the MkIVs featured that subtle lip spoiler, there wasn't really much to separate the 1500 from its predecessor – aesthetically. The big news was under the bonnet as well as in the cabin.

The Italian-market 1500 looks very much like those supplied for UK buyers. Except it
had just a two-speed gearbox; one for flat-out and another for stationary...

PAINT AND TRIM OPTIONS

All Spitfire 1500s built up to February 1977 could be ordered
with the following colour schemes:

White	Black or beige
French Blue	Black
Delft Blue	Black or beige
British Racing Green	Black or beige
Java Green	Black or beige
Carmine Red	Black or beige
Pimento Red	Black
Maple Brown	Black or beige
Mimosa Yellow	Black or beige
Topaz Orange	Black or beige

The final Spitfire 1500s, made between March 1977 and
August 1980, were offered with an almost entirely different
set of paint and trim colours from before, comprising of:

Leyland White	Black or beige
Pageant Blue	Black or beige
Brooklands Green	Beige
Carmine Red	Beige
Vermilion Red	Black
Russet Brown	Beige
Inca Yellow	Black

PRESS REACTION

Unsurprisingly, the British press tested the 1500 later than their US counterparts: *Autocar* reported on the new arrival in its 7 December 1974 edition, but didn't test the car until March 1975. Almost all of the first page of the review focused on the extra power and higher gearing of the 1500, as well as how jolly marvellous it all was, aside from a bit less flexibility than was ideal in overdrive top. Still, that meant the car was much more relaxing to drive at sustained high speeds. The test focused very much on the car's dynamics, which generally got the thumbs up aside from the lack of ride comfort, but there were a few observations about the car's usability – and lack of it. To be fair, the car was considered to be generally well thought through, but the ventilation wasn't and neither was the glove box, which was not lockable. Still, according to the reviewer, 'the handbrake has a pleasingly shaped hand grip', which was nice…

Autocar was clearly keen on the Spitfire 1500, as they also group-tested it against thirteen potential rivals, including the Jensen Healey, Lotus Europa, MGB, Morgan 4/4 and Datsun 260Z. Despite its age, one reviewer (Maurice Smith) still chose the Triumph as his car of the day, proving that perhaps it wasn't that long in the tooth.

The same magazine's Peter Windsor also ran a Spitfire 1500 as a long-term test car. Unsurprisingly, a year in the car simply reinforced the verdict of the original road test: that this was a car that had been usefully updated and improved and which still looked good, despite the age of the Spitfire marque. However, clocking up 12,000 miles in that year showed that Triumph still couldn't screw together its cars particularly well. Not only did the car reek of petrol after refuelling, but the exhaust proved fragile, the rear hub bearings had to be repacked and the ignition system overhauled – and all within the first 6,000 miles.

Road & Track got its hands on a 1977 Spitfire 1500 and came away impressed by the car's honesty, economy and interior design. In his report, Thomas Bryant said: 'The Spitfire is still a kick to drive on a sunny day with the top down and a clear, winding road stretching before you. The fully independent suspension is better now than it was on the first Spitfires as the swing axles at the rear are kept under better control to prevent jacking up in hard cornering… The Spitfire is an ideal choice.'

However, the same magazine had been less keen on the Spitfire when it had compared a 1500, a year earlier, with the Fiat 124 Spider, Fiat X1/9, MGB Roadster, MG Midget and Triumph TR7. Although it was the Midget that came last, the Spitfire fared little better – at least its stablemate the TR7 proved more popular. *Road & Track*'s testers felt that: 'There's little hope for the three other British cars (Midget, B, Spitfire) despite how much we enjoyed the Spitfire. The only thing left is for British Leyland to start all over with a clean sheet of paper.'

As the final curtain drew near for the Spitfire, it was still appearing occasionally in the press, if only to remind everyone how outdated it had become. Triumph was clearly milking the car for all it could. Newer rivals had come along, putting the car in the shade with its separate chassis and poor packaging.

Perhaps one of the most damning reviews was by Steve Cropley in the May 1979 issue of *Car*. Much of the article contained his reminiscences of growing up in Australia, with a Spitfire-owning cousin who was clearly a menace behind the wheel – something that obviously wasn't the Spitfire's fault. However, that had been back in 1965 – a decade and a half later, the Triumph was clearly getting very long in the tooth.

With an opening line of: 'The Triumph Spitfire is as awful today as it ever was', the reader was left in no doubt from the outset about what *Car* thought of the Spitfire. The rest of the article was taken up with Cropley quoting extracts from the 1500's brochure, then spelling out in no uncertain terms why it was all marketing hype: 'The Spitfire's engine is an undistinguished four… that has all the properties you can absolutely rely on in an old-time Leyland four – the roughest of idles… and enough racket and harshness at the top to make sojourns to the 6,000rpm red line an endurance test rather than any part of the pleasure of driving a responsive motorcar'. Not a lot of ambiguity there then but, to be fair, by 1979 the Spitfire was getting rather long in the tooth…

It had become traditional for British carmakers to unveil their new models at their home motor show: the Earls Court extravaganza which took place every October. However, British Leyland chose not to take the wraps off its Spitfire 1500 at the 1974 show, opting instead to introduce the car at the Turin salon in November. For some odd reason the decision was made to keep quiet about the whole thing, with the media told very little in advance about the arrival of the new car.

Things were not helped by the fact that the new car looked much like the old one. Indeed, aside from fresh badging proclaiming the fitment of a 1500 engine – that badging being in the form of stickers rather than actual badges – the only other giveaways were details that would be lost on the typical onlooker. The wheel centres were now silver instead of black while the trim surround on the rear panel was now finished in black instead of chrome. Other than that, it was visually business as usual – BL's designers hadn't clocked up much overtime updating the Spitfire's design for its swansong.

Once again, road testers were generally keen on this last incarnation of the Spitfire when it appeared, but less so as production drew to a close.

MARKETING

Triumph Spitfire 1500

...rever your activities take you, ...fire's versatile image will be ...target. It is, in fact, a sports car for every occasion, equally at home in the multitude of roles that you demand of it. You can choose between the standard soft-top and tonneau model, or the detachable hard-top version. The latter features a snug fitting, fully trimmed and easily removable steel top that effectively converts your open sports car into a closed coupe. It's styled to complement the Spitfire's sleek lines, and features hinged anti-draught rear quarter vents. You pay your money and take your choice. And at the rear, there is a sensibly shaped luggage boot of 7 cu. ft. capacity, which is automatically illuminated when the lid is raised. Rain or shine, the Spitfire gives you more fun and enjoyment per mile and per £ than anything else on wheels.

Triumph had always shown the Spitfire's getaway-from-it-all nature within its brochures, but it was taken to new heights with the 1500. This was a trend that had started in the early 1970s generally, showing people enjoying various pursuits which, by association, marked them out as successful.

TRIUMPH Spitfire 1500

GRW 976N

🔵 Triumph

RACER

Spitfire's looks and specifications are enough to stir just about everybody who enjoys driving. Consider its hard-won racing credentials: more Sports Car Club of America class championships than any other imported sports car!
To underscore the point, young Steve Johnson is the SCCA's current F Production champion. When he wheeled his Spitfire into victory circle, it was his first title—and Spitfire's fourteenth!
Perhaps you ought to try racing yourself... right down to your Triumph dealer.

Spitfire—the sports car that looks and acts the part. Italian styling gives it a purity of line. And its crisp response comes from rack and pinion steering, front disc brakes, fully independent suspension, and the pairing of a 1500cc engine with a 4-speed gearbox.
And the moment the top goes down, driving takes on an entirely new dimension. In this era of boxy sedans and pseudo sports cars there's really only one word for Spitfire.

RACY

Call 800-447-4700 for the name of your nearest Triumph dealer. In Illinois call 800-322-4400. Jaguar Rover Triumph Inc. Leonia, New Jersey 07605

156 LYF

SPITFIRE
JUST FOR THE FUN OF IT.

GRW 976N

Introducing the Triumph Spitfire 1500.

Win after win. Race after race. 30 times last year the Triumph Spitfire showed the world what a championship sports car is made of.

That was last year.

This year we have even bigger things in mind. And better.

This year's Spitfire has more engine than last year's racing champion. It's now a full 1½ litres.

To go along with the greater power,

this year's new 1500 has a 2 in. wider rear track, a higher axle ratio (3.89 to 1) and a larger 7¼ in. clutch.

All of which means more traction, more stability, and more getaway power.

And to give you an even sportier sports car for your money, this year's Spitfire comes with a new racing style steering wheel, walnut dash and adjustable headrests, not to mention

other less obvious... improvements.

We know you don... by resting on your la...

You'll know it too... moment you test dri... new Spitfire 1500.

Triumph Sp...
We make sports ca...

Sexism was alive and well in the PR department in 1977. Well, the Spitfire was getting rather long in tooth by this point, so something was needed to spice things up a bit...

OPTIONS

Dealer-fit options

Soft-top conversion kit	£51.00
Hard-top kit	£77.22
Skid plate	
Headlamp conversion mask	
Oil cooler	
Radio, aerial and speaker installation	£60.00
Mud flaps	
Touch-in paints	
Wooden gear knob	
Hood stowage cover-for use with hard-top	
Rubber floor mats	
Workshop manuals and parts list	

Factory-fitted options

Overdrive	£135.08
Laminated windscreen (standard from 1978)	£19.07
Front upper ball joint with grease nipple	
Competition DS11 brake pads	
Luxury pack (standard after FH 80000 on non-US cars)	£39.78

To boost power and allow more relaxed cruising thanks to a higher final drive ratio, the 1296cc engine was stroked to become a 1493cc unit.

because there was now a useful 71bhp on tap in place of the previous 63bhp. More importantly, there was also 82lb ft of torque on offer, whereas the 1500's predecessor offered just 70lb ft. When this was combined with a raising of the final drive ratio from 3.89 to 3.63:1, the Spitfire 1500 felt quite a lot more relaxing to drive than the MkIV.

Although there was a new gearbox – one that BL would roll out across as many of its cars as possible – the ratios weren't changed compared with the Spitfire MkIV. Overdrive was still an optional extra at £135, and it was still a Laycock J-Type unit: when this was specified, thanks to the taller gearing and extra power, the Spitfire could finally break the 100mph (160km/h) barrier.

Whereas those early North American editions of the Spitfire featured a single Stromberg carburettor and a 7.5:1 compression ratio, the full-fat edition as sold everywhere else was fitted with a pair of 1.5in (3.8cm) SUs and a 9.0:1 compression ratio.

Any other updates over the Spitfire MkIV were hardly what you could call far-reaching. Stiffer coil springs for the front suspension were joined by a rev counter that was now controlled electrically rather than mechanically, while the dash now featured a warning lamp that flashed up if the seat-

belts weren't being worn. A tonneau cover was also standard for the first time, while the dash also featured a switch for the hazard warning lights; to finish things off, the treadplates were now finished with a polished aluminium cover.

Although British Leyland's PR department didn't appear to be especially switched on at this point, its marketing bods appeared to have grasped the basics of getting punters to part with a bit of extra cash by offering something called the Luxury Pack. While there was a raft of individual extras available, listed separately and individually, those who opted for the Luxury Pack got head restraints, a driver's door mirror, inertia-reel seatbelts (the standard belts were still static items), a central arm rest and a map light for the passenger. Ordered as one extra, this Luxury Pack offered a useful saving over ordering each item separately.

The 1500 Evolves

Although the 1500 would prove to be the biggest selling and longest lived of all the Spitfire variants, this was not because it was necessarily a particularly good car in period. Indeed, with little money to develop the car much beyond ensuring

FEDERAL 1500s

Although Triumph did its best to minimize market-led specification differences for its cars, Spitfire 1500s produced for North America were different from those built for other markets. While the bodyshell and interior were barely altered, there were some minor external differences. In line with US regulations, marker lights had to be fitted to the front and rear wings, while the final cars (those built in the 1980) were fitted with ugly impact-resistant over-riders and extra brightwork for the wheels.

There were bigger changes under the skin, however, as a dual-circuit braking system was fitted to all North American 1500s, from the start. Of more importance to Triumph's buyers were the powerplants fitted – powerplant being something of a misnomer in most instances. Initial examples of the 1500 were fitted with a single Zenith-Stromberg carburettor and a 7.5:1 compression ratio that enabled the unit to peak at a weedy 57.5bhp – although at least the 75lb ft torque peak wasn't quite so disastrous, especially as this could be delivered from just 2,000rpm.

From 1977 all US-bound 1500s were fitted with a catalytic converter; this was in response to California demanding such

equipment, with Triumph opting to build a US-spec version of its car rather than one just for a single state. With the compression ratio raised to 9.0:1, power and torque were reckoned to be the same as before – so barely enough to stimulate the senses then.

When the emissions regulations were tightened up once more in 1980, Triumph reduced the compression ratio to just 7.5:1 again, cutting power to 53bhp and torque to 69lb ft in the process. When California tightened the screws even further in 1980, Triumph simply couldn't get the 1493cc engine to comply with the new rules, so it withdrew the car altogether. Thank God for that! If Triumph could have got the car through the tests, no doubt we would have seen a 40bhp Spitfire in the price lists!

Sadly, withdrawing the car from California jeopardized the model's viability: Triumph was dependent on the US market and especially the state of California. Without any American sales, it wasn't viable to keep the car in production because Triumph wouldn't have had the necessary economies of scale. Therefore, California's tighter emissions regulations led to the demise of the Spitfire as a whole – but then it had enjoyed a decent innings, with production lasting almost two decades.

The US-market Spitfire looked ungainly and lacked power – much like many of its contemporaries.

PRODUCTION CHANGES

FH 76285   The hood cover press studs now plastic-coated brass.

FH 78674   The front light lenses now flatter, the same as the MGB's.

FH 80000

(Jan 1976)   The Luxury package option becomes standard, the door mirror and windscreen wiper arms now painted black, the rocker cover securing nuts changed to slotted screws, and the inside of the battery box no longer painted black. The battery box side brackets also reduced in height, the negative battery cable no longer yellow, and all cars get brake master cylinders with plastic reservoirs; US cars already fitted with these for several years.

FH 84398   The seatbelt lock now all black so there is no chrome edge to it.

FH 85802   Waxstat Jet carburettors now fitted and the air filter box gets a BL logo.

FM 95001   US cars get rubber bumper covers.

FH 100020

(Mar 1977)   The door handles now painted black, there are chrome trim rings fitted to the road wheels (only to FH 100447 though) and from hereon there are TR7-style steering column stalks, incorporating the windscreen wash/wipe controls. Meanwhile, a cigarette lighter added to non-US cars, there's a redesigned, solid-spoked steering wheel without a horn button, the turn signal indicator light moved to below the hazard light switch, and there are now hound's-tooth cloth seats.

FH 105278   Non-US cars get another carburettor revision (shorter dashpots, different Waxstats and needles, different float chamber tops and overflow pipe).

FH 105734

(Jan 1978)   Non-US cars get the viscous fan already fitted to Federal-market cars.

FH 113678   The interior vinyl changed to a 'smooth' pattern, while the hound's-tooth trim revised slightly.

FH 114523   The carpet material changed from a tufted pile to a looped pile (including the lower door panel), while there's also a thinner seat reclining lever.

FH 116000   The bumper-mounted rear number plate lights replaced by a Triumph-branded light bar on non-US cars.

FH 127151   Revised air filter box with staggered air inlets.

FH 130000

(Jan 1979)   The wheel rims increase to 13 x 5J, notches added to the wheel nuts to help prevent the chrome from flaking off, non-US cars get the tandem brake master cylinder already fitted to federal cars and there's another steering wheel redesign along with a new speedometer (now marked to 110 mph). There's also now a passenger side interior light and door switch.

VIN 001198   Some cars get factory-fitted fog lamps at the rear and door-mounted mirrors for the passenger side. Some also get bonnet catches painted body colour along with plastic boot lid trim instead of metal.

Changes made by date rather than VIN:

Oct 1975   British Leyland square badges (on bonnet by catches) omitted from the passenger side.

1976   Emissions label fitted under the bonnet, while the windscreen washer bottle no longer has a 'Tudor' label. Also, from hereon there are square holes in the wheels of US cars.

Dec 1977   Bonnet bracing bar simplified, extra bonnet bracing added to prevent the bonnet from hitting the windscreen in the event of a frontal crash: this is chiefly for US cars but some UK cars featured it too.

1978   Laminated windscreen standard, and a plastic tool bag replaced the canvas roll.

Mid-1978   Moto-Lita steering wheel now fitted, with a leather-covered rim.

Oct 1979   VIN number plates replace the previous commission number plates; later a small VIN plate welded to the right-hand side of the boot rain channel.

SPITFIRE 1500 SPECIFICATIONS

Build dates	Nov 1974 – Aug 1980
Commission numbers	FH 75001 – TFWAD5AT 009898
Engine prefix	FM (starting at 28001)
Gearbox prefix	FR
Differential prefix	FR
Total produced	95,829
Basic price	£1,290
On the road price	£1,509.30

Performance

0-30mph	3.8sec
0-50mph	8.8sec
0-60mph	13.2sec
0-80mph	25.3sec
Max speed in first gear	31mph (49.88km/h)
Max speed in second gear	50mph (80.46km/h)
Max speed in third gear	78mph (125.52km/h)
Max speed in overdrive third	97mph (156.10km/h)
Top speed	101mph (162.53km/h)
Standing 1/4 mile	19.1sec
Power to weight ratio	87.9bhp/ton
Typical fuel consumption	34mpg (8.32ltr/100km)

Dimensions, weights and capacities

Length	12ft 5in (3785mm)
Width	4ft 10in (1486mm)
Height overall	3ft 9in (1206mm)
Ground clearance	5in (120mm)
Wheelbase	6ft 11in (2108mm)
Front track	4ft 1in (1245mm)
Rear track	4ft 0in (1219mm)
Dry Weight	1780lb (808kg)
Engine oil	8 pints (4.7ltr)
Gearbox oil	1.5pt (0.9ltr)
Overdrive gearbox oil	2.7pt (1.6ltr)

Compared with the Spitfire MkIV, the Spitfire 1500 introduced few significant changes stylistically – but it was still a significantly improved car.

Differential	1pt (0.6ltr)
Cooling system	8pt (4.7ltr)
Fuel tank	7.25gal (33ltr)

Engine

Maximum power	71bhp at 5,500rpm
Maximum torque	82lb ft at 3,000rpm
Displacement	1493cc
Bore	73.7mm
Stroke	87.5mm
Compression ratio	9.0:1
Oil pressure	50psi at 2,000rpm
Tappet clearance	0.010in
Fuelling	Twin SU 1.5in HS4 carburettors
Firing order	1-3-4-2
Spark plugs	Champion N-9Y (N-12Y from FM 33738)
Spark plug gap	0.025in
Distributor	Lucas 45 D4 – 41449
Contact breaker gap	0.015in
Dwell angle	38°/40°
Ignition timing – static	10° BTDC
Centrifugal advance	0° at 600rpm 6°/10° at 1,400rpm 12°/16° at 3,200rpm
Vacuum advance	0° at 2inHg 10°/14° at 18inHg
Ignition coil	Lucas 15.C6

Transmission

Clutch	Diaphragm
Clutch diameter	7.25in (18.4cm)
Clutch output shaft	20 splines
Master cylinder diameter	5/8in
Slave cylinder diameter	7/8in
Gearbox	Single-rail
Synchromesh	All gears
Gear ratios	4th = 1.0 3rd = 1.39 2nd = 2.16, 1st = 3.5 R = 3.99
Optional overdrive	Laycock J-type
Overdrive ratio	0.797

Overdrive gear ratios	4th = 0.797; 3rd = 1.1
Final drive ratio	3.63:1

Brakes and steering

Front	9in solid disc
Calliper type	Girling 14.LF
Swept area	150sq in
Rear	7 x 1.25in drum
Swept area	55sq in
Wheel cylinder diameter	5/8in (0.7in from FH 80000)
Master cylinder diameter	5/8in (0. 7in from FH 80000)

Steering

	Rack and pinion
Turning circle	24ft 2in (7.36m)
Turns between locks	3.75

Suspension, wheels and tyres

Front suspension	Double wishbone
Spring rate	180lbf/in
Camber angle (unladen)	+3° ± 1°
Castor angle (unladen)	4° ± 1°
King pin inclination	5.75° ± 1°
Toe	1/16in – 1/8in toe in
Rear suspension	Swing spring
Number of leaves	5
Leaf width	1.75in
Leaf thickness	0.38in, 0.25in (bottom two leaves)
Spring rate	110lbf/in
Toe (unladen)	1/32in – 3/32in toe out
Camber angle (unladen)	–1° ± 1°
Wheel size	Steel 13 x 4.5 J
Tyres	Dunlop SP68 or Goodyear G800
Tyre size	155SR 13
Tyre pressure	Front: 21psi Rear: 26psi

Electrics

Earth	Negative
Alternator	Lucas 16ACR
Max current output	34 amps
Starter motor	Lucas M35J
Headlights	60/45w

it complied with the latest US emissions regulations – which got tighter every year – the Spitfire became really quite stale as the 1970s progressed. With around four out of every five Spitfires built being sold to an American buyer, keeping the model legal in the US was essential – but also a big drain on Triumph's resources. As a result, development of the car was sporadic and not especially far-reaching.

The first thing to change during the 1500's development was its badging: early cars featured a BL badge on each front wing, which was cut to just one on the driver's side from October 1975. At some point in 1976 these badges were deleted altogether, leaving just Triumph references on the car's bodywork; even British Leyland had been forced to accept by this point that its brand was not one with which its customers necessarily wished to be associated.

Around the same time, BL started to increase the amount of standard equipment fitted to the Spitfire, to boost its showroom appeal. First came a driver's door mirror and laminated windscreen, then from January 1976 the Luxury Pack was fitted to all cars at no extra cost. Later that year the carpet was upgraded, while detail changes included the fitment of black wiper arms and door mirrors, along with tamper-proof carburettors to meet new European regulations.

The biggest changes, however, arrived in March 1977, as part of a mid-life refresh. The switchgear was updated to the latest TR7-style design, while the ignition barrel was finally moved so that it was more accessible. The interior trim was also improved: there was now hounds-tooth check in beige or black while the steering wheel design was altered so there were no slots in the spokes – but barely a year later this would change again to one that was reminiscent of those produced by Moto Lita, and before long there would be a further change to a less slender design. Under the bonnet there was now a viscous coupling for the engine-driven cooling fan. Other improvements were larger cylinders for the rear brakes, fresh speedometer markings and redesigned lighting for the rear number plate.

From this point on, there was virtually no development of the Spitfire, as the end was now in sight for the model. Wider 5in wheels became standard on 1979 model year cars, while from January 1979 there were dual-circuit brakes. The last few cars featured twin door-mounted mirrors and rear fog lamps. The final Spitfire was built in August 1980, marking the end of an era. By the conclusion of the year, the TR7

would also be dead, along with the Canley factory, leaving just the Acclaim – a rebadged Honda – to carry on the Triumph name: a sad end for a once-illustrious marque.

SPITFIRE 1500 CHASSIS NUMBERS

Whereas things were pretty simple for earlier editions of the Spitfire, there was a major upheaval in terms of chassis numbers, towards the end of 1500 production. While 1500 chassis numbers had carried an FH prefix from the outset (or an FM prefix for American cars), the system was changed completely in October 1979, when the industry standard was adopted, of 14 digits. This new VIN (Vehicle Identification Number) coding featured eight initial digits that gave various pieces of information about the car, with the final six numbers being the Spitfire's serial number.

All 1500s had a VIN that started T (for Triumph) then F (for Spitfire). Next came the market for which the car was produced (A for European, L for Canada, V for North America and Z for California). All cars then had a D (for Drophead) and a W (for the 1493cc engine), but then it got a little more complicated. A number denoted where the steering wheel sat and whether or not overdrive was fitted (1 for RHD and non-O/D, 2 for the LHD equivalent. 5 was for RHD with overdrive and 6 denoted LHD with overdrive). Next came an A to say the car was built in 1979/80 while the final T denoted the car having been built in Canley. After all this came the car's serial number.

So, taking the final car's serial number as an example, we have:

T	Triumph
F	Spitfire
A	European market car
D	Drophead
W	1493cc engine
5	Right-hand drive with overdrive
A	Built in 1979/80
T	Produced at Canley
009898	The car's serial number

GT6 MkI (1966–1968)

It was no secret that when Triumph launched the Spitfire, the company's finances were in pretty poor shape; the car had to succeed. However, before it was even launched, thoughts were turning to developing the model to increase sales volumes. Standard-Triumph's engineers were being kept busy with a whole raft of new cars to launch, from the 2000 and TR4 to the 1300 FWD and a revised Herald. However, Harry Webster was still keen to put a hatchback Spitfire into production.

Although there was a factory hard top available for the Spitfire, enabling greater levels of comfort and security, Webster envisaged a car that also offered far greater practicality: a tailgate to allow easier access to the luggage bay plus more carrying capacity. The idea was to produce a mini GT for those who wanted performance but rated practicality over exposure to the elements. The Spitfire GT would have a fixed steel roof, a hatchback and rakish lines to attract buyers.

Webster introduced the idea of a Spitfire GT to Triumph's board in August 1963 and again a few months later. Although no decision was made on whether or not to proceed with the project, Webster instructed Michelotti to start thinking about how the open-topped Spitfire could be translated into a closed edition, carrying over as many panels as possible.

At this early stage, it was assumed that the GT would be little more than a closed version of the regular Spitfire. Mechanically it would be identical, while forward of the A-pillars there would be no body changes either. Indeed, with so many parts shared between the open and closed editions of the Spitfire, it would cost Triumph a minimal amount

Most of the Spitfire's panels were carried over in the transition to GT6, helping Triumph to keep development costs to a minimum.

The bonnet bulge was necessary to clear the straight-six now sitting underneath.

to put the new car into production, while the development process would also be extremely short. So easy would the development of the new car be, that during a December 1963 board meeting, it was suggested that the car should be ready for an October 1964 launch. Sadly, things wouldn't prove quite so easy in reality…

To streamline the development process, the Spitfire prototype X691 (registered 4305 VC) was despatched to Turin for Michelotti to reclothe as a closed Spitfire. In terms of translating the roadster into a hatchback, things went pretty smoothly. The fuel tank had to be redesigned and relocated so the luggage bay could be used, but most of the panels were carried over along with all of the mechanicals – something that would prove to be this early prototype's downfall.

As autumn turned to winter, the running prototype was ready for testing – and what a disappointment it was. It's not known which engine was fitted to the car at this stage, other than that it was a four-cylinder unit. One must suppose that it was an 1147cc unit, and perhaps tuned in some way, but

this is nothing more than an educated guess. Whatever was fitted, the closed Spitfire's performance was somewhat underwhelming, thanks to the much greater weight of the new bodyshell.

With production costs for the closed car being significantly higher than for the open edition, there was no way Triumph could charge a premium for a car with less performance, so a rethink was required. It didn't take Webster long to hit upon the idea of fitting the 1596cc straight-six which had recently been introduced in the Vitesse. Smooth and compact, this would turn the closed Spitfire into a true GT – except it didn't. In standard form the straight-six produced just 70bhp and 92lb ft of torque while the 1147cc unit was capable of pushing out 63bhp and 67lb ft of torque. So while the six-cylinder engine would ensure the closed car was more accelerative, it still wouldn't be capable of taking the car to a top speed much (if any) higher than the 1147cc edition. Another rethink was needed, but it didn't take long to come up with an answer: a larger edition of the straight-six.

This picture shows why comparisons with Jaguar's E-Type were common; the GT6's proportions were well and truly perfect.

However, we're jumping slightly ahead of ourselves here because the initial six-cylinder installation was of a 1.6-litre unit, which was fitted early in 1964. Compared with the four-cylinder prototype that had been transported from Turin the previous year, this revised car only differed in its motive power along with the profile of the bonnet. Because of the greater length of the six-cylinder engine compared with the four-cylinder unit, the bonnet had to be modified to accommodate it. In time there would be a power bulge, but for now there was simply a scoop cut into the top panel.

As already mentioned, it didn't take long to establish that the 1596cc engine would not provide the sort of performance Webster had been hoping for, but the solution already lay in Triumph's armoury. The 1.6-litre engine was a small-bore version of the 1998cc powerplant introduced in the 2000 in 1963. So, if the Spitfire GT could accommodate the smaller engine, it could also easily accommodate the larger one.

Until this point, X691 had been fitted with the 4.11:1 rear axle usually found in the Spitfire, but a significantly higher ratio could be accommodated (and indeed would be required) for a more performance-focused GT. Again the solution was obvious: fit the stronger, 3.89:1 rear axle from the Vitesse.

The GT6 is Born

The next step was to build a pair of test vehicles, each equipped with the 1998cc engine and the stronger Vitesse

rear axle, along with an all-synchromesh gearbox of the type developed for the works Spitfires. These were the first prototypes built which shared the same specification as the showroom-ready GT6s. The car wouldn't go on sale until 1966, but the first prototype, numbered X742 (and later registered EVC 375C), was completed in April 1965. This was built with right-hand drive, but a left-hand drive prototype was also constructed, numbered X746 (later registered FWK 319D) and completed in November 1965.

These test cars featured the same mechanicals as the production cars while the bodywork had also been further refined since the early prototype had been constructed. Gone was the lashed-up bonnet scoop to clear the straight-six: in its place was a power bulge of the type that would be carried over to customer cars. Because of the extra heat generated by the six-cylinder engine, when compared with the four-cylinder unit, there were now louvres in the top of the bonnet to help the powerplant keep its cool.

It wasn't just the engine that was in danger of overheating though: the cabin was also prone to getting very hot. So, in a bid to stop the occupants from roasting there were now opening quarter lights, while the rear side windows could also be tilted open to improve airflow through the passenger space.

The extra power available from the six-cylinder engine, and the greater weight of the car, also necessitated a stronger braking system. As a result, there were now 9.7in discs at the front in place of the Spitfire's 9in items, while the drums at the rear measured 8in across instead of the 7in for the Spitfire.

OPTIONS

Dealer-fit options

Bonnet lock	£1 15s 0d
Brake servo kit	From £13 0s 0d
Cigarette lighter (push down)	10s 8d
Cigarette lighter (pull out)	£1 10s 0d
Continental touring kit	
Double-gauge instrument mounting panel	
Electric windscreen defroster	£1 15s 0d
Emergency windscreen	
Fire extinguisher	
Fog lamp	From £3 19s 6d
Fuel tank filter	
Head-rest	
Heated rear window	
Hub cap medallion	
Level Master wheelbrace	
Mud flaps with Triumph motif	From £1 7s 6d
Oil cooler kit (from KC 5001)	
Plugmaster spark plug spanner	
Radio (Smiths Radiomobile)	
Roof rack	From £7 0s 0d
Seat belts	From £4 4s 0d
Sill protectors	
Single-gauge instrument mounting panel	
Spot lamp	From £3 19s 6d
Steering wheel glove; brown leather	
Steering wheel glove; simulated brown leather	
Touch-in paints	
Tow rope and luggage rack strap	
Tow bar	
Warning triangle	
Windscreen anti-frost shield	
Wing mirrors	From 19s 6d
Wire wheels	£36 17s 6d
Wood-rim steering wheel	From £7 10s 0d

Factory-fitted options

Alternator-11ACR	
Competition brake pads and shoes	
Front upper ball joint with grease nipple	
Heater kit	£13 10s 5d
Laminated windscreen	
Leather seats	
Leather trim	
Overdrive	£58 7s 8d
Skid plate	
Steering column lock	
Track rod end with grease nipple	

The wraps were taken off the GT6 at the 1966 Earls Court Motor Show, where the car was very well received.

Decades after it went out of production, the GT6 still looks right from every angle.

Differential ratios were also revised, with ultra-long 3.27:1 gearing for cars not fitted with the optional Laycock de Normanville D-type overdrive; anyone who ticked the overdrive option box received a car fitted with a 3.89:1 ratio. This was because of the much greater torque on offer from the straight-six; the extra weight of this engine also meant a less direct steering rack had to be fitted – if only Triumph's engineers could have chosen a power-assisted set-up from the parts bin…

One of the areas that needed particular attention was the cooling system, as the radiator had to sit quite a lot further forward than in the Spitfire, while the bonnet line also had to be kept as low as possible. Not only this, but with a 6-cylinder engine to cool instead of the Spitfire's 4-cylinder unit, the cooling system had to be as efficient as possible. The six-bladed Vitesse-style cooling fan was moved to the crankshaft pulley, but despite the relatively poor airflow around the sump, there was no need to fit an oil cooler. Meanwhile, the sealed cooling system was a little more complicated than usual, due to the fact that the header tank sat lower than the top of the cylinder head. Combined with a water-heated inlet manifold, this resulted in a need to incorporate a pair of pipes from the thermostat housing to the header tank, in a bid to eradicate any air locks.

Although the GT6 was fitted with the same straight-six as the 2-litre Vitesse, the two models didn't share the same gearbox. This four-speed all-synchromesh gearbox used many of the same components as the one fitted to the Vitesse, but a new casing was designed to accommodate the rearranged gears and first-gear synchromesh. On the Vitesse gearbox, first gear and reverse are engaged by sliding the non-synchronized mainshaft gear into mesh with the appropriate train, while the GT6's first gear is in constant mesh, but free to rotate on the mainshaft to which it's connected by the dog teeth of the synchromesh mechanism.

While the rest of the transmission would have looked familiar to owners of the contemporary Herald, Spitfire and

PAINT AND TRIM OPTIONS

From launch until its replacement in January 1967, the same colour combinations were offered for the GT6 Mk1 as for the final Spitfire Mk2:

Paint	Interior trim
White	Black or red
Royal Blue	Black or Midnight Blue
Wedgwood Blue	Midnight Blue
Conifer Green	Black
Signal Red	Black

Whereas all factory-built Spitfires were fitted with a 4-cylinder engine, all GT6 variations got an extra pair of cylinders.

Vitesse, it featured a significantly higher ratio of 3.27:1 – at least if the car was ordered without overdrive. To help boost reliability levels, stronger output flanges were also fitted, with thicker bolts for the half-shafts.

The rest of the running gear would also have been familiar to owners of contemporary separate-chassis Triumphs, with a rack-and-pinion steering set-up for all cars. The suspension was also carried over from the Spitfire, albeit with adjustments to the spring and damper rates to account for the different weights over each of the axles.

Importantly, while the GT6 turned out to be more than a fastback Spitfire, Triumph succeeded in carrying over much of the bodywork of the latter, in a bid to keep expenditure to a minimum. The floorpans, bulkhead and doors were the same, as were most of the external panels including the bonnet – although, as mentioned, this had to be fitted with a bulge to clear the six-cylinder engine. The fuel tank, however, was completely redesigned: instead of sitting underneath the boot floor, it was now sited in the nearside (on a right-hand drive car) rear wing, its capacity increasing by 1.5gal (6.8ltr) in the process.

The GT6's interior would also have been familiar to Spitfire owners, although the instruments were now grouped in front of the driver rather than in the centre of the dash, while there was also a full-width walnut dashboard. There was still a collapsible steering column but, despite the pre-mium nature of the GT6, there was no ammeter or oil pressure gauge, although the padded leather steering wheel was as good to use as it was to look at. At 15in (38.1cm) across, it was an inch smaller than the Spitfire's wheel but, because the steering rack was also geared slightly lower, there was little difference in feel between the two cars. Crucially though, the GT6 was every bit as manoeuvrable as the Spitfire, as both cars shared the same 25ft (7.62m) turning circle.

The GT6's cockpit was also more luxurious than the Spitfire's, with carpeting throughout, padded door trims and much more comfortable bucket seats that held the car's two occupants in place when the car was being driven with enthusiasm. While seatbelts were optional, all cars were fitted with the relevant mountings; all GT6s also featured sun visors as standard where they were merely optional on the contemporary Spitfire.

The biggest change however was, of course, the fitment of a fixed roof, which not only raised cabin temperatures significantly, but also increased the car's luggage carrying capacity. The GT6 offered a useful 14.2 cubic ft (0.40 cubic m), accessed via a top-hinged tailgate that opened more easily thanks to the assistance of a torsion bar.

The usefulness of the load bay was increased by the refusal to fit rear seats: Triumph's engineers realized that they would be so small as to be useless to anybody except amputee dwarfs, so sensibly opted for a carpeted platform

GT6 MkI PRODUCTION CHANGES

KC 1040	Seatbelt mounting moved forward, while the handbrake cable now passed through a metal tube rather than a rubber grommet.
KC 3762	Reversing light switch moved inside the gearbox.
KC 4232	Bonnet stay now attached to a bracket welded to the suspension turret (on earlier cars it was attached to a bolted-on bracket).
KC 4799	Door locks now double-entry key items.
KC 5000	Stronger crankshaft, main bearings all the same width (two thinner middle bearings fitted before), and fuel pump top changed from glass to metal.
KC 7279	Rear brake wheel cylinders reduced from ¾in to ⅝in.
KC 11503	Green ignition leads with straight connectors replace earlier black items with right-angled connectors.
KC 21737	Door locks now stronger.

In keeping with its compact luxury/sporting brief, the GT6's interior featured high-quality materials, which included a wooden dash.

that ran from the tailgate edge right through to the back of the front seats. There could have been even more space available if this platform hadn't been so high: it was designed to cover not only the spare wheel but also the fuel tank, jack and tool kit.

Testing and development of the GT6 continued over the following weeks and months, but few changes were required thanks to the basic (Spitfire) formula being such an effective one. As a result, it was deemed that by early 1966 the car was ready for production. By July 1966, the first cars were being built, ready for an Earls Court launch in October.

The GT6 was in a class of its own, and few ever tried to emulate its beautiful lines. It wasn't a coupé or a hatchback as such, but it offered elements of both.

MARKETING

Sunset boulevardier: The Triumph GT6s from its most familiar angle.

All the world wants the new Triumph GT6

The GT6 puts a new class of car within the reach of the world. Until last October's Motor Show, if you wanted a very fast two-seater saloon with a smooth big 6-cylinder engine, it cost you a small fortune, wherever you lived. Now, anyone who can afford a medium 2-litre saloon can indulge himself with the low, sleek, 100-mph plus GT6.

The GT6 gets its sweeping fastback from the Le Mans Spitfires but is second in their class). But it gets its verve from the 6-cylinder Triumph 2000 engine. Almost without trying, this engine develops 95-BHP, and sweeps the

16-cwt GT6 from 0 to 50-mph in 7.8 seconds. **You have control** Each wheel on the GT6 is individually sprung to ensure that this power and the road keep in close harmony. Rack-and-pinion steering makes the front wheels as responsive as your own fingers. **Export expertise** Last year, Triumph was to the fore of Britain's export drive—Triumph export 50%, of their output. Result, the Queen's Award to Industry to both Standard-Triumph International and the Leyland Motor Corporation. Already the world is itching for the new Triumph GT6. This

beautiful car will catch up and overtake most things—not least its own waiting list.

However, Triumph success in world markets does not depend on one car—or even just on sports cars. There are other exciting Triumphs. Names and profiles are below. Your Triumph dealer will be pleased to tell you more about any of them.

Triumph TR4 World famous sports car in the grand manner.

Triumph Herald The most talented light car (and the prettiest).

Triumph 2000 2-litre, 5-seater, leather upholstery, full-flow ventilation.

Triumph 1300 Voted 'Car of the Year' by *Car* Magazine.

Standard-Triumph Sales Ltd
Berkeley Square, London W1
England G/R/Dealer: 8050

Here's where the suitcases stretch out

GT6 drivers and passengers have lots of room. So why shouldn't the suitcases? The luggage area is 42in. wide by 41in. deep, three brilliant. The rear slopes 34in. Additional accommodation: a parcel shelf beneath the luggage platform. This is one sports car where luggage isn't limited to hand brush and comb.

18

A 2-litre
from Tri
continued

Space at the back for hiding cameras and various odds and ends.

telescope on impact, is incorporated in the rack-and-pinion system and an attractive three-spoke wheel with leather-covered rim is used. From lock to lock involves 4½ turns, which sounds very low-geared for a car of this type—but is not because of the very small turning circle of 25 ft. 3 in. between kerbs; wheel movement for normal turns is more reasonable.

The body is an example of racing experience being put to practical use in a subsequent production model. Styled by Giovanni Michelotti of Turin, the steel-panelled body is a development of the Spitfire but with a new bonnet top and a gently curved roof which slopes down in a single sweep from the top of the curved windscreen to the tail. It has a very large rear window in a 34-in.-wide, top-hinged, counter-balanced rear door giving access to the luggage space behind the seats. This luggage floor is 41½ in. from front to rear and 42 in. wide, with a maximum height above it of 24 in. The result is to give 14.2 cu. ft. of luggage space.

Beneath the rear part of the luggage floor are the tank on one side and the spare wheel, lying horizontally, on the other. Access to the wheel is by a removable panel secured by two screws and a pair of clips, and there is room round the wheel for tools and similar oddments. Below the forward portion of the luggage floor and accessible from behind the seat squabs is a useful parcel shelf which supplements the front parcel shelves under the facia board.

Apart from a slight obstruction caused by the rear quarter panels, vision is very good but a user who regularly carried much luggage would probably need to fit an external mirror. The door windows are of the winding type and a good point is that the rear quarter lights are pivoted for

How it all fits together. Note the spare wheel and fuel tank side by side to give a flat rear floor, the separate chassis members and suspension units. Practically every part of the engine and its ancillary units is instantly accessible for servicing.

The rakish hardtop has a really large rear window and the sides have a decidedly aircraft look about them.

ventilation as well as the hinged panels on the leading edges of the doors.

Inside, the body is compact but not cramped. Doors 29 in. wide at waist level, with burst-proof latches, give access to an interior 45 in. wide between doors and 38 in. high, of which 34 in. represents headroom above the seat cushion. The seats themselves are of the rally type and measure 20 in. fore and aft and 19½ in. in width. The usual fore-and-aft adjustment is provided and both squabs tilt forwards for access to the luggage space. Ambla material is used to
Continued on the next page

The lift-up front cowling gives splendid access to the six-cylinder engine which fits snugly in place with only a slight bulge on the bonnet top to give away its presence.

Specification

Engine	
Cylinders	6 in-line with 4 bearing crankshaft
Bore and stroke	74.7 mm x 76 mm (2.94 in x 2.99 in)
Cubic capacity	1,998 c.c. (122 cu. in)
Piston area	40.7 sq. in
Compression ratio	9.5:1
Valvegear	In line o h v operated by pushrods and rockers
Carburation	Two Stromberg 1.50 CD sidedraught carburetters, fed by mechanical pump, from 3½-gallon tank
Ignition	12-volt coil, centrifugal and vacuum control 14 mm Champion sparking plugs
Lubrication	Eccentric lobe pump. AC full flow filter
Cooling	Water cooling with pump, fan and thermostat; 11 pint water capacity
Electrical system	12 volt 48 amp. hr battery charged by 300 watt generator
Maximum power	95 b.h.p. net at 5,000 r.p.m. equivalent to 124 b. sq. in b.m.e.p. at 2490 ft /min. piston speed and 2.33 b.h.p. per sq. in of piston area

Maximum torque	117.3 lb. ft. at 3,000 r.p.m. equivalent to 145 lb./sq. in. b.m.e.p. at 1,490 ft. /min. piston speed

Transmission	
Clutch	8½ in. diaphragm type
Gearbox	4-speed with synchromesh on all forward gears
Overall ratios	3.27, 4.11, 5.82 and 8.98, reverse, 10.15 (With optional overdrive: 3.89 (O/D 3.12); 4.88 (O/D 3.89); 6.92 and 10.30 (reverse 12.08))
Propeller shaft	
Final drive	Inboard-mounted hypoid bevel and swing axles

Chassis	
Brakes	Girling hydraulic, disc front/drum rear
Brake dimensions	Front 9.7 in dia discs; rear 8 in dia x 1¼ in wide drums
Brake areas	60.2 sq. in of lining (22.2 sq. in. front plus 38 sq. in. rear) working on 260 sq. in. rubbed area of discs and drums
Front suspension	Independent, by coil springs and wishbones with Girling telescopic dampers and anti-roll bar

Rear suspension	Independent by transverse leaf springs, radius arms and swing axles. Girling telescopic dampers
Wheels and tyres	Steel disc wheels with 4J rims and 155-13 SP 41 tyres
Steering	Alford and Alder rack-and-pinion with adjustable collapsible column

Dimensions	
Length	Overall 12 ft. 1 in. wheelbase 6 ft. 11 in.
Width	Overall 4 ft. 9 in. track 4 ft. 1 in. at front and 4 ft. 0 in. at rear
Height	3 ft. 11 in. ground clearance 4 in. laden
Turning circle	25¼ ft.
Kerb weight	17 cwt. (with fuel, oil, water, tools spare wheel, etc.)

Effective gearing	
Top gear ratio	20.15 m.p.h. at 1,000 r.p.m. and 40.2 m.p.h. at 1,000 ft /min. piston speed with optional overdrive 18.8 m.p.h. (O/D 21.0 m.p.h. and 33.6 m.p.h. (O/D 42.1 m.p.h.)

Understandably, Triumph was keen to cash in on its motorsport investment as much as possible, which is why it dropped in references to Le Mans at every opportunity, making the link between the GT6 and the Le Mans Spitfires. However, there were also plenty of references to the car's practicality and usability.

Bred at Le Mans

to put you safely ahead!

Triumph's incredible new GT6

GIVES RACE-BRED PERFORMANCE WITH GRAND TOURING COMFORT AND SAFETY

The power bulge on the bonnet of the GT6 is not there for show. It makes room for a big 1998 cc, 6-cylinder engine. Standing room for a big 1998 cc, this race-bred beauty is just over 17 seconds.

The GT6 develops a smooth 95 BHP. It can reach 46 in 7 seconds in first. Do an easy 96 in third. A vivid 0–50 in 7.8. And top gear times—like 40–60 in 7.5—cut overtaking time so dramatically that GT6 motoring is not only one of the most exhilarating ways to travel, but one of the safest.

Built-in safety to match its power

The GT6, cruising at 70, is a safer car than many of today's family saloons at 30.

It inherits its low, sleek shape from the fastback Spitfires that took first and second places in their class at Le Mans. The same all-independent suspension gives the GT6 race-proved stability and road holding.

It has the same strong, double-backbone steel girder chassis. The same big front-wheel disc brakes. It has also been given some other safety features. Like rack and pinion steering with adjustable and collapsible steering column; burst-proof door locks; a forward hinged bonnet that cannot fly up while the car is moving; and a 25' turning circle that makes the GT6 more safely manoeuvrable than any other make of sports car on the road.

Grand touring comfort for two

Under the bonnet the GT6 is all guts. Inside it is all comfort. A grand tourer, with deep pile carpeting, adjustable seats that are soft to sink into, tailored to support you, shaped to hold you firm on corners. There's a centre arm rest, too, which neatly houses the 'Fly-Off' hand brake. A racy leather-covered steering wheel, and a short, cranked gear lever. Under the fascia (with padded cowl, of course), a deep parcel shell holds your odds and ends, and in the back is luggage space enough to let you travel a long way from home.

For £1124.6.1 the GT6 is a lot of car for the money. Its nearest 6-cylinder rival would cost you nearly £150 extra—and you still wouldn't get all the advantages of the GT6. Visit your Triumph Dealer and arrange a test run.

Standard-Triumph Sales Ltd
Berkeley Square, London W1
Telephone: 01-499 0000

TRIUMPH

TRIUMPH PUTS YOU SAFELY AHEAD

iumph's lusty newcomer, the GT6—may look familiar

...ere by the winning post at Le Mans it ...will. Because the GT6 takes its breeding from ...mph Spitfires that came first and second in ...s. One significant difference, the power is ...y a 95 bhp version of the Triumph 2000 ...t the body, chassis, independent suspension ...disc brakes are of the same stamp as the ...odels.

...time

1 of the GT6 is well above British limits ...that. But its acceleration, properly used, ...safe machine indeed. Figures like 40–60 ...in 8.5 mean you overtake decisively with ...reassuring margin. Another impressive figure: a

turning circle of 25 ft. 3 ins. that is about 7 feet less than its rivals.

GT comfort

In spite of the performance there's nothing hairy about the GT6. Deep-pile carpet goes with 68 in second. There's walnut on the facia, leather on the steering wheel and the seats are as welcoming at the end of a long ride as they were at the beginning.

GT6 in detail

Engine, 6 cylinder, 1,998 cc. Performance—top gear acceleration : 30–50 in 7.4 seconds, 40–60 in 7.5 seconds; Through the gears: 0–50 mph 7.8 seconds, 0–60 mph 11.2 seconds. Standing ¼ mile: 17.7 seconds.

Chassis: double backbone, channel section with outriggers. Instruments: speedometer, tachometer, temperature gauge, warning lights for headlamp main beam, oil pressure, ignition and direction indicators. Dimensions: Length 12 ft. 1 in. Width 4 ft. 9 ins. Height 3 ft. 11 ins. Luggage accommodation: parcel tray, large luggage compartment behind seats with storage pockets underneath.

Triumph GT6 - Born in Le Mans

PRESS REACTION

Intriguingly, when *Sporting Motorist* got its hands on the first GT6 test car in November 1966, it constantly referred to the car as a hatchback Spitfire 6, failing to make the distinction between the two separate model ranges. Clearly confusing the GT6 with Jaguar's E-type, *Sporting Motorist*'s scribe asserts that there's a side-hinged tailgate (it was actually top-hinged of course), which doesn't inspire confidence in the rest of the review. Still, at least the article was positive, with the thumbs up given to the GT6's performance, handling, practicality, looks and luxurious cabin.

When *Car* (October 1966) got its hands on GWK 884D, it was equally impressed. As is typical with this thinking enthusiast's magazine, it analysed just what Triumph had done to create the GT6 from a range of parts already available within the company's existing model ranges, demonstrating that rationalization is nothing new. Crucially though, *Car*'s testers also discovered that they: 'were startled to find how entirely different the GT6 feels from the Spitfire on which it is based – a much greater difference, for example, than between a Herald and Vitesse… Thanks to fatter tyres and much greater front-end weight, and in general the whole car feels solider (sic) and more substantial'.

Autocar was just as positive about Triumph's new baby when it was tested in October 1966. Comparing the handling to Jaguar's E-type, the car was praised for its engine's flexibility, overall refinement and the performance too. The magazine concluded: 'With so much performance at such reasonable cost, we can foresee long waiting lists long before home allocations begin in six months' time.'

Road & Track first reviewed the GT6 in November 1966, making the inevitable comparisons with Jaguar's E-type. Tester Joe Lowrey got behind the wheel of a pre-production prototype, so minor irritations such as the stiff gear change would hopefully be engineered out by the time customer-ready GT6s started to roll off the production lines. Lowrey commented: 'This little car is geared to use torque rather than rpm. Also, because it has such a smooth and quiet six-cylinder engine geared to run at low rpm, the GT6 does not feel as fast as it is.'

When *Road & Track* printed a more comprehensive test of the GT6 in its April 1967 edition, complete with full performance figures, the verdict was generally positive, although there were one or two riders. Fitting the six-cylinder

engine had clearly been a good move: 'We liked the 2-litre six in the 2000 and we like it even better in the GT … This straightforward overhead valve unit is one of the quietest and smoothest sixes to be found anywhere.'

Praising the transmission, engine flexibility and dynamics ('we found that the GT6 could not be faulted on its handling'), the only real downside to the GT6, according to *Road & Track*'s testers, was the ergonomics. The instrumentation wasn't easy to read, the switchgear was laid out confusingly and for tall drivers the car was uncomfortable on long journeys. However, Triumph must have been very pleased with the magazine's summary: 'The GT6 is a great improvement over the Spitfire from which it's descended. Not that the Spitfire is bad, it's just that the GT6 is so much better. It has no parallel and it's worth the money.'

Just a few weeks before the Mk2 GT6 was unveiled, *Car* magazine's Mike Twite drove a Mk1 from London to Madrid as quickly as possible – and came away feeling somewhat underwhelmed by the experience. Covering the 1,100 miles in twenty-three hours (including two hours of breaks), the car had averaged 52.5mph (84.4km/h), which wasn't slow.

Reporting in the July 1968 edition of the magazine, Twite commented: 'A big engine in a small chassis usually gives benefits in acceleration, top speed and a lower noise level. Where it can fall down is in the way it affects handling, steering, ride and braking. Alas, this is just where the GT6 suffers, for it is fairly obvious that dropping a two-litre 95bhp six into what is virtually a Triumph Herald chassis is going to be exciting to say the least.'

As if this wasn't enough, Twite went on to say: 'Although the GT6 has a cruising potential of 100mph (160.9km/h) or more, I seldom let it go much above 80mph (128.7km/h) on the continent as it was just not controllable.' Sounds like Triumph desperately needed to launch a revised GT6 to tackle such criticisms – which is exactly what it did less than three months later.

The GT6 got a big thumbs up from most who drove it, but not everyone loved it.

A 2-litre GT from Triumph

Modified 2000 engine in a Spitfire derivative—

NEW CARS

NEW from Triumph is a two-litre six cylinder GT model using a high-compression version of the 2000 engine in a chassis and body developed from the Spitfires which ran so well at Le Mans in 1964 and '65. Named the Triumph GT6, its three-figure total price of £985 1s. and unique specification place it in a class of its own. Its maximum speed is given by the makers as 107 m.p.h.

Also notable in the Triumph range for '67 is the latest Vitesse which now has the same high-compression, two-litre version of the 2000 six cylinder engine as the GT6 instead of the special under-bored 1,596 c.c. edition used to date. In this case, a maximum speed of 100 m.p.h. is claimed. Although the total price of the saloon (at £838 15s. 7d.) is some £67 higher than that of the 1.6-litre model (now super-seded), the increase covers improvements to the clutch, gearbox, brakes and body details as well as the bigger engine—and still leaves the Vitesse the cheapest six cylinder car on the British market by a margin of more than £100. As before, there is a convertible and the total price in this case is £883 0s. 7d.

The GT6 in detail

The new GT6 is a typically Triumph enterprise in the sense that it offers something not found in any other maker's catalogue: a two seater closed body of the GT type, independent suspension all round and a six-cylinder engine—all at a total price of under £1,000. To obtain a similar combination elsewhere it is necessary to pay a much higher price.

The GT6, in fact, is a sort of "business-man's express" for the less-affluent business-man. Some might think that the 70 m.p.h. limit does not apply in most overseas markets, and one time to introduce such a car. There are several answers to that. One is that our new antiquated limit does not apply in most overseas markets, for which the first six months' production is in any case being reserved; another is that British people do take their cars abroad (and will go on doing so even on £50 a head plus £25 for the car); and a third point is that the new model should get to the legal limit in Britain very quickly indeed and hold it with a lot in hand.

So far, our actual experience of the new model is confined to a short trial with no opportunities for taking performance figures (see the editor's impressions at the end of this description) but the following figures issued by the makers give a clue to the sort of performance to be expected: top-gear acceleration from 20 to 40 m.p.h., 7.5 secs.;

by half a [...] to increase the output [...] net at the same speed (5,000 r.p.m.), [...] the maximum torque virtually unchanged. With the relatively high gearing made possible by the power/weight ratio, 1,000 engine r.p.m. is equivalent to 20.15 m.p.h., giving 101 m.p.h. at peak revs., while maximum torque (at 3,000 r.p.m.) occurs at just over 60 m.p.h.

The high-compression GT6 engine is distinguished by a chromium-plated valve cover and drops neatly into a new chassis frame of similar general configuration to that of the Spitfire but modified to cope with the extra size, weight and output of the 2000 unit, still leaving room for an overdrive when required. A slight "power bulge" is necessary in the bonnet top, but this is not so pronounced as to spoil either appearance or forward vision. As on the Spitfire and

the six-cylinder engine and re-positioned radiator. In fact, competition Spitfires have been run with considerably thinner frames with no ill-effects on roadholding or strength. As on the related Vitesse, the 6-cylinder engine is a tight fit under the bonnet. Its radiator is short and squat, being relatively much farther forward in the chassis than that of the Spitfire. The new gearbox is little bulkier, so no changes to body floor or gearbox tunnel have been necessary.

Apart from its raised compression ratio (9·5 instead of 9·0 to 1) the 1,998 c.c. engine is exactly the same as that fitted to the Triumph 2000. Power is increased from 90 to 95 b.h.p. (net) at 5,000 r.p.m. Closed circuit crankcase breathing, using a Smiths valve, is standard, in order to minimize the

[...] applied [...]nience [...]cause [...] come [...]-mounted [...]wer to the [...]res on 4·1J

[...] also follow [...]priate adjust-

ments for weight and so on) but the Girling disc/drum brakes are up in size from Type 12 to Type 16, which have 9.7-in. discs (in place of 9-in.) and 8-in. rear drums in place of 7-in., giving an increase in total rubbed area of just over 30%. The central hand brake, which juts out neatly from the central arm-rest and is conveniently close to the gear lever, has a fly-off ratchet.

The now almost traditional Triumph feature of a steering column adjustable for length (to the extent of 4 in.) and designed to

Continued on the next page

The power bulge on the bonnet top is a genuine one!

The GT6 brought with it a healthy dose of practicality; there was no rear seat because it would never be of any use. Note the aftermarket slip-on headrests fitted here.

Well before the unveiling though, Triumph's marketing team made a crucial decision, which was to drop any references to the Spitfire for the new car. By doing this the GT6 could be sold as a distinct model, for which the company would be able to charge a premium. With a power-to-weight ratio of 117bhp per ton, the GT6 had good performance and looked the part; thankfully for Triumph, that's the verdict most reviewers would reach.

The GT6 Evolves

The GT6's development had been pretty thorough, and while that's not to say there was no room for improvement, Triumph got the formula basically right. As a result, there wasn't that much development of the GT6 Mk1; Triumph left most of the changes for the Mk2 edition that went on sale in 1968.

However, there were a few modifications made during the life of the GT6 Mk1, largely mirroring those made to the Spitfire Mk3. That's why the door locks were strengthened fairly early in the model cycle, while the braking balance was improved with the fitment of smaller rear wheel cylinders. The handbrake was also changed from a fly-off type to a conventional system, and the engine's durability was improved with the fitment of larger main bearings and a stronger crankshaft.

PERIOD MODIFICATIONS

Unsurprisingly, it was SAH which led the way when it came to tuning options for the early GT6s. Perhaps the most impressive product offered by the company was a Tecalemit Jackson mechanical fuel injection set-up, with a kit costing £95. Capable of taking the GT6 to beyond 120mph (193 km/h), the fuel injection system was available as part of SAH's stage three kit; when *Hot Car* put SAH 136 through its paces in its April 1968 issue, the car proved effective and impressive. Offering much more low-down torque along with far greater fuel efficiency, the car showed the way forward for tuning companies – not that they would embrace such technology especially readily, thanks to its cost and complexity. SAH offered five stages of tune for the GT6 Mk1:

Stage 1   Optimized cylinder head, hotter camshaft, six-branch exhaust manifold and upgraded carburettors to give around 120bhp.

Stage 2   Everything in the stage one kit plus larger inlet valves, balanced and polished cylinders and ports, a 10.5:1 compression ratio.

Stage 3   Everything in the stage two kit plus Tecalemit Jackson fuel injection, to give around 145bhp.

Stage 4   Everything in the stage two kit plus three Weber carburettors and a spicier camshaft.

Stage 5   As stage three, but with a wilder camshaft.

As well as these mechanical upgrades there was a raft of cosmetic alterations also available, such as a Le Mans-style bonnet with faired-in headlights, which reduced the car's kerb weight by a useful 40lb (18.14kg) thanks to its glass fibre construction. Also offered from early 1968, Minilite alloy wheels, which allowed the fitment of wider (165x13) tyres.

Motor tested SAH 136 as well, concluding that the various modifications to the car made it a more complete animal rather than one that merely highlighted the standard car's shortcomings. The magazine also pointed out that the various improvements to Syd Hurrell's own car pushed its cost up to a hefty £1,432. At the time, it was possible to buy a new TR5 for less. That didn't make the GT6 any less impressive though, with its greater grip and more predictable handling plus extra urge and sportier sound.

70

CONVERTED CAR TEST

The SAH Triumph GT6

External changes are confined to the Minilite wheels with 5½ rims on the back and 5J on the front; note the different offsets which increase the rear track quite markedly.

MOTOR week ending October 28 1967

The second conversion on this car was simply a replacement of the fuel injection system by triple Webers. Normally, this is a SAH stage 4 conversion, which uses an SAH 47 cam (40,70,70,40 degrees), but the 26 cam was retained for our test. This conversion is fully developed and gave usefully more power at the top end than the T-J system but below 3,000 r.p.m. it was not as good. We had to estimate the top speed from a comparison of the acceleration times, since the fuel pump couldn't keep up with the Webers demands if full throttle were maintained for a whole lap at MIRA, but on the open road the car should reach very nearly 125 m.p.h.

A stage 4 conversion on the Triumph 2000 only reduced the fuel consumption from 23.5 m.p.g. to 21.0, so one can expect around 20 m.p.g. from the Weber layout on a harder driven GT6. Although on paper the stage "3½" with Webers looks a better buy than the stage 3 with T-J injection we would expect a little further development to give the edge to the injection system. On the brake this gives another 5-10 b.h.p. at the rear wheels also the injection is quieter but some people like to hear that throaty gobble of Webers changing to a harsh roar when the engine climbs up onto the cam. The choice however is yours.

Suspension

Our original road test car was fitted with 155-13 Dunlop SP41s on 4½J rims; it held the road quite well but it had the usual nasty habit of the tail coming out as soon as the throttle was released in a corner. Not that this is ever likely to be a great embarrassment on the roads; it can even be used to advantage if you just ease the throttle gently to help the car line up for the straight, but it doesn't make it particularly swervable if you are faced with an emergency.

The SAH car was rather better in this respect and rather had 165-13 Cinturatos on 5½J wheels at the rear and ... wheels had different offsets as well as ... to have a puncture although

Injection or multi-c...

TO start with, the GT6 is quite a fast car; our road test example, fitted with overdrive and consequently the lower final drive, reached 60 m.p.h. in just over 10 seconds. A lot of this credit goes to astute choice of ratios since the maximum power and maximum speed are very similar to those of the arch rival, the MGB GT, but the acceleration is rather better. It needs quite a useful power increase to make such a car noticeably faster, but on Syd Hurrell's own GT6, which we tried in two stages of tune, there really was an obvious improvement. In the first stage with triple Webers, the 0-60 m.p.h. time was reduced from 10.5 seconds to 8.4 and the maximum raised from 107.8 m.p.h. to an estimated 120. We also tried the same car equipped with Te calcmi Jackson fuel injection (known as the T-J system); this is not yet fully developed and better figures are hoped for but it still reached 60 m.p.h. in 8.9 seconds and a maximum of 116.5 m.p.h. on the banked MIRA track. Lest it be thought that such a power increase might not suit the standard chassis and suspension, we'd better say here and now that the SAH GT6 had modifications in the roadholding department as well, with wider wheels, including a wider track offset, and stiffer dampers. The roadholding is certainly improved although the front and rear felt rather less co-ordinated than before with the firmer damping.

Both states of tune cost the same, a fairly expensive £238, but the car as we tested it with the conversion, overdrive, electric fan, dual exhaust system, Minilite wheels and Cinturatos, Armstrong dampers, brake servo, and oil pressure and temperature gauges comes to a rousing £1,432 or thereabouts—rather more than a TR5. Both conversions can, of course, be applied to either the Triumph Vitesse 2-litre or the Triumph 2000, or with the comprehensive SAH catalogue you can select your conversions to suit your pocket at some intermediate state.

Engine

Our first test was in fact on the T-J equipped car; this corresponds to the stage 3 tune with the larger valved head, six-branch exhaust manifold oil cooler kit, SAH "26" camshaft and all the bits and pieces which go to make up the fuel injection system. This system is still under development but it differs from the racing type conversions that are mostly seen in that the throttle is just a simple butterfly valve on the end of a tubular collector box, which of course avoids the minor complication of arranging all the individual throttles to work together, and is thus better suited to a road conversion.

It is some time since *Motor* ... 1964): basically, fuel enters ... through a restrictor ... directly propor... rail fr...

valve at ... according ... cam whi... the size ... major d... then ... pump ... compl... contr... nozz... ator... sup... furt... th...

they are nominally interchangeable. Adjustable Armstrong dampers at the rear were firm enough to stop the curious side-step or hip wobble on undulating straight roads. These mods may not sound particularly significant but they certainly made the car feel a lot more swervable and much more fun to drive far and fast with safety. The only "moment" we had was on MIRA's road circuit; the cornering power was sufficiently great to get the inside rear wheel off the deck on one corner so that we couldn't get any power on to the road when it was needed and the tail went even further, but we didn't spin. However a limited slip differential, available for all Triumphs from SAH, would cure even that problem; suffice to say then that the cornering power is a lot ... er than before even if the increased offset of the wheels makes ... steering feel a little unpleasant at first with a lot of kickback. ... u still have to make up your mind before the corner how you ... going to get through, either power all the way or trailing ... itually, but the SAH will be faster. If you try to go through with ... series of throttle dabs the car feels like a gangling, untrained colt.

Some conversions show up the weakness in a car's design, particularly the gearbox, but these two SAH conversions make the GT6 into a much nicer car.

Squatting down on a fast take-off, the SAH GT6 shows off its swing axle rear suspension.

Performance

	With T-J injection	With Webers	Standard
			Road test October 29 1967
Maximum speed	116.5 m.p.h.	120* m.p.h.	107.8 m.p.h.
Standing starts	sec.	sec.	sec.
0– 30 m.p.h.	3.7	3.6	3.6
0– 40	5.0	5.0	5.6
0– 50	6.9	6.9	7.4
0– 60	8.9	8.4	10.5
0– 70	11.7	10.9	13.7
0– 80	14.4	13.5	18.8
0– 90	18.2	17.2	26.6
0–100	26.2	22.8	—
S.S. ½m	17.0	16.5	18.1
Acceleration in upper ratios			
	Top Third	Top Third	Top Third
	sec. sec.	sec. sec.	sec. sec.
20– 40	7.5 5.4	9.0 7.0	6.2 4.6
30– 50	7.1 5.4	7.6 6.1	6.7 5.1
40– 60	6.3 4.9	6.3 4.8	6.7 5.2
50– 70	6.8 5.0	6.8 4.8	7.6 5.9
60– 80	6.9 6.1	7.0 4.9	9.1 9.0
70– 90	8.3 —	7.0 —	11.6 —
80–100	12.1 —	7.8 —	— —
Overall fuel consumption	21.2 m.p.g.	—	26.3 m.p.g.

SPECIFICATIONS: GT6 Mk1

Build dates	July 1966 – Sept 1968
Commission numbers	KC 1 – KC 13752
Engine prefix	KC
Gearbox prefix	KC
Differential prefix	KC
Number built	15,818
Basic price	£800
On the road price	£985 1s

Performance

0-30mph	3.6sec
0-50mph	7.4sec
0-60mph	10.5sec
0-80mph	18.8sec
Max speed in first gear	33mph (53km/h)
Max speed in second gear	56mph (90km/h)
Max speed in third gear	80mph (128km/h)
Top speed	107mph (172km/h)
Standing 1/4-mile	18.1sec
Power to weight ratio	117bhp/ton
Typical fuel consumption	26.3mpg
	(9.31ltr/100km)

Dimensions, weights and capacities

Length	12ft 1in (3683mm)
Width	4ft 11in (1448mm)
Height (unladen)	3ft 11in (1194mm)
Ground clearance (laden)	4in (100mm)
Wheelbase	6ft 11in (2108mm)
Front track	4ft 1in (1245mm)
Rear track	4ft 0in (1219)
Dry vehicle weight	1793lb (813kg)
Engine oil	8pt (4.7ltr)
Gearbox oil	1.5pt (0.9ltr)
Overdrive gearbox oil	2.375pt (1.4ltr)
Differential	1pt (0.6ltr)
Cooling system	11pt (6.4ltr)
Fuel tank	9.75 gal (44.3ltr)

Engine

Maximum power	95bhp @ 5,000rpm
Maximum torque	117lb/ft @ 3,000rpm
Displacement	1998cc
Bore	74.7mm
Stroke	76.0mm
Compression ratio	9.5:1
Oil pressure	50psi at 2,000rpm
Tappet clearance	0.010in
Fuelling	Twin Stromberg 150CD carburettors
Firing order	1-5-3-6-2-4
Spark plugs	Champion N-9Y
Spark plug gap	0.025in
Distributor	Delco Remy D202
Contact breaker gap	0.015in
Dwell angle	40°/42°
Ignition timing – static	13° BTDC
Centrifugal advance	0° at 500rpm
	9°/13° at 2,400rpm
	15°/19° at 5,000rpm
Vacuum advance	0° at 3.8/6.2inHg
	22 at 20in Hg

Ignition coil	Lucas HA12	Turning circle	25ft 3in (7.69m)
		Turns between locks	4.3
Transmission		Front suspension	Double wishbone
Clutch	Diaphragm	Spring rate	200lbf/in
Clutch diameter	8.5in (21.5cm)	Camber angle (unladen)	+2.75° ± 0.5°
Clutch output shaft	10 splines	Castor angle (unladen)	3.5%° ± 0.5°
Master cylinder diameter	5/8in	King pin inclination	6° ± 1°
Slave cylinder diameter	1in	Toe	1/16in – 1/8in toe in
Gearbox	3-rail	Rear suspension	Swing axle
Synchromesh	All gears	Number of leaves	8
Gear ratios	4th = 1.0	Leaf width	1.75in
	3rd = 1.25	Leaf thickness	0.25in
	2nd = 1.78	Spring rate at wheel	86lbf/in
	1st = 2.65,	Spring camber (free)	+2.38in
	R = 3.10	Toe (unladen)	1/16in – 1/8in toe out
Optional overdrive	Laycock D-type	Camber angle (unladen)	0° ± 1°
Overdrive ratio	0.802		
Overdrive gear ratios	4th = 0.80	**Wheels and tyres**	
	3rd = 1.0	Wheel size (steel)	13 x 4.5 J
Final drive ratio	3.27	Optional wire wheels	13 x 4.5 J
	(3.89 with overdrive)	Tyres	Dunlop SP41/
			Goodyear G800
Brakes and steering		Tyre size	155 SR-13
Front	9.7in solid disc	Tyre pressures	Front: 20psi
Caliper type	Girling		Rear: 24psi
Swept area	197sq in		
Rear	8 x 1.25in drum	**Electrics**	
Swept area	63sq in	Earth	Negative
Wheel cylinder diameter	0.75in	Dynamo	Lucas C40L
	(5/8in from KC7279)	Max current output	25 amps
Master cylinder diameter	0.7in	Starter motor	Lucas M35G
Steering	Rack and pinion	Headlights	60/45w

CHAPTER EIGHT

GT6 Mk2 (1968–1970)

Two years after the original GT6 had been unveiled, Triumph took the wraps off a heavily revised car at the 1968 Earls Court Motor Show. Stylistically, this Mk2 edition of the GT6 incorporated the same changes as the Spitfire Mk3 compared with its predecessor. That meant a raised front bumper with combined sidelight/indicator units directly below, while at the back the quarter bumpers also sat higher, with larger indicators positioned underneath. There were also new Rostyle wheel trims, in line with various other models in the Triumph range but, for those who preferred something more tasteful, there was still the option of painted wire wheels.

Other details less likely to be spotted at a casual glance were wipers set more widely apart (the same as the later Spitfire Mk3), a cream enamel GT6 badge in place of the previous chrome item, and an exhaust that featured a trans-

versely-mounted silencer just ahead of the rear valance – a feature which would also be used on the Spitfire MkIV.

Of more significance, however, was what Triumph had done under the skin – and particularly to the rear suspension. The GT6's swing axle rear suspension was always going to be a compromise, and while it would never hamper the GT6 to the same degree that it affected the Herald and Vitesse, it certainly held the car back dynamically. The answer was to graft in the same rotoflex rear suspension design that Triumph fitted to the Vitesse 2-Litre Mk2.

The usual fix for reducing lift-off oversteer on cars fitted with swing axles was to fit stiffer suspension. While this had the effect of reducing roll in corners, it also tended to wreck the ride, and there was only so much that anti-roll bars could do. What was needed of course was a redesign of the suspension altogether, and while the GT6 Mk2 didn't offer

The GT6 Mk2's nose was taken straight from the Spitfire Mk3 (or was it the other way round?), with a full-width raised bumper. However, the Spitfire didn't have the GT6's humped bonnet of course, while it also didn't get Rostyle wheels.

The biggest news with the GT6 Mk2 was the adoption of rotoflex rear suspension, which truly transformed the car dynamically. The lifespan of the rubber couplings used could be a bit of an issue, but this was a small price to pay for so much more driving pleasure.

that, it did give the next best thing. The move to a rotoflex design was the result of testing by Triumph's competitions department, and had been inspired by a 1950s Cooper Formula One suspension set-up.

Although the transverse leaf spring of the GT6 Mk1 was retained, it became the upper wishbone in what was effectively a double-wishbone set up. The lower wishbone was made of cast iron, and it was fitted back to front – that is, with the single pivot attached to the chassis and a pair of pivots at the base of the vertical link. Whereas the Vitesse had been forced to endure a conversion to lever arm dampers at the back, the GT6 retained its telescopic shock absorbers all round, but they were relocated to clear the new vertical links.

The final alteration was a move to a half-shaft which incorporated a rotoflex coupling: a rubber ring that joined the inner driveshaft (from the differential) to the outer driveshaft (to the hub). Not only did this allow a certain amount of axle articulation, but it also acted as a driveline damper to reduce torsional shocks.

The overhauled rear suspension transformed the GT6's manners through the bends – as was to be expected considering the car now effectively featured double-wishbone suspension at each end. The redesign reduced the roll height of the rear suspension by 6.5in (16.5cm), so the car could now be driven enthusiastically through bends without any risk of the rear wheels tucking under – the transformation really was complete.

THE AMERICAN GT6 Mk2

While the rest of the world got the same specification of GT6 Mk2 as each other (albeit in left or right-hand drive forms of course), Triumph made a special effort to keep its American customers happy – and to comply with federal regulations. To that end, US-market GT6s (badged GT6+) were fitted with whitewall tyres as standard, along with marker lights on the front and rear wings.

Inside, there were integrated head restraints for the front seats, which were now trimmed in perforated vinyl. There was also a leather-trimmed gear knob and, for those who preferred wire wheels, they were now an extra-cost option – as were eight-spoke alloy wheels. Those who didn't want to spend extra cash had to settle for steel wheels, with nasty spoke-effect wheel-trims, which frankly didn't suit the car. Still, many thought that the Rostyle-effect items fitted to GT6 Mk2s sold elsewhere were equally grim, so it's not as though the Americans necessarily got the short straw.

As well as the suspension redesign there were other mechanical changes for the GT6 Mk2, most notably to the engine and transmission. Although the Mk1 GT6's engine worked well, there was still room for improvement – especially when it came to allowing it to breathe better. The answer was to fit a redesigned cylinder head, with larger inlet and exhaust valves, as installed on the new TR5 and TR250. Although the engine fitted to these models was a 2.5-litre unit, that powerplant was little more than a long-stroke version of the 2-litre unit fitted to the GT6. As well as the cylinder head, the GT6 also adopted the TR250's inlet manifold: the TR5 was fitted with Lucas mechanical fuel injection, so that featured a different manifold.

While Triumph was at it, the company took the opportunity to incorporate a few other revisions to the straight-six. A revised crankshaft ran in larger bearings, and a slightly spicier camshaft gave greater lift and more overlap. Even though the compression ratio was lower than before, there was a ten per cent jump in power from 95bhp to a useful 104bhp, and there was also a very handy 117lb ft of torque.

The other key mechanical alteration was to the back axle ratio, which was raised to 3.27:1 for all models, whether equipped with overdrive or not. Mk1 editions of the GT6 had featured this tall gearing only if the car was supplied without overdrive. If it was specified, the ratio was dropped to 3.89:1. The result was gearing in top that was barely different between cars with overdrive and those without, the only benefit being an extra ratio for those who spent the extra cash.

Triumph's solution was to fit the taller ratio as standard on all cars, but for those who preferred it, the 3.89:1 diff could be specified instead – and there were plenty of buyers who opted to take this route. The reason was the car's lack of acceleration in overdrive top, because the gearing was too high; cruising was relaxed, but perhaps too much so for those who didn't sit at the same speed all day.

PRODUCTION CHANGES (FROM THE COMMISSION NUMBER GIVEN)

KC75031   Reclining seats fitted, together with redesigned steering wheel. Also more cockpit padding and stronger bulkhead (for crash safety).

OPTIONS

Dealer-fitted options

Bonnet lock (pair)	
Brake servo (Girling Powerstop)	£13 0s 0d
Cigarette lighter (push-in)	10s 8d + purchase tax
Cigarette lighter (pull-out)	£1 10s 0d + purchase tax
Continental touring kit	
Electric windscreen defroster	£1 15s 0d
Emergency windscreen	
Fire extinguisher	
Fog lamp	From £13 9s 0d
Fuel line filter	
Head rest	£3 19s 0d
Luggage strap	
Mud flap kit	£1 7s 6d
Oil cooler kit	
Radio (Smiths Radiomobile)	
Roof rack	From £6 19s 6d
Seat covers	
Sill protectors	
Spark plug spanner	
Spot lamp	From £13 9s 0d

Touch-in paints	5s 0d
Tow bar kit	From £5 10s 0d
Tow rope and luggage rack strap	
Warning triangle	
Wheelbrace	
Windscreen anti-frost shield	
Wing mirrors	From 19s 6d
Wire wheels (hexagonal spinner only)	£38 6s 8d
Wood-rimmed steering wheel	From £7 10s 0d

Factory-fitted options

Competition DS11 brake pads and shoes	
Front upper ball joint with grease nipple	
Heated rear window	£11 10s 0d
Laminated windscreen	
Leather seats	
Leather trim	
Occasional rear seat	£19 3s 6d
Overdrive	£60 13s 11d
Skid plate	
Steering column lock	
Track rod end with grease nipple	

This modified GT6 Mk2 sports aftermarket alloy wheels, and is also fitted with a Webasto cloth sunroof to keep the cabin cool.

PAINT AND TRIM OPTIONS

Throughout the life of the GT6 Mk2, it was offered with the same paint and trim options as for the contemporary Spitfire Mk3, which meant buyers could select from:

Paint	Interior trim
White	Black, tan or Matador Red
Royal Blue	Black or Shadow Blue
Wedgwood Blue	Black or Shadow Blue
Valencia Blue	Black or tan
Conifer Green	Black or Matador Red
Signal Red	Black or tan
Damson Red	Black or tan
Jasmine Yellow	Black or tan

little short of unbearable on a hot day: a few hours behind the wheel was like sitting in a mobile sauna.

Even the interiors of the earliest GT6 prototypes had shown a tendency to get uncomfortably warm, but Triumph had put the car into production without adequately addressing the problem – the development of the Mk2 was an opportunity to put things right.

The only way of undertaking a long summer journey in a MkI GT6 was to open the front quarter lights and hinged rear side windows, to allow air to flow through the cabin. But this could be noisy and it wasn't always convenient to have the windows open. Triumph's solution was to fit a two-speed heater fan plus air ducts in the footwells and dash, with eyeball vents as already seen in its 2000 Saloon and Estate. That got the air into the cabin – it was then extracted through the fitment of louvred vents in the C-pillars, aft of the rear side windows. The solution was just what the doctor ordered: the GT6's occupants were no longer likely to be hit with a nasty dose of heat stroke on a long journey.

There were other interior changes too, such as the use of a satin wooden dash: until now there had been a gloss finish to it. The switchgear was also new: it was flush-fitting (the same as the TR5's), while the gauges featured black bezels in place of the previous chromed items. Extra headroom was gained by reducing the amount of padding in the seats, while three-point seat belts were also now standard for those in the front. Speaking of which, until now there had been no rear seat option, but the Mk2 brought one with it, in a bid to compete more closely with the MGB GT. This rear seat was definitely only of the occasional variety, and suitable merely for small children, but it was at least a nod towards greater practicality.

While the mechanical upgrades were generally welcome, Triumph also needed to address other issues with the GT6 Mk2, especially the poor cabin ventilation. With that hefty six-cylinder engine up front, and little in the way of through-flow ventilation, the heat build up in the GT6's cabin could be

The Mk2's interior benefitted from a raft of improvements such as more modern switchgear, the adoption of three-point seatbelts, plus a new satin-finish wooden dash.

MARKETING

Triumph started to move towards a more lifestyle-focused pitch for the marketing of the GT6 Mk2, showing people getting away from it all, or indulging in pursuits such as motorsport. Unsurprisingly, there was also a lot of attention paid to the more capable chassis of the Mk2, with various references to the revised rear suspension.

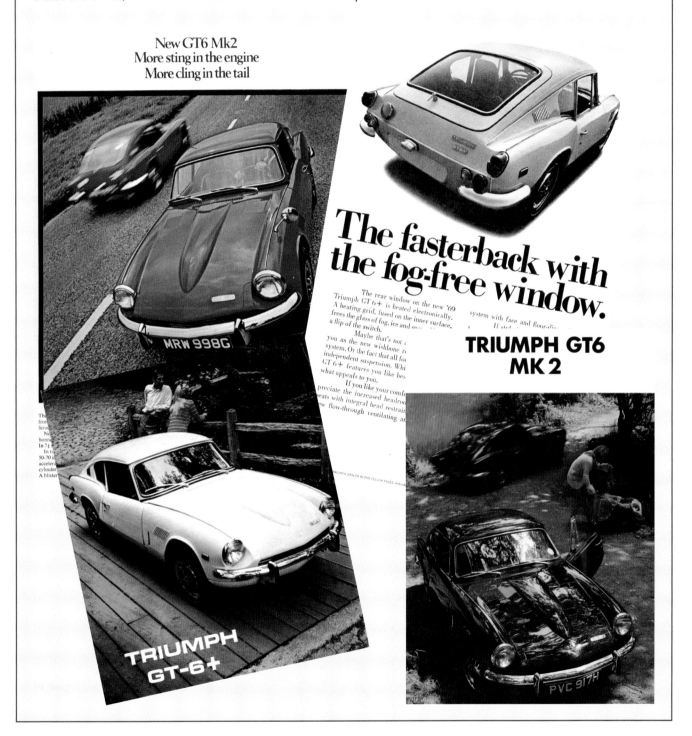

PRESS REACTION

True to form, *Autocar* and *Motor* were first out of the blocks with their coverage of the GT6 Mk2 in September 1968, but neither would test the car until well into 1969. Both magazines opened with the line that the Mk2 was a 'much improved' car compared with its predecessor, thanks to the revised suspension design that gave much more secure handling without destroying the ride. Both titles were also impressed by the GT6's economy and value, but *Autocar* felt the steering was too slow while *Motor* focused on the poor top-end refinement.

Car magazine tested the Mk2 GT6 in its October 1968 issue, which because it was a motor show edition didn't go into any more detail than absolutely necessary to spell out what Triumph had done with its baby. Although the piece was generally somewhat objective (perhaps disappointingly so for

this usually more analytical magazine), at least the news was good, with the mechanical changes proving highly effective.

It was a similar story when *Road & Track* put the GT6+ through its paces in its February 1969 issue, with the article proving disappointingly descriptive; much of what was in there could have come from Triumph's press release. However, R&T did discover that despite offering more power, the GT6's fuel consumption hadn't increased, while the steering was light and precise. It also commented on the fact that Triumph recommended tyre pressures front and rear of 24psi – but increasing this to 30psi at each corner improved things enormously – not that they had to worry about boring things such as tyre life of course…

Sports Car Graphic also tested the GT6+, slating its excessive throttle pedal travel and hating a defect in the windscreen that made everything look rippled – not ideal! However, the rest of the magazine's review was far more positive, the testers

NEW FOR '69 MK 2 TRIUMPH GT6

New rear suspension, more power and revised styling details

Once again the coverage was almost universally positive for this first refresh of the GT6.

falling in love with the Triumph's lines, (predictably) comparing them with those of Jaguar's E-type. Also getting the thumbs up were the car's ergonomics, ventilation, brakes, handling and performance, as well as the practicality. Result.

MOTOR ROAD TEST No. 28/69

Triumph GT6 Mk.2

M MOTOR TESTED

Much improved

New rear suspension greatly improves roadholding and handling; good performance and excellent economy made still better by changes; engine rather noisy at high revs.

As on the Spitfire, the front bumper has been raised to meet American safety regulations.

Seats have been thinned down to increase headroom but they are still comfortable. Leather-covered steering wheel has a thinner rim than before.

High-speed mobile greenhouse: one of the many uses for the rear luggage space. Note extractor louvres in rear quarters.

PERIOD MODIFICATIONS

Although SAH didn't offer a massive choice of tuning options when the GT6 was launched, it didn't take long for the company to broaden its range. By the time the Mk2 was launched towards the end of 1968, there were no fewer than four stages to which the GT6 could be taken, with a multitude of other options also available.

The entry-level package was the stage one kit, costing £132 10s and offering around 120bhp. This was achieved by fitting an exchange cylinder head, hotter camshaft, new valve springs and spark plugs plus a six-branch exhaust manifold, Stromberg 175CD carburettor and fresh air filters. If this wasn't enough, for £188 17s there was a stage two kit offered, capable of generating around 135bhp. This consisted of everything in the stage one kit, but with a sports coil and oil cooler along with a more heavily reworked cylinder head.

By the time the Mk2 was launched, the stage three kit had been discontinued, but there was a stage four offering, taking

maximum power to around 145-150bhp in exchange for £263 10s. This kit took everything available in the lesser ones, adding a hotter camshaft that allowed revving to 7,000rpm, twin silencers for the exhaust system plus a trio of Weber 40DCOEs.

As mentioned in the previous chapter, there was also the option of choosing fuel injection instead of the Webers, with the costs of each conversion being broadly similar. The results were also much the same in terms of maximum power and top speed, but the injection system offered a much better spread of torque at the bottom end. As well as these packages, SAH also offered various items on a pick-and-mix basis:

• Stage three cylinder head	£40
• Six-branch exhaust manifold	£18
• High-lift camshaft	£15
• Oil cooler kit	£15
• Kenlowe thermostatic fan	£17 11s
• Weber manifold for triple carbs	£15 15s
• Links and couplings for above manifold	£3 10s
• Weber 40DCOE carburettor (each)	£26
• Brake booster kit	£16 15s
• Competition brake pads (set of four)	£5 5s
• Competition shoes (set of four)	£4 6s
• Minilite alloy wheels (set of four 4.5x13)	£82 18s
• Dunlop steel wheels	£4 15s
• Le Mans bonnet with faired-in headlamps	£53

Hurrell used to have a demonstrator on hand to prove just what he could do to the GT6. The car was registered SAH 4, and it featured a stage 3-cylinder head, a trio of Weber 40DCOEs and a cast alloy rocker cover. That cylinder head boasted reprofiled combustion chambers, bored out inlet and exhaust ports, competition valve springs and the whole lot was polished for optimum gas flow.

Unusually, there were no enlarged inlet or exhaust valves, but the head was skimmed to achieve a 10.5:1 compression ratio – which was about as far as the six-pot engine could be taken without a danger of detonation. To finish the straight-six off there was a high-lift camshaft, to get the fuel mixture in and out of the combustion chambers as quickly as possible.

GT6 owners could buy this stage three kit for £278.50, which included all the parts as well as the labour to fit them. Also included in the kit were a six-branch tubular exhaust

manifold (complete with twin silencers), an oil cooler, sports ignition coil and a set of NGK spark plugs. For those who wanted even more it was possible to specify a whole raft of extras such as auxiliary lighting, alloy wheels and revised suspension.

When *Car* magazine got its hands on SAH 4 (September 1971) it was highly impressed with Hurrell's work – the car was not only much faster than the standard edition, but it was also far more surefooted. Despite changing up at 6,500rpm (Hurrell recommended a 7,500rpm red-line), *Car*'s testers managed to get to 80mph (128km/h) from a standing start in just 14sec, with 100mph (160km/h) being despatched in 24.9sec – and this was despite a slipping clutch. Not only this, but a useful 125mph (201km/h) was squeezed from the car; what's not recorded is how much fuel it took to achieve these figures. You can bet it was plenty!

SPECIFICATIONS: GT6 Mk2

Build dates	July 1968 – Dec 1970
Commission numbers	KC 50000 – KC 83397
Engine prefix	KC
Gearbox prefix	KC
Differential prefix	KC (KD if fitted with overdrive)
Number built	12,066
Basic price	£879
On the road price	£1,158 5s 6d

Performance

0-30mph	3.5sec
0-50mph	7.2sec
0-60mph	10.0sec
0-80mph	18.2sec
Max speed in first gear	37mph (59.5km/h)
Max speed in second gear	54mph (86.5km/h)
Max speed in third gear	77mph (123.9km/h)
Max speed in overdrive third	93mph (149.6km/h)
Max speed in fourth gear	94mph (151.2km/h)
Max speed in overdrive fourth	107mph (172.1km/h)
Standing 1/4-mile	17.3sec
Power to weight ratio	116bhp/ton
Typical consumption	28mpg (9.9ltr/100km)

Dimensions, weights and capacities

Length	12ft 3in (3734mm)
Width	4ft 9in (1448mm)
Height	3ft 11in (1194mm)
Wheelbase	83in (2108mm)
Front track	4ft 1 in (1245mm)
Rear track	4ft1 in (1245mm)
Dry weight	1793lb (813kg)

**A GT6 Mk2 tackles Prescott hill climb, sporting Minilite alloy wheels
and an optional sliding cloth Webasto sunroof.**

Engine oil	8pt (4.7ltr)
Gearbox oil	1l7pt (0.9ltr)
Overdrive oil	2.375pt (1.4ltr)
Differential oil	1pt (0.6ltr)
Cooling system	11pt (6.4ltr)
Fuel tank	9.75gal (44.3ltr)

Engine

Max power	104bhp @ 5,300rpm
Max torque	117lb ft @ 3,000rpm
Max BMEP	144psi @ 3,000rpm
Displacement	1998cc
Bore	74.7mm
Stroke	76.0mm
Compression ratio	9.25:1
Oil pressure	50psi at 2,000rpm
Tappet clearance	0.010in
Fuelling	Twin Stromberg 150 CD carburettors
Firing order	1-5-3-6-2-4
Spark plugs	Champion N-9Y
Spark plug gap	0.025in
Distributor	Delco Remy 0200
Contact breaker gap	0.015in
Dwell angle	400/420
Ignition timing – static	100 BTDC
Centrifugal advance	00 at 400rpm 200 at 4,400rpm
Vacuum advance	00 at 3.8/6.2inHg 110 at 20in Hg
Ignition coil	Lucas HA12

Transmission

Clutch	Diaphragm
Clutch diameter	8.5in (21.25cm)
Clutch output shaft	10 splines
Master cylinder diameter	5/8in
Slave cylinder diameter	1in
Gearbox	3-rail
Synchromesh	All gears
Gear ratios	4th = 1.0
	3rd = 1.25
	2nd = 1.78
	1st = 2.65
	R = 3.10

Optional overdrive	Laycock D-type
Overdrive ratio	0.802
Overdrive gear ratios	4th = 0.80
	3rd = 1.0
Final drive ratio	3.27 (3.89 with overdrive)

Brakes and steering

Front brakes	9.7in solid disc
Calliper type	Girling
Swept area	197sq in
Rear brakes	8 x 1.25in drum
Swept area	63sq in
Wheel cylinder diam	5/8in
Master cylinder diam	0.7in
Steering	Rack and pinion
Turning circle	25ft 3in (7.62m)
Turns between locks	4.3

Suspension, wheels and tyres

Front suspension	Double wishbone
Spring rate	200lbf/in
Camber angle (unladen)	+2 3/40 ± 1/2°
Castor angle (unladen)	3 1/2° ± 1/2°
King pin inclination	60 ± 10
Toe	1/16-1/8in toe in
Rear suspension	Rotoflex
Number of leaves	6
Leaf width	1.75in
Leaf thickness	0.234in
Spring rate	93lbf/in
Toe (unladen)	0 ± 1/32in
Camber angle (unladen)	0 ± 1°
Wheel size (steel)	13 x 4.5 J
Optional wire wheels	13 x 4.5 J
Tyres	Dunlop SP41/SP68
Tyre size	155 SR-13
Tyre pressure	Front: 24psi
	Rear: 28psi

Electrics

Earth	Negative
Alternator	Lucas 15 ACR
Max current output	28 amps
Starter motor	Lucas M35G
Headlights	60/45w

CHAPTER NINE

GT6 Mk3 (1970–1973)

Although the GT6 had proved to be a winner for Triumph, by 1968 sales had started to wane, forcing some kind of facelift. The answer was simple: to restyle the car along the same lines as the Spitfire MkIV, which meant a heavily restyled nose and tail, along with a far more modern interior. Making its début alongside the Spitfire MkIV at the Turin Motor Show of October 1970, the Mk3 was the most accomplished of the GT6 breed; conversely, the MkIV would go on to be the runt of the Spitfire litter as far as the car's collectability is concerned.

The Mk3's slimline bumpers ensured the GT6 now looked sleeker, but the most obvious change was at the back of the car, where the new corporate tail design had been adopted. Gone were the dainty tail lights which had stood proud of the rear corners of the bodywork: instead there were much bigger, flush-fitting units that sat in a Stag-like chrome surround that ran the whole width of

the car's rear.

There was still a bonnet bulge to accommodate the 1998cc straight-six, but it was now flatter and wider, so it looked more discreet and less of an add-on. Gone were the louvres that previously adorned the front wings, while the door handles were now flush-fitting units that looked rather sleeker than before.

For the last few months of production (February-November 1973) there was an increase in the number of combinations offered, with all of the previous chart options still being available. New to the range was Magenta with black trim or Mimosa Yellow with black or Chestnut trim.

Alongside all this detailing which updated the GT6's aesthetics, some of the cosmetic elements of the redesign went deeper. For example, the rear side windows were reshaped so they integrated far better with the car's profile, while the louvres that sat behind for cabin ventilation were also

The most striking styling change for the Mk3 GT6 was its redesigned rump, which now sported the Triumph corporate look.

OPTIONS

Dealer-fit options
Continental touring kit
Headlamp converter mask (Lucas)
Headrests (from KC 20000 only)
Luggage straps
Occasional rear seat
Oil cooler
Tow bar
Wire wheels-bolt-on   £47.50
Wooden gear knob
Special order (factory-fitted) options
Front upper ball joint with grease nipple
Laminated windscreen   £8.75
Leather trim panels-up to KE 20000 only
Leather seats
Overdrive   £68.75
Skid plate
Sundym glass-standard after KE 20000
Track rod ends fitted with grease nipple

PAINT AND TRIM OPTIONS

The GT6 Mk3's colour options mirrored those of the contemporary Spitfire MkIV. This meant that until December 1971, the choices were:

Paint	Interior trim
White	Black, tan, Shadow Blue or Matador Red
Sapphire Blue	Silver Grey or Shadow Blue
Wedgwood Blue	Black or Shadow Blue
Valencia Blue	Black or tan
Laurel Green	Black, tan or Matador Red
Signal Red	Black or tan
Damson Red	Black, tan or Silver Grey
Sienna Brown	Black or tan
Saffron Yellow	Black or tan

A colour range overhaul between January and August 1972 meant buyers could choose from:

White	Black, tan or Shadow Blue
Sapphire Blue	Black, Silver Grey or Shadow Blue
Emerald Green	Black, or Silver Grey
Damson Red	Black, tan or Silver Grey
Pimento Red	Black
Sienna Brown	Tan
Saffron Yellow	Black

There was yet another overhaul of the colour options for the period running between September 1972 and January 1973. Buyers could now choose between:

White	Black, Chestnut or Shadow Blue
Sapphire Blue	Black or Shadow Blue
French Blue	Black
Emerald Green	Black
Mallard Green	Black or tan
Carmine Red	Black or tan
Pimento Red	Black or Chestnut
Sienna Brown	Black or tan

restyled. Now painted body colour, rather than chrome-plated, they were less of a stylistic feature but more efficient thanks to also being longer than before.

The windscreen was also now deeper, to match the Spitfire MkIV's – additionally, it was available in laminated form, while those with even deeper pockets could specify green-tinted Sundym heat-resistant glass for the screen, along with the rest of the cabin's glass.

Earlier GT6s had featured a fuel filler neck in the rear panel, but for the Mk3 this was moved to the nearside (on right-hand drive cars) rear wing; there was also a flush-fitting cap in place of the previous racing-style item.

Alongside these major changes there was a range of minor adjustments too, with items such as badging and wheels being redesigned. Rectangular badges were fitted front and rear, denoting the fact that this was now the GT6 Mk3, while the wheels were much more nicely finished. Still 4.5in wide, they dispensed with the previous cheap-looking plastic trims, sporting a painted finish instead. Still wearing centre caps with the GT6 logo, these standard pressed-steel items could be replaced by wire wheels at the factory when the car was ordered, although in place of the previous knock-on units, Triumph had by now moved over to bolt-on rims instead.

Meanwhile, the rear window's heating elements now ran horizontally instead of vertically (although some early Mk3s used up stocks of the earlier glass) and there was a more effective catch for the tailgate release.

There were interior changes too, which were overdue as the GT6's cabin was starting to show its age. Out went the previous toggles to be superseded by flush-fitting rocker switches, while there were now modified heater controls and an ignition barrel that featured a locking mechanism. While this last feature was no doubt a move forward, the fact that Triumph's designers sited it somewhere under the dash so it was largely inaccessible to anyone over four feet tall was not such a good move. However, those same designers redeemed themselves (at least partly) by moving the overdrive switch to the gear knob, allowing the driver to change gear and flick out of overdrive with just one hand movement.

Mechanical changes for the GT6 Mk3 were slight, the focus being on improving refinement and efficiency rather than boosting power. Indeed, on paper the new model was less powerful than the old one, but the reality was that this was purely down to how the power output was measured, rather than there being any actual reduction in the number of horses on tap.

A pair of emission-controlled Zenith-Stromberg 150CDSE carburettors was now fitted, operated by a cable linkage instead of the previous rod affair. There was a fresh design of intake for the air filter box and a new plastic cooling fan was now fitted, which was claimed to be lighter and quieter than before. The exhaust system was overhauled, with a centre silencer fitted in conjunction with the transverse silencer that had débuted on the GT6 Mk2.

The **GT6 Mk3** incorporated a raft of changes over its predecessor, from new rear lights to redesigned wheels. The cabin ventilation louvres were now painted to match the rest of the bodywork, while flush-fitting door handles also made an appearance.

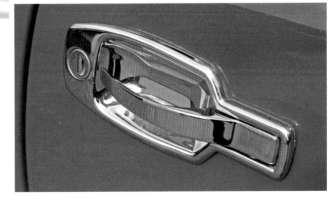

The engine was carried over unchanged from the Mk2, but there were revisions to some of the ancillaries, such as the air filters and carburettors.

The result of all these changes was supposedly a reduction in power and torque from 104bhp and 117lb ft to just 98bhp and 108lb ft, although as already mentioned, there was no change in reality – or at least not for UK cars. Unfortunately though, there were some very real reductions in power and torque for US-market GT6s, and it was these alterations that would ultimately prove to be the car's downfall. That's because the early seventies saw the introduction of strict emissions regulations for the federal market, many cars suffering from huge power drops in a bid to clean up engine emissions. That was certainly the case for the GT6, which saw its power output drop to just 79bhp for the 1972 model year, thanks to the adoption of emissions control equipment

Incidentally, while the GT6 Mk2 had been marketed in the US as the GT6+, the arrival of the Mk3 edition heralded a return to the same GT6 badging and marketing for the federal market as for everyone else.

There was fresh switchgear for the Mk3, while cars fitted with overdrive now featured a switch on the gear knob.

PRODUCTION CHANGES

GT6 sales had begun to slide in 1968 and the introduction of a Mk3 edition did nothing to halt the decline. In a bid to save money, British Leyland elected to rationalize its 6-cylinder engine range, and as a result the GT6 was fitted with the 2000's cylinder head from January 1972, from engine number KE10001. With its deeper combustion chambers and domed pistons, the compression ratio dropped from 9.25:1 to 9.0:1. At the same time, a milder camshaft was introduced in a bid to reduce fuel consumption, and hence emissions. Unfortunately, all this had an effect on the power and torque outputs – and this time it wasn't just on paper.

Power was down from 98bhp to 95bhp while the peak torque dropped from 108lb ft to 106lb ft.

The GT6 soldiered on throughout 1972. Then, in 1973, Triumph introduced a whole raft of revisions, in a final bid to increase sales. Buyers no longer had to spend extra money to purchase a new GT6 with Sundym glass or a brake servo, as these were now standard. There was also a more powerful alternator, revised switchgear and a steering wheel that looked much like the TR6's, which meant it not only looked neater, but was also much nicer to use as well.

Although the GT6 still looked great (arguably better than ever), it no longer had the performance of a sports car, which is why US buyers stayed away. Triumph was depend-

A BRAVE NEW WORLD

Although the Mk3 GT6 was a clear evolution of the breed, it might not have been so if this design study had become reality. Proposed in the late 1960s, this proposal aimed to inject a bit of radicalism into the GT6, with its pop-up headlamps – although the key changes are all in the nose.

Look closely and you'll see that each side of the car is different, with louvres behind the offside headlamps, but on the nearside those louvres sit just forward of the base of the windscreen. There's also a slight hump on the nearside too, but it's pretty slight, meaning the whole bonnet has been raised to clear the straight-six that sits underneath. Interestingly, there are still seams along the top of each wing; these were dispensed with when the real Mk3 arrived. Sadly, this unconventional proposal was overlooked, with a rather more predictable design being used instead.

Two Mk3 prototypes were constructed in the end, numbered X797 and X799. The former was a right-hand drive car, which was registered PHP 439H and carried engine number X1257E, while the latter was left-hand drive and was fitted with engine number KD 78921E; it was never road registered.

This proposal could have breathed new life into the GT6 formula, but instead it was mothballed.

ent on the federal market for the GT6 to remain viable, and with global registrations for the model plummeting to just 2,745 in 1973, it no longer made sense to keep building the car. As a result, the final GT6 was produced in November 1973 – a full seven years before the last Spitfire was built.

GT6 buyers flush with cash could still specify a range of extras, one of the key items being a pair of very neat detachable head restraints. These could be attached to the front seats, which were now finished in corded brushed nylon, a material that British Leyland was introducing across all of its models on account of it being more durable and far more comfortable than the vinyl previously fitted.

Although few buyers would realize it, the revised GT6

THE GT6 MkIV

Triumph may have killed off the GT6 in 1973, but that didn't stop the model from being revived – albeit only very briefly – in 2002. The man behind the revival was Wayne Westerman, who was a Swedish fan of the Triumph marque. An ex-Saab apprentice, Westerman penned a proposal for a super-sleek fastback with hints of the Jensen SV-8 around the nose.

Nearly three decades after the GT6's demise, this proposal for a successor was penned. We're still waiting...

Mk3 also featured a more significant change under the skin: the disappearance of rotoflex rear suspension. Though very effective, this suspension was costly to build and since the demise of the Vitesse in 1971, British Leyland's sole car to feature it was the GT6.

It made no sense to buy in the components for a single model that by now was selling in small numbers, so the axe was wielded and the rotoflex design bit the dust, to be replaced by the cheaper swing-spring set-up as used on the Spitfire MkIV. It's doubtful any buyer ever noticed the difference – especially as few would have had the chance to drive the two GT6 variants back-to-back. The GT6 still handled tidily, but it wasn't this that would cause British Leyland problems with the model.

Westerman approached BMW design head Chris Bangle to ask about the possibility of reviving the Triumph marque, but predictably, it wasn't a part of BMW's strategy. Although Westerman sought backing to go it alone with the project, things never got beyond a quarter-scale model. Thus details such as powerplants and transmissions were never pinned down; indeed, one of the few details settled upon was the wheel/tyre size, which was set at 235/35 18.

Compared with some of the completely barking proposals dreamed up by car designers, the GT6 MkIV was surprisingly sane and superbly proportioned and detailed. It's a shame the car never got as far as a running prototype, because it would have looked great. Maybe one day…

MARKETING

For this 1972 brochure, Triumph got all creative, coming up with something that resembled a storybook, which was somewhat suggestive of GT6 owners being international men and women of mystery. It was contrived to say the least, but at least it attempted to offer something new.

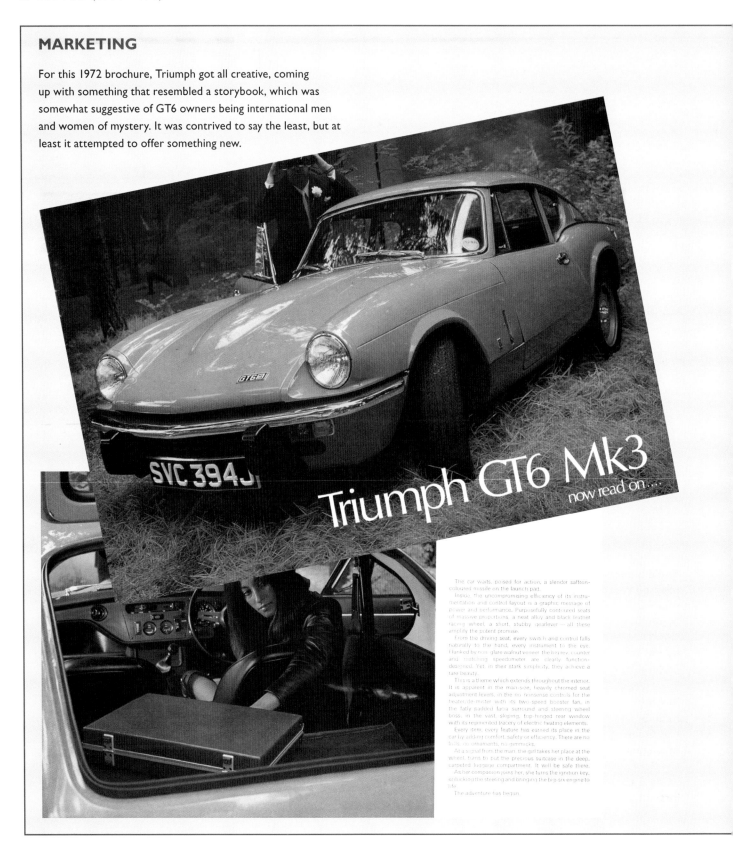

Triumph GT6 Mk3

now read on....

The car waits, poised for action, a slender saffron-coloured missile on the launch pad.

Inside, the uncompromising efficiency of its instrumentation and control layout is a graphic message of power and performance. Purposefully contoured seats of massive proportions, a neat alloy and black leather racing wheel, a short, stubby gearlever — all these amplify the potent promise.

From the driving seat, every switch and control falls naturally to the hand, every instrument to the eye. Flanked by non-glare walnut veneer the big rev. counter and matching speedometer are clearly function-designed. Yet, in their stark simplicity, they achieve a rare beauty.

This is a theme which extends throughout the interior. It is apparent in the man-size, heavily chromed seat adjustment levers, in the no-nonsense controls for the heater/de-mister with its two speed booster fan, in the fatly padded facia surround and steering wheel boss, in the vast, sloping, top-hinged rear window with its regimented tracery of electric heating elements.

Every item, every feature has earned its place in the car by adding comfort, safety or efficiency. There are no frills, no ornaments, no gimmicks.

At a signal from the man, the girl takes her place at the wheel, turns to put the precious suitcase in the deep, carpeted luggage compartment. It will be safe there.

As her companion joins her, she turns the ignition key, unlocking the steering and bringing the big-six engine to life.

The adventure has begun.

You'd be hard-pressed to find much in the way of advertising for the GT6 Mk3; by the time it arrived, Triumph appeared to have lost interest in its baby sports car, focusing more heavily on the Stag and its various saloons instead, as well as the TR6.

PRESS REACTION

When *Car* pitched a GT6 Mk3 against an MGB GT (February 1971), its reviewers didn't seem especially enamoured with either car, claiming that both were long in the tooth – with the MG appearing especially so. What's of more interest is the opening paragraph in the article: 'The whole concept of the open sports car is pretty well dead. The end will not come, unless by legislation, so long as there are a few long-suffering diehards around to demand that they should be buffeted by wind, irritated by draughts and alternatively chilled or frozen – and always deafened – as they drive along increasingly crowded and polluted roads.' And this was in 1971 remember…

Autocar was more positive about the redesigned GT6, reckoning that it was an improvement in pretty much every way over its predecessor. Aside from a braking system that didn't inspire confidence, most aspects of the GT6 got the thumbs up from *Autocar*'s testers. Intriguingly, the magazine

also claimed that specifying overdrive wasn't worthwhile, because a car without it would not only offer much the same performance (thanks to the higher final drive ratio) but the overdrive-equipped car would return inferior fuel economy to a car without it.

Motor Trend was also very positive about the Mk3; once again, the magazine tested a car without overdrive. Acknowledging that the GT6 was a small car for Americans, *Motor Trend* was still enthusiastic about the car's performance, handling, interior and styling – as well as its value at $3,424. The magazine claimed that: 'The GT6 is one of the better values for money in the wonderful world of Grand Touring. Strong, fast, solid, with excellent handling characteristics it will go like, feel like and do like a number of cars costing considerably and significantly more and sip gasoline at the rate of around twenty-five miles to the gallon in day-to-day urban and suburban running while doing all these things. Asking more for the money would be sheer greed.'

Although the GT6's days were numbered, this last iteration still received largely enthusiastic reviews.

having the double jointed drive shafts and other mechanical gubbins which make it a far more sanitary car than the swing axle Mk1. The power of the standard engine went up from the 95bhp at 5000rpm of the Mk1 to the current 104bhp at 5300rpm of the Mk2 and Mk3.

The stage three unit on the test car is just about as hot as it is advisable to go on a road car without intractability rearing its ugly head. Of course, for racing use considerably more power is available—at a price. As soon as the forward hingeing bonnet is raised, part of the reason for the greatly improved performance is revealed, for no less than three enormous 40DCOE Weber car-

The other main mechanical change on the GT6 is a new cam,

returned the car to SAH that we could have used 7500rpm and that the clutch was an experimental one they were testing. With a good clutch and using 7500rpm there's no doubt we could have knocked a couple of seconds off that zero to 100mph time. The performance is accomp⋯⋯ ⋯ir amount of ⋯⋯ ⋯e begins to ⋯rsh sort of ⋯ and the ⋯usual suck-⋯ng noises; ⋯st system ⋯ce period ⋯ a crackle ⋯inhibited ⋯t others ⋯raucous,

PERIOD MODIFICATIONS

Although uprated mechanicals were still popular when the Mk3 GT6 was current, more fashionable were cosmetic and comfort modifications, in a bid for personalization. Companies such as the Car Hood Company would be happy to trim a GT6's roof in whatever shade of vinyl the owner wanted, while there was a raft of outfits happy to cut a big hole in the roof to fit a sliding cloth sunroof: these included Golde, Tudor Webasto and Weathershields, the first two based in London with the last in Birmingham – prices started at £44. Something more intriguing though was the service offered by Kent-based Lenham, which was happy to cut a hole in the GT6's roof panel and bond in a sheet of perspex, to let more light into the cabin. Let's just say it probably looked good at the time…

GT6 Mk3 SPECIFICATIONS

Build dates	Oct 1970 – Dec 1973
Commission numbers	KE 1 – KE 24,218
Engine prefix	KE
Gearbox prefix	KE
Differential prefix	KC (KD for cars with overdrive)
Number built	13,042
Basic price	£1,002
On the road price	£1,254.38

Performance

0-30mph	3.9sec
0-50mph	7.7sec
0-60mph	10.1sec
0-80mph	18.4sec
Max speed in first gear	46mph (74km/h)
Max speed in second gear	68mph (109km/h)
Max speed in third gear	96mph (154km/h)

**The GT6 Mk3 retained its predecessors'
perfect proportions and all the practicality too,
but now there was a sharper exterior design
that brought the lines right up to date.**

The Mk3 would be the last iteration of the GT6 to come from Triumph; production finished a full seven years before the final Spitfire was built.

Top speed	112mph(180km/h) (110mph (177km/h) from KC 10000)
Standing 1/4-mile	17.4sec
Power to weight	111.6bhp/ton (108bhp/ton from KC 10000)
Typical fuel consumption	28mpg (9.9ltr/100km)

Dimensions, weights and capacities

Length	12ft 5in (3785mm)
Width	4ft 10.5in (1486mm)
Height overall (unladen)	3ft 11in (1194mm)
Ground clearance (laden)	4in (100mm)
Wheelbase	6ft 11in (2108mm)
Front track	4ft 1in (1245mm)
Rear track	4ft 1in (4ft 2in from KC 10000)
Dry Vehicle Weight	1936lb (878kg)
Engine oil	8pt (4.7ltr)
Gearbox oil	1.5pt (0.9ltr)
Overdrive gearbox oil	2.375pt (1.4ltr)
Differential	1pt (0.6ltr)
Cooling system	11pt (6.4ltr)
Fuel tank	9.75 gal (44.3ltr)

Engine

Maximum power	98bhp @ 5,300rpm (95bhp @ 5,200rpm from KC 10000)
Maximum torque	108lb ft @ 3,000rpm (106lb ft @ 3,000rpm from KC 10000)
Displacement	1998cc
Bore	74.7mm
Stroke	76.0mm
Compression ratio	9.25:1 (9.0:1 from KC 10000)
Oil pressure	50psi at 2,000rpm
Tappet clearance	0.010in
Fuelling	Twin Stromberg 150 CDSE carburettors
Firing order	1-5-3-6-2-4
Spark plugs	Champion N-9Y
Spark plug gap	0.025in
Distributor	Delco Remy 0200 (0204 from KC 10000)
Contact breaker gap	0.015in
Dwell angle	40°/42° (38°/40° from KC 10000)
Ignition timing – static	10° BTDC (6° BTDC from KC 10000)
Centrifugal advance	0° at 400rpm
	22° at 4,400rpm (22° at 5,000rpm from KC 10000)
Vacuum advance	0° at 3.8/6.2inHg
	11° at 20inHg (14° at 20inHg from KC 10000)
Ignition coil	6 volt Lucas 16C6 (Lucas 15C6 from KC 20000)

Transmission

Clutch	Diaphragm
Clutch diameter	8.5in (21.5cm)
Clutch output shaft	10 splines
Master cylinder diameter	5/8in
Slave cylinder diameter	1in
Gearbox	3-rail
Synchromesh	All gears
Gear ratios	4th = 1.0
	3rd = 1.25
	2nd = 1.78
	1st = 2.65
	R = 3.10
Optional overdrive	Laycock D-type
Overdrive ratio	0.802
O/D Gear ratios	4th = 0.80
	3rd = 1.0
Final drive ratio	3.27 (3.89 with overdrive)

Continued on page 130

Continued from page 129		Number of leaves	6 (5 from KC 20000)
Brakes and steering		Leaf width	1.75in
Front	9.7in solid disc	Leaf thickness	0.23in (2 x 0.31in/3 x 0.375in
Calliper type	Girling		from KC 20000)
Swept area	197sq in	Spring rate (at wheel)	93lbf/in (from KC 20000 only)
Rear	8 x 1.25in drum (8 x 1.5in from	Toe (unladen)	0 ± 1/32in (1/16in ± 1/32in toe
	KC 20000)		out from KC 20000)
Swept area	63sq in (75.5sq in from	Camber angle (unladen)	0 ± 1° (-1° ± 1° from
	KC 20000)		KC 20000)
Wheel cylinder diameter	0.7in, (7/8in from KC 20000)	Wheel size (steel)	13 x 4.5 J
Master cylinder diameter	0.7in, (3/4in from KC 20000)	Optional wire wheels	13 x 4.5 J
Steering	Rack and pinion	Tyres	Dunlop SP68
Turning circle	25ft 3in (7.62m)	Tyre size	155 SR-13
Turns between locks	4.3	Tyre pressures	Front: 24psi
			Rear: 28psi
Suspension, wheels and tyres			
Front suspension	Double wishbone	**Electrics**	
Spring rate	200lbf/in	Earth	Negative
Camber angle (unladen)	+2 3/4° ± 1/20	Alternator	Lucas 15 ACR (Lucas 16ACR
Castor angle (unladen)	3 1/2° ± 1/20		from KC 20000)
King pin inclination	6° ± 1°	Max current output	28 amp (34 amp from
Toe	1/16in-1/8in toe in		KC 20000)
Rear suspension	Rotoflex (swing spring from	Starter motor	Lucas M35
	KC 20000)	Headlights	60/45w

PRODUCTION CHANGES (FROM THE COMMISSION NUMBER GIVEN)

KE10001 Lower compression cylinder head (from 2000 Saloon), 9:1 domed pistons, milder cam, longer push rods.

KE11829 Overdrive inhibitor switch and bracket changed.

KE12389 Brake callipers revised to accept metric fittings (and now painted black)

KE20000 Swing spring replaces Rotoflex rear suspension, Girling brake servo added, cloth seats, new TR6-derived steering wheel, revised instruments, wood dash gets slightly darker finish, revised speedometer, temperature and fuel gauges, and the tachometer is now redlined between 6,000 and 7,000rpm. Also, the eyeball vents get chrome edges, the sun visors now black. Stiffer rear spring and front anti-roll bar while new mounting brackets fitted to the steering rack. Brake master cylinder bore increased from 11/16in and the rear wheel cylinder bore was increased from 11/16in to 7/8in. Wider brake drums at rear and, from hereon, self-adjusting brakes adopted.

CHAPTER TEN

BUYING A SPITFIRE OR GT6

Hopefully by now you'll need no persuading that the Spitfire and GT6 each make a great classic buy, as they're cheap to acquire and run as well as easy to maintain. However, low values mean these cars are often bought and run on a tight budget, with bodges rife, so you need to have your eyes wide open before diving in. Here's what you need to be on the lookout for.

Bodywork

Corrosion is the main enemy of the Spitfire: it can strike in the bodyshell as well as the chassis and, although it is not of monocoque construction, the sills are essential to the car's strength. Many owners restore their Spitfires at home and don't brace the bodyshell when the three-piece sills are

While this early GT6 is obviously too far gone for economical restoration, many rough cars can't be so easily identified as such. Make sure you buy with your head rather than your heart.

Any mechanical maladies can be put right, usually on a DIY basis and often fairly cheaply. Bodywork is a different matter though, and corrosion is highly likely.

replaced, twisting the shell in the process. The cars' low values also ensure there are plenty of cash-strapped owners who nurse their cars from one MoT to the next, investing in the bare minimum of maintenance. However, there are also lots of really superb Spitfires that have been cherished and which have had really good restorations, so don't assume they are all dogs.

Start by looking at the integrity of the sills: the area where

they meet the rear wings is where corrosion is most likely, and once rot takes a hold, long-lasting repairs will require skill. Also take a look at the leading edge of each sill: there's a good chance of holes here, after constant bombardment by road debris. Once there are holes in the steel, water will get in, wreaking havoc throughout the length of the sill.

There are plenty more rot spots to inspect too: the rear quarter panels, door bottoms, boot floor and the windscreen frame can all corrode badly. So too can the A-posts, wheel arches (inner and outer) plus the headlamp surrounds and front valance. The last is double-skinned, so corrosion often spreads from the inside out; check for any signs of bubbling, because what you can see is likely to be just the tip of the iceberg.

Floorpans also corrode, sometimes because rot spreads from the sills and sometimes because the footwells have been allowed to fill up with water, which is then forced to eat its way out. The area behind the seats is likely to be particularly bad, as it's rarely inspected very often; the front footwells also give problems, so lift the carpets and see what state the metal is in underneath.

Next check the door shuts, which should be even all the way down. If a car has been badly restored, with the shell twisted in the process, the door fit will not be flush all the way down, and the shut lines won't be even. Putting this right is a huge job that, if done professionally, will cost more

Remove any covering in the boot floor and check the metal underneath; it's often full of holes.

The chassis needs to be checked for corrosion as well as accident damage. The outriggers rot where they join the main rails while the crossmember that runs across the car's nose gets kinked by parking nudges.

than the car is worth because the whole structure needs to be realigned.

Accident damage is also a strong possibility, as these cars often appeal to inexperienced drivers who want some cheap fun. If the car has been in a major shunt, the damage will be obvious; any prang big enough to distort the main chassis will have wrecked the car's delicate panels. It's the small knocks that are likely to cause you the most problems, as they may be harder to spot. However, if the panel fit is all over the place at the front, there's a good chance the front chassis rail, to which the valance attaches, has been knocked out of true.

It's a similar story for the GT6; unless the example you're looking at has been really cherished, it will have had some remedial work performed on it at some point. That's no problem if it has been done properly, but if a full-scale restoration has been attempted, and the body and chassis have not been separated, the work clearly has not been done properly. It's not so much the bodyshell that's the problem, as the chassis. The rear can be easily repaired, but ensure the front is all aligned as it should be. The bonnet mountings are the most important here, because if they're not lined up correctly you'll never get the bonnet to line up properly.

Like the Spitfire, the GT6's bodywork consists of two main sections: the front end (bonnet top, nose and front wings) and the main bodyshell (a tub made of the roof, floorpans and rear wings). The tailgate and doors attach to the tub and it's all put together like an overgrown Meccano kit – very handy for taking apart and putting back together.

Although it's a good idea buying a bodyshell that is not full of holes, it's the chassis that gives the GT6 most of its strength. Thanks to the engine having a tendency to spray the underside of the car with oil, there's a good chance that the metal has been reasonably well preserved towards the front. It's worth buying replacement outriggers to patch up the chassis if the main rails are sound. If the frame has rusted away comprehensively, you'll be better off getting a replacement – you won't find a new one anywhere, but usable second hand ones can be picked up cheaply. Bear in mind that everything is based around the chassis, so if it needs replacing you're going to have to remove the brakes, steering, suspension and bodywork – and you can bet you'll end up finding problems with some of those along the way.

Even if the chassis doesn't need any work, there's a good chance the bodywork will. The first areas to check are the sills, floors and wheel arches. The GT6's sills are structural and if these, together with the floorpans, have not been

replaced yet, the chances are they will need renewing before long. Nearly all panels are available new and are fairly easy to fit but if somebody else has already done this, make sure the panels line up – putting right somebody else's bodge is far harder than starting from scratch.

Check under the false boot floor where the metal floor meets the arch – the passenger side is hidden under the petrol tank but the off-side will give a good idea of condition. All versions have a habit of corroding between the rear lights, and as new panels are not available you'll have to be handy with the MiG welder. Some of the most rot-prone parts of the car are the doors, which can rust very badly once moisture has got trapped in the seam between the shell and the skin. Thankfully the door shells usually remain sound, needing only a new skin.

Other rot spots include the bottom of the hatch aperture, which fills with water, then rots out, and the double-skinned leading edge of the roof where it meets the windscreen surround – condensation collects in the seam and rots from the inside out. As if all this isn't enough, it's quite common for the master cylinders on the bulkhead to leak brake fluid onto the metal panels below. Once this has stripped the paint, corrosion will follow, but the use of a silicone-based brake fluid will avoid this happening.

Even if there is no discernible rust anywhere, the car may have been in an impact at some point. Poor shut-lines are common on otherwise well-restored GT6s because aligning the panels can be very tricky. The easiest way of telling if the car has been shunted is to look at the chassis rails in front of the engine; they may be crumpled. Even if the car has been in a fairly big accident, if the chassis has been repaired properly or replaced, along with the necessary panel work, there's no need to worry. That's the beauty of not having a monocoque – although if you do need to replace the bonnet, you'll need to have a fair chunk of cash at the ready.

Finally, some GT6s were fitted with a full-length sliding cloth sunroof, which needs to be tensioned properly and lubricated so it opens and closes smoothly. Obviously the fabric itself needs to be checked for splits and tears, and you must also make sure the plastic deflector is fitted at the front of the aperture, to reduce buffeting on the move.

Engine

There were three different engines fitted throughout the life of the Spitfire, with each one also used in other models

**Triumph engines are reasonably long-lived as long as they're properly maintained.
When a rebuild is due, it's an easy enough job to do at home.**

in the Triumph range. Because the Spitfire was generally the most highly tuned of the lot, you need to make sure the engine fitted is the one that belongs there, as less powerful units are often substituted from other Triumph models. All Spitfire engine numbers start with an F: FC in the case of the MkI/MkII, FD for the MkIII, FH for the MkIV (but FK for US cars) and FH for the 1500 (FM for US cars). However, there's a good chance that something else will be fitted, such as an engine with the prefix G (Herald), D (Dolomite) or Y (1500 saloon).

MkI and MkII Spitfires were fitted with an 1147cc engine, but because these early cars are rare, you are unlikely to find a car with one of these relatively gutless powerplants. Even if you do find a first or second-generation car, the chances

are the engine will have been swapped for a later unit by now. The MkIII featured a 1296cc engine, which was carried over to the MkIV, but with less power because of emissions control equipment.

The 1147cc and 1296cc engines are very durable, but all Spitfire engines must have the correct oil filter fitted if they're not to expire prematurely. This filter features a non-return valve to stop the oil draining back into the sump when the car is left; if there's much rattling when the engine is started, it's because the crankshaft's big-end bearings have had it, probably because the correct type of filter hasn't been fitted. Once this has happened, a bottom-end rebuild is necessary: it's an easy enough job that you could do at home, but it's also a big task.

These two smaller engines will usually clock up 100,000 miles (160,000km) without problems, with the first sign of wear usually being a chattering top end because of erosion of the rocker shaft and rockers. The engine will keep running happily enough for thousands of miles, but it's always best to budget for a top end rebuild sooner rather than later.

A problem that affects the 1296cc engine all too often is worn thrust washers, given away by excessive fore-aft movement of the crankshaft. The easiest way to check this is to push and pull on the front pulley: any detectable movement means possible disaster as the crankshaft and block could ultimately be wrecked if the thrust washers fall out. MkIV Spitfires are especially prone to these problems because the crankshaft was larger, placing more load on the thrust washers. Listen for rumbling from the bottom end as the engine ticks over.

The 1493cc engine fitted to the Spitfire 1500 has problems of its own, as the crankshaft can wear badly, along with the pistons and rings. That's why you need to listen out for rattling when starting up and look for blue smoke as you accelerate through the gears. If the engine has had it, your best bet is to fit an exchange rebuilt unit or find a decent used one.

The 1500 engine also suffers from faulty waxstats in the carburettors, which is why many cars have had various carburettor conversions – or the fitment of fixed jets to overcome the problem altogether. If the car runs badly, it could be for a multitude of reasons (such as badly balanced carbs or a tired ignition system), but there's a good chance it's because the waxstat jets have had it if they're still fitted.

The 1500 engine can also suffer from a cracked cylinder head because of overheating problems. Cars so afflicted will suffer from the same symptoms as those with a blown head gasket – which is the coolant and oil mixing. Remove the oil filler cap and look for signs of a white emulsion on its underside; if there's a build up of a mayonnaise-like substance, things could be on the verge of getting expensive.

The 6-cylinder engines can suffer from the crankshaft's thrust washers falling out; the same fate can befall the 1296cc engine of the Spitfire Mk3 and MkIV.

The GT6's straight-six is renowned for its smoothness as well as its low-down torque. It's also famed for its oil leaks, and rattles at start-up. But thankfully these 'characteristics' can be engineered out without too much difficulty or expense. All GT6s were fitted with a 1998cc straight-six and, if looked after with oil changes every 6,000 miles (9,600km), it'll last 100,000 miles (160,000km) between rebuilds without any problem.

All parts are readily available, and it's an easy engine to cut your teeth on if you're buying a restoration project. Renew all oil seals while you have it apart, as it'll save taking the engine out again later. If the engine has had it and you don't fancy rebuilding it yourself, a running unit can be picked up cheaply.

If the original canister type of oil filter is still fitted, it's worth investing in a spin-on conversion, which will allow you to fit a modern type of filter with a non-return valve on it, so the bearings won't be starved of lubricant when you start it up, eliminating that initial rattle.

Where overdrive is fitted, it tends to be reliable. Most issues are down to faulty electrics, so check those first, before taking the transmission apart.

Transmission

The first three generations of Spitfire featured the same four-speed manual gearbox, with synchromesh on all gears except first. The MkIV was fitted with the same transmission, but with synchromesh on all ratios, while the 1500 received a Marina-derived unit, which is the most durable of all the gearboxes. All of these transmissions are reasonably long-lived, but high mileages will lead to rebuilds being necessary – although that's nothing to worry about in terms of cost or difficulty.

Synchromesh is usually the first thing to go, so check if there's any baulking as you go up and down the gears. Also listen for whining, indicating that the gears have worn, or rumbling, which signifies the bearings are on their way out. If there's any sign of trouble, your best bet is to budget for a rebuilt gearbox, which shouldn't prove especially costly. Even better, replacing a gearbox is surprisingly easy as it just pulls out from inside the car, once the seats and gearbox cover have been removed.

Many Spitfires have overdrive, which can also give problems. The first thing to check in the event of non-engagement is that the electrics are working properly: they're often the main cause of problems. If there's continuity in the circuit, the next most likely cause of trouble is an oil level that's fallen below the minimum required for the overdrive to operate. Fixing this is easy; you simply add some EP90 to the gearbox and all should work once more. However, if the gearbox is leaking, there's clearly a problem to be addressed. If the oil is up to the level and the electrics are working fine, the overdrive unit probably needs cleaning out. If you budget for the worst – a rebuilt overdrive – you won't go far wrong. Exchange units aren't that costly, although you would really want to opt for a rebuilt gearbox and overdrive combined, which pretty much doubles the price.

The rest of the transmission is simple, which means cheap and easy to repair – but there are various problems that can crop up. Most of these relate to wear in components such as universal joints or a propshaft that needs balancing, but these are nothing to worry about. If the propshaft is out of balance, there'll be a vibration at a certain road speed, which disappears once you accelerate. Worn universal joints are given away by clonks as the drive is taken up when moving off in forward or reverse.

Clutches don't give any particular problems, so just check for slipping as you accelerate, or juddering as you let the clutch out. The former is simply a worn clutch that needs renewing while the latter suggests there's oil on the pressure plate. This will also mean the clutch needs to be renewed, but there's also the issue of where the oil is coming from: Triumph engines aren't renowned for their ability to seal perfectly.

The final potential weak spot is the differential, which will whine when it's worn. Even when things sound really bad,

Differentials are readily available on an exchange basis; expect lots of whining once around 100,000 miles have been racked up – or potentially significantly less if the car has been thrashed.

Transmission problems are common, because of worn universal joints, or through the propshaft being out of balance.

the rear axle will just keep going, but it's obviously not a good idea to just put up with the racket. A rebuilt unit isn't expensive, but while replacement is easy enough, it can get quite involved if you also find that the rear suspension needs work when you take everything apart.

The GT6's weakest link is its final drive, although if it's well looked after there's no reason for it to leave you stranded. The problem lies with the universal joints and diff, which can struggle to cope with the 2.0-litre engine's torque. They're an evolution of the Herald units – which in turn had evolved from Standard units of years before. The first Heralds had generated less than 40bhp and all GT6s put out more than double that so, if an owner has been over-enthusiastic with the throttle, there may be rather more play in the system than there should be. Make sure the diff and gearbox aren't especially noisy – the gearbox is usually sturdy, but the diff will whine loudly if it's getting tired.

If there's clonking from the transmission as you manoeuvre backwards and forwards it's probably because some of the universal joints need replacing. New joints are cheap, and replacing them isn't tricky, but you might have to do all four if things are really bad. If it's got to that stage, there's probably a fair bit of vibration once cruising, so check all four to see how much play there is. There's one on each driveshaft and one on each end of the propshaft, all of which are accessible from underneath.

The plastic bushes in the remote gear change mechanism wear out eventually, but fitting a new set is cheap and easy. No GT6 had overdrive fitted as standard, but it was available as a factory-fitted option. Few Mk1 owners ticked the box but it became increasingly popular and most Mk3s owners specified it. A lot of cars have it nowadays because it's easy enough to retro-fit – and overdrive is worthwhile because it's more relaxing driving a car so equipped if you raise the final drive ratio at the same time.

Unusually, when new a GT6 with overdrive was no more relaxing to drive than one without. That's because the final drive ratio of cars not equipped with it was lowered to 3.27:1 from the previous 3.89:1, to improve acceleration rather than make high-speed cruising more relaxed. If overdrive is fitted but it's not working, the chances are that it's only an electrical connection somewhere that's playing up, or a lack of oil pressure because the unit's internal filter needs a clean. If it's anything more serious, rebuilds are best left to a specialist but, if it has called it a day, you can buy a rebuilt overdrive on an exchange basis.

If the car is fitted with a rubber doughnut rotoflex coupling, make sure the coupling isn't about to disintegrate. Even the genuine Metalastik couplings last no more than 35,000 miles (56,000km); cheaper ones will disintegrate a lot faster than that. If the car doesn't have rotoflex couplings, things are a lot simpler as you've then only got to be concerned with the rear bearings, which last well and are very cheap to replace.

Steering and Suspension

The rack-and-pinion steering is unlikely to have any problems, as it isn't under much strain, despite the fabulously tight turning circle. Aside from worn track rod ends or split rubber gaiters, which can affect any car, there's little to watch out for. However, as with any mechanical item, steering racks do wear out so check for lots of play, signifying a replacement rack is needed. It's hardly a disaster if one is required, as replacements are cheap to buy and easy to fit – although you'll need to remember to have the tracking checked once the work is done.

Thanks to the flip-up bonnet, the front suspension of the Spitfire and GT6 is simplicity itself to work on. That's just as well because there are various bits that can give trouble

The rubber steering rack gaiters perish then split, especially after being soaked in engine oil. But they're easily and cheaply replaced.

The front suspension works brilliantly, but it needs to be kept oiled; EP90 should be pumped into the trunnion periodically to prevent corrosion.

There are ball joints at the top of each wishbone. They feature a rubber gaiter that has a tendency to split, allowing dirt to get into the joint.

– but it's all very cheap and beautifully simple to put right, especially if you can do the work yourself.

The nylon bushes in the brass trunnions can wear, so feel for play with a crowbar. Fresh bushes are cheap, and even if the trunnion is past its best this is no disaster: they're also cheap to replace. The main problem with the trunnions is wear of the threaded brass at the bottom, if EP90 oil hasn't been pumped in every six months or so. Without this, water gets in and corrodes the lower portion of the vertical link, weakening it and leading to the suspension collapsing when the wheels are turned at low speed. Replacement vertical links are available, but they're costly.

There are various other rubber bushes throughout the suspension, all of which will perish at some point – but they're cheap to buy if somewhat involved to replace if you want to fit a complete new set. Some repro stuff isn't especially durable and there are mixed views about the polyurethane items that are available. Some claim they make the ride too hard while others disagree; if yellow or blue bushes are in place, they're made of polyurethane so you might want to pay particular attention to how hard the ride is when you take the car on a test drive.

The anti-roll bar links can also break, but are cheap and easy to replace, so that's nothing to worry about. The same goes for the rest of the front suspension: there are all sorts of potential weak spots but they're all quickly and cheaply fixed. The wheel bearings can wear, as can the track rod ends, steering rack and upper ball joints that locate the top wishbone. The rubber steering rack mounts can also perish, usually after they've been marinated in leaked engine oil. Your best bet is to feel for play by getting underneath, but when driving the car it'll be obvious if things are really bad.

The rear suspension can also give problems, but it's generally easy to overhaul, with one key exception: the wheel bearings. These wear out and are difficult to remove as a press is needed. The problem is the bearings act directly on the driveshaft so, if left, the driveshaft can be scrapped as well as the bearings. The only other likely problem, apart from worn or leaking shock absorbers, which are easy to replace, is a sagging leaf spring. If the top of the wheel has disappeared above the wheel arch, the spring definitely needs to be renewed. A fresh one isn't expensive, but without the correct spring lifter, fitting it will be a pig of a job.

As far as the GT6 is concerned, all of the Spitfire's weaknesses also apply. The basic suspension design is the same, front and rear, although exact specifications vary in detail between the various iterations of the Spitfire and GT6. One key thing to bear in mind is that if you're looking at a swing spring (late Mk3) car, it will probably only need new rubber pads between the leaves. There's also a rubber bush at each end of the leaf spring along with bushes in the radius arms, which locate the back axle and in each of the dampers. By the time the damper rubbers have gone, the damper itself is likely to need replacing, but this isn't anything to worry about.

Wheels and Brakes

Pressed steel wheels were fitted to all Spitfires and GT6s as standard, but by now many have been swapped for alloys or

If wire wheels are fitted, look for rusty or broken spokes. Also check for wear in the splines.

wires. Because these cars have an unusual offset, it's easy to buy wheels that suffer from clearance problems, so if aftermarket wheels are fitted, check that they're not rubbing. Even if wheels with the correct offset are fitted, it's possible to fit wider rims than the car can really cope with. So, if some lunatic has put 205s onto the one you're looking at, be very wary – the widest tyres that will comfortably fit are either 175 or 185-section, depending on the model in question. Even if all looks alright with the car stationary, by the time it's moving and the wheels are rising and falling (plus turning at the front), there could be rubbing in all sorts of places where you really don't want rubbing...

If wire wheels have been put on, make sure that the spokes haven't broken and that the splines have not worn. Your best bet is to lift each wheel off the ground and with somebody holding the footbrake on, try to rock the wheel top to bottom. Significant movement suggests the wheel splines have worn – which generally means throwing the wheel away and starting again.

The brakes should prove to be equally trouble-free: they're completely conventional so you just need to be on the lookout for leaking rear wheel cylinders, sticking calliper pistons and seized handbrakes. If any work is needed, it's easy and cheap to do, as all parts are available and access is good for anything that needs to be replaced.

Electrics and Trim

Neither the electrics nor the trim should pose any significant problems. Although there's a good chance that some sort of electrical problem will be present, it's usually only down to poor earths, dodgy bullet connectors or the failure of some cheap-to-replace component. Everything is available and there isn't anything that's a problem to fit – and most of it is very cheap to buy too. If the wiring has been hacked about, you can buy a new loom, while the few ancillaries that are fitted, such as the wiper motor, dynamo/alternator and starter motor, are cheap and easy to buy.

The trim shouldn't pose any problems as it's generally hard-wearing, but if any parts have worn out, it's possible to fit well-made remanufactured trim. Some bits for early cars are impossible to get hold of, such as rubber mats or the early type of dash surround, but seat covers and carpet sets are available for most models. You're especially well-served if you're looking at a MkIV or 1500 because everything is

Expect electrical problems because of perished wiring and poor connections. Everything is available though, including replacement wiring looms.

The interior trim, including headlinings, seats, door cards and carpets are all fairly durable. Good quality reproduction parts are available though, to keep any interior looking smart.

available for these cars, so you don't need to fret about missing or damaged parts.

Seats tend to sag after a few years, but they can be re-stuffed, recovered or even replaced altogether. What's more problematic is if the mounting holes in the floorpan are damaged: they can become elongated, which means repairs can get involved.

Dashboards and their surrounds can fade or discolour after years of exposure to the sun, and while the materials used are generally tough, problems can crop up: holes being cut in the dash face (for extra instruments or radios) is a common phenomenon. Usually the only solution is to replace the dash altogether: they're available on a new or used basis, but there's a lot of work involved in transferring the switchgear and instruments.

Everything that applies to the Spitfire also goes for the GT6, as you can also source remanufactured trim for all models, including moulded carpet sets, seat covers and trim panels – and they're very well made too. While the GT6 features a headlining instead of a cloth roof, it's still possible to renew it: the originals tend not to sag so replacement is only likely to be required if any damage has occurred.

Specialists

Anglian Triumph Services, Norfolk. 01986 895 387, www.angserv.demon.co.uk

Canley Classics, Coventry. 01676 541 360, www.canleyclassics.com

Chic Doig, Fife. 01592 722 999, www.chicdoig.com

David Manners, Midlands. 0121 544 4444, www.davidmanners.co.uk

Jigsaw Racing, Kettering. 01536 763 799, www.jigsawracing-services.co.uk

Mick Dolphin, Leicester. 01530 271 326, www.mickdolphin.co.uk

Moss Europe, London. 0208 867 2020, www.moss-europe.co.uk

Quiller Triumph, London. 0208 854 4777, www.triumph-shop.co.uk

Rimmers, Lincoln. 01522 568 000, www.rimmerbros.co.uk

Southern Triumph Services, Dorset. 01202 423 687, www.southerntriumph.com

Triumph Spares Worcester, 01905 345 222, tinyurl.com/nxa4x8

CHAPTER ELEVEN

MODIFYING

Thanks to superb club and specialist support, you're spoiled for choice when it comes to uprating your Spitfire or GT6. There's a massive range of goodies on offer, so whether you want to improve the handling, make it more comfortable, faster or simply more reliable, you've got no shortage of options. However, as with anything, spending money on an upgrade often has ramifications, while sometimes things aren't all they're cracked up to be.

This chapter aims to guide you through the options available to you and whether or not they're worth considering. What this chapter is not, is a technical guide on how to perform upgrades to your car – that's a whole book in itself. This also isn't a definitive guide to what you can do: engine and transmission swaps alone could fill this book because

there are so many options. Instead, this is an overview of the sorts of modifications that are possible, based on the most popular routes that owners have been taking.

The key thing to bear in mind is what you'll use the car for. If you're after a track day special your focus will be on performance, handling and stopping power and comfort won't really enter into the equation. However, if you're preparing a car for track use, the cost will invariably stack up pretty swiftly because you'll need to upgrade so many areas. It's also a very specialist area – which is why the focus here is on upgrades for road use, whether that's to make the car faster or simply better to drive.

On this note, before embarking on any changes, you need to ask around to see whether what you have in mind really

You don't have to stick with a Triumph engine to power your Spitfire or GT6. Over the years there have been numerous Fiat, Ford and Rover units installed instead.

This MkI GT6 has been uprated only mildly, but the investment has been in the right areas: lightening and balancing, a freer-breathing exhaust manifold and some more efficient air filters.

will improve your Triumph, or whether it'll make things worse. Talk to specialists, join a club or two and get stuck into some of the many online forums – benefit from the experiences of others. It's only by doing this that you might be able to save yourself a load of grief and expense by altering your Triumph in a way that makes it worse rather than better.

Engine

Given that the GT6's straight-six is a large and heavy engine, swapping it for pretty much anything you like is feasible – and especially if it's modern because it'll invariably be lighter and more compact. The same goes for the Spitfire, although you may end up having to fit the GT6's humped bonnet to obtain the clearance that you need – but such conversions are both easy and popular. Bearing in mind that the possibilities are just about endless in terms of which engines you could fit, we'll stick with Triumph units here, to keep things relatively simple. However, powerplants that have been fitted over the years include various Vauxhall, Rover and Ford units, including the brilliant Zetec lump.

Perhaps the most obvious swap is to fit a GT6 engine to a Spitfire, to create a GT6 convertible (or Gitfire). You'll need

to upgrade the brakes and suspension while you're at it, because of the extra grunt and weight, but it's not a conversion that should pose too many problems. See the separate panel for more on this.

If upping the cylinder count of your Spitfire by 50 per cent doesn't appeal, you don't have to go that far to enjoy some extra power. You could tune the existing engine or you could also simply upgrade to a later powerplant, assuming you're not starting with a 1500 of course. Few early Spitfires are still fitted with their 1147cc engines, but if you have such a beast and it's not quick enough for you, the 1296cc or 1493cc units can be fitted without too much difficulty.

If you indulge in engine swapping, it's normal to also transplant the relevant gearbox while you're at it. However, you don't have to do this, because you can stick with the original gearbox and simply fit the correct clutch to make it all work. The 1296cc engine is mated to a gearbox with a ten-spline input shaft while the equivalent 1493cc shaft has twenty-two splines.

If swapping to a later engine sounds appealing, and you want to enjoy a trouble-free conversion (or as close to as possible), your best bet is to carry all the ancillaries over while you're at it – especially the carburettors and exhaust.

If your start point is a GT6 and you want something even pokier, you can either tune the lump you've already got, or if you want a quick and cheap route to more horses you could slot in a 2.5-litre engine. The 2.5-litre straight-six, as seen in the TR5 and TR6 along with the 2500, was simply a long-stroke version of the 2-litre unit. As a result, you can slot in the larger unit with a minimum of effort, although the 2.5-litre powerplant does have a deeper sump, which can lead to clearance problems with the crossmember. The answer is to reshape the sump so it clears both the crossmember and the con-rods; something that's easy, if a little fiddly.

This larger engine isn't as free-revving as the 2.0-litre unit, thanks to its longer stroke, but it has a lot more torque. As a result, you can look forward to fewer gear changes if you're after a relaxing cruiser, but if you want to drive with more urgency you'll probably need to upgrade the transmission to cope, as well as the brakes.

Whatever your start point – and certainly if it's a Triumph engine – it's worth paying attention to the basics such as balancing everything dynamically, lightening where possible and tuftriding the crank. The first will improve the smoothness, the second will make the powerplant more free-revving – while the third will improve durability.

Cylinder Head

As with any sixties engine, a bit of porting and polishing won't go amiss when it comes to trying to extract more horses, but such skills are getting increasingly hard to find – and as a result they're very expensive. It doesn't help that the Triumph cylinder heads are cast-iron, ensuring that the removal of any metal is a very laborious process. As a result, this is one of the most costly things you can do to a Triumph engine and it doesn't always yield the power gains you might hope for. At least there are no downsides in terms of usability or reliability, but undertaking headwork could prove to be a costly folly if you're not careful.

Whether or not you opt for a modified head, you generally need to stick with the same item that was originally fitted. For example, the TKC1155 Spitfire head can be swapped for a TKC1156 Dolomite item, and it'll fit perfectly well – but you'll invariably suffer lots of pinking. However, there are certain swaps which are fine, and if you don't want to resort to having costly work undertaken on your cylinder head, you might simply be able to resort to doing a bit of swapping. For example, post-1973 Spitfires and Toledos featured a big-valve head that can be fitted to earlier Spitfires, to aid breathing.

You're also likely to suffer from pinking if you have the head skimmed too much, to increase the compression ratio. For everyday use you're best to stick with a compression ratio of no more than 10:1; much more will lead to detonation, with melted pistons guaranteed. Skim the head exces-

This GT6 cylinder head has been treated to the stage three treatment, with plenty of porting and polishing plus hardened valve seats.

There are various aftermarket air filters available. **K&N** is perhaps the best known of the lot, but there are also **Pipercross** and **ITG**.

sively and you're also likely to suffer from blown head gaskets on a regular basis – especially if you end up having to slot in two gaskets because you've removed too much metal.

With unleaded petrol having made an appearance in the UK as long ago as the mid-1980s, there's a chance that your Triumph's engine is already set up to run on it. The bottom line is that any engine rebuild should involve the fitment of hardened valve seats, so you don't have to use additives or worry about the spectre of valve seat recession.

Fitting hardened inserts isn't a DIY job; your local machine

shop will need to do it. However, once the work has been done you'll need to set the engine up properly – although this doesn't usually involve anything more than retarding the ignition by a couple of degrees to prevent pinking.

Incidentally, if you buy a Triumph that hasn't got an unleaded-friendly head fitted, don't rush into forking out for a top end rebuild. You can use additives, but you could also simply use unleaded fuel and see how quickly it takes for valve seat recession to become an issue: you might find you're waiting a long time. Cars used only occasionally, and not run under load for prolonged periods, often don't suffer from valve seat recession at all – or at least not for many years.

Whether or not you undertake any cylinder head work, it makes sense to aid the engine's breathing by installing a decent filter set. The conventional paper cartridge filters are alright up to a point when new, but even when fresh out of the box they don't allow the engine to breathe as freely as a decent aftermarket set-up. The best known of these is K&N, but there's also Pipercross; fit one of these and your powerplant can breathe more freely, allowing it to produce more power. Also bear in mind that some of these performance air filters need periodic cleaning instead of replacement – something that's often overlooked.

Camshaft and Valves

The standard camshaft for all these cars does a perfectly good job of getting the air/fuel mixture into the combustion chambers, then out again at the right point. However, that's not to say there's no room for improvement, and if you're after extra power, something a little spicier is usually worthwhile. However, you have to be very careful what you fit because if you install something designed more for track use you're going to end up with a powerplant that's very peaky and pretty much undrivable on the road.

If you do opt for something fruitier than standard, to get the best out of it you really need to lighten and balance the engine – the crankshaft, pistons, con-rods and flywheel. You also ought to consider fitting a more free-flowing exhaust and while you're at it, larger valves are usually a good idea too. They're not always practical though; if you've got a Spitfire Mk3, it's an easy change because the MkIV's head will go straight on, and this has bigger valves.

Ignition

The problem with points is that they're prone to wear or simply going out of adjustment – which is guaranteed to result in a less efficient engine. If the distributor shaft is badly worn there's no substitute for a new one, but you can mitigate its effects by fitting electronic ignition; this is especially a problem with Delco distributors, which wear more readily than their Lucas equivalents.

There's a variety of systems on the market, some of which mount inside the distributor so you'd never know they were there; others involve the fitting of a box on the bulkhead, feeding the distributor via a pair of wires. Whichever system you go for it's a worthwhile move, because the engine will stay in tune for a lot longer.

While a standard engine should be fitted with NGK BP6ES

FINAL DRIVE RATIOS

3.27:1
Swiss Spitfire 1500 (1980 model)
GT6 non O/D
German GT6 with overdrive

3.63:1
Non-US Spitfire 1500

3.89:1
Non-US Spitfire Mk4
US Spitfire Mk4 (1971 only)
US Spitfire (1973-79)
GT6 with overdrive
Vitesse 2-litre
Toledo 1500

4.11:1
Spitfire Mk1-3
US Spitfire Mk4 (1972)
US Spitfire Mk4
Herald 1200 (which used two different input shafts throughout production)
Vitesse 1600
Toledo 1300
Dolomite 1300

4.55:1
948cc Herald coupe, convertible and twin-carb saloon

4.875:1
948cc Herald saloon

spark plugs, a modified powerplant should have NGK BP7ES items fitted, opened up to 0.030–0.035in (0.76–0.89mm) to improve combustion efficiency and hence reduce the likelihood of fouling.

Having said all this, there are some who prefer a good old-fashioned points system, because it's cheap, easy to adjust and if the engine starts to misfire you can substitute the fitted points for a replacement set to see if it makes any difference. Points are not inherently unreliable, so don't be too anxious to modernize.

Fuelling

There are numerous options available to you if you want to alter your engine's fuelling, ranging from mild to wild. Electronic fuel injection is possible for any engine nowadays, but it's very expensive and has to be set up on a bespoke basis. If ultimate power and efficiency are what you're after, and you've got very deep pockets this might be the solution for you.

However, if you're using a 2.5-litre Triumph straight-six, you could always opt for the Lucas mechanical fuel injection that was fitted at the factory. Although the system had a reputation for fragility when it was current, as with most sixties technology there has been continuous development to the point where there's now no reason why the set-up

should give you any problems. Set up properly the system is inherently more efficient than any carburettor installation – but you've got to have a 2.5-litre Triumph engine for it to work.

If you'd prefer to stick with carburettors, there's a multitude of routes you can take, from larger versions of whatever was originally fitted (Strombergs or SUs) to something completely different such as twin-choke Webers (usually 40DCOEs).

All Spitfire and GT6 engines featured a pair of carburettors as standard; one of the most popular tuning routes is to go up a size, such as from 1.25 to 1.5, or 1.5 to 1.75. It's a neat solution that works well, but there are alternatives – not least of all switching to three carburettors. This can be a triple-SU set-up, but more common is a three-Weber system.

While a triple-Weber set-up looks impressive, don't assume that it's an automatic route to massive power, because it isn't. Properly set up, a decent twin-SU system can produce just as much power, as long as attention has been paid to other key areas such as the cylinder head, exhaust and decent air filters.

Also bear in mind that if you do opt for the three-Weber route, you'll need to fit an electric fuel pump, as the standard mechanical item can't cope with the carbs' thirst. You'll also need to fit an in-line mechanical fuel pressure regulator so the carbs aren't overcome with petrol – but perhaps the

It's possible to fit a trio of Weber carburettors to the GT6; this is a Vitesse engine bay, but the set-up for the GT6 is much the same.

If you fit three Webers to your GT6, you'll have to ditch the original mechanical fuel pump and switch to an electric item instead. Note the fuel pressure regulator also fitted.

THE GT6 CONVERTIBLE

Triumph missed a trick by not offering the six-cylinder engine in a roadster bodyshell; as a result you could enjoy top-down motoring or fabulous smoothness and torque but not both. As a result, many Triumph fans have created their own GT6 convertibles, which isn't as complex as it sounds.

Thanks to the Meccano-like nature of these cars, it's easy to mix and match parts between the various iterations of the Spitfire and GT6 – although using a non-rotoflex GT6 does simplify things. As a result, fitting a Spitfire body to a GT6 chassis isn't a very difficult proposition; if you know what you're doing it can be done in a weekend.

A six-cylinder engine can be slotted into any Spitfire; if converting an early car you'll need to stick with the GT6 MkI or Mk2 bonnet, while the later Spitfires use a GT6 Mk3 front end.

The biggest problem is finding a suitable GT6 chassis complete with running gear; most tatty GT6s have been restored by now or are still too good for cannibalizing. However, all is not lost because it's possible to stick with your Spitfire and transplant the six-cylinder engine into its nose.

Whatever route you take you'll need to use a GT6 bonnet for the required clearance, and if you do fit the straight-six lump you'll definitely need to upgrade the brakes and suspension to suit – although Spitfire rear brakes are best retained for optimum balance. However, if you're undertaking a major rebuild anyway, installing the beefier GT6 parts while you're at it shouldn't pose any problems – other than financial ones potentially.

The final way of helping to keep under-bonnet temperatures down is to fit an oil cooler. Bearing in mind that oil helps the engine to get rid of around 30 per cent of its heat, you shouldn't underestimate the value of an oil cooler. There are two basic types: thermostatic and open circuit. The former, as the name suggests, only starts to cool the oil once it's up to temperature, while the other cools the oil as soon as the engine is up to pressure. As with the cooling system, it makes sense to go for the thermostatic option because it's only working when needed; naturally it's a bit more costly but it's ultimately cheaper than having to overhaul the engine early.

biggest consideration before forking out major money on a fancy multiple-carb set-up is keeping everything running properly. Any decent back-street garage can balance a pair of carbs, but once you start adding to that number you'll have to find a specialist who can keep everything ticking over properly. That usually means finding a good rolling road, and that's when things start to get costly.

Lubrication

Lubrication is a bit of an issue for these engines, for both the top end as well as the bottom. In the case of the former, a poor oil feed to the cylinder head leads to premature wear of the rockers as well as the rocker shaft; things are made worse if the oil isn't changed regularly or if the engine is revved from cold. Once the rockers and their shaft have worn, the problem will be transferred to the camshaft and valves, so it's important that things are caught in time – and it's even better if the original problem is eliminated in the first place.

One way of doing this is to fit a rocker shaft oil feed kit, which takes its supply from the fuel pump take-off – but don't be too eager to fit one of these as there are certain consequences. The key one is a significant boost in oil pressure at the top end, leading to oil creeping past the valve guides and into the combustion chambers. The result is clouds of oil smoke from the exhaust when the lubricant is burned; it's always worst when firing up the engine and as things warm up the air will clear, but not necessarily com-

A spin-on oil filter conversion is essential with any Spitfire or GT6, to protect the big-end bearings from oil starvation.

pletely. Also, these engines aren't easy to seal, and once the pressure has been increased in various places, the chances are that lubricant will start escaping from all over the place.

As far as oil starvation at the bottom end is concerned, the solution is even simpler; just fit a spin-on oil filter that incorporates a non-return valve. The standard filter doesn't have this valve, so overnight all the oil drains back into the sump, leading to oil starvation as the engine is cranked over. The fitment of the correct filter will ensure the oil is retained while the engine is standing, so that when you fire the engine up it's properly lubricated from the outset.

If things have been allowed to deteriorate there'll be lots of rattling from the top end, which no amount of tappet adjustment will reduce. Catch it early enough and you might get away with replacing just the shaft while reusing the rockers, but don't count on it. Once the valve guides have worn, oil will be drawn into the engine and burned, leading to pinking when pulling away. There are two possible solutions to this; the fitment of phosphor-bronze guides or phosphor-bronze sleeves, the latter option being the cheaper of the two. Phosphor-bronze dissipates heat better than steel, and it's also more compatible with the stainless steel inserts which prepare a cylinder head for the use of unleaded petrol.

An electric fan runs only when the engine is up to temperature and the point at which it cuts in can be adjusted – or you can fit an over-ride switch if you want to keep it on all the time.

Cooling

If you want an engine that generates more power, you're almost certainly going to need to upgrade the cooling system if you don't want it to all end in tears. Often the most effective way of improving the cooling capacity is to have

Wrapping the exhaust manifold (as shown here) or applying a ceramic coating can dramatically reduce under-bonnet temperatures.

There are lots of more free-flowing exhaust systems available for all versions of the Spitfire and GT6. Invariably made from stainless steel, they provide a sportier sound and should increase power output too.

the radiator re-cored; this should be done every decade or so because the system invariably gets clogged up with silt. While you're at it, it might be worth having a high-gain core fitted, which is more efficient so you'll be less likely to suffer from overheating if caught in traffic. However, if you over-cool your engine it won't run efficiently, so don't get carried away.

Another way of helping the engine bay to dissipate heat is to fit vents or louvres on the top of the bonnet or in the wings. It's the former that will prove the most effective, but it's not as easy as it sounds because access to the bonnet top is tricky, because of the wings getting in the way. If the wings weren't in place things would be a lot easier, so if your car is undergoing a complete restoration that entails much panelwork, this may be something to think about while the car is dismembered.

Another popular way of aiding the cooling, while also improving engine efficiency is to fit a thermostatic fan. Perhaps the best known manufacturer of these is Kenlowe, but there are others, including Facet. The idea of these fans is to cut in only when the coolant temperature has reached a certain point, reducing drag on the engine while also helping the engine to reach operating temperature that much faster.

Exhaust

There are three key reasons to swap the exhaust on your Triumph: to boost performance, to improve the sound and to move over to a long-life stainless steel system, which

won't rot. Choose carefully and you can enjoy all three benefits – but it's also easy to get it wrong.

Whichever Spitfire or GT6 you have, it's worth fitting a tubular exhaust manifold so your engine's spent gases can escape more freely. Most systems are now made of stainless steel so you can fit and forget – but bear in mind that this material generally produces a more tinny sound than a mild steel installation.

Also consider that if you go for one of the popular twin-pipe systems you'll lose 5bhp compared with an equivalent big-bore, single-pipe set-up. This latter system is inherently more efficient, and while that term 'straight-through' might conjure up images of needing ear defenders because of the racket, this needn't be the case if you choose carefully.

A couple of other things worth considering are whether or not there'll be any clearance issues and how well matched the system is to your cylinder head. On the former point, as roads become ever more infested with speed humps, wrecking your costly exhaust system is becoming ever more likely every time you take your car out. On the latter point, if the exhaust manifold can be matched to the exhaust ports of the cylinder head, it'll help smooth the flow of gases so they can escape more quickly – but this is a fiddly and time-consuming exercise that's invariably costly as a result.

Transmission

One of the Triumph's weakest areas, the transmission can struggle to deal with even standard power outputs when

It's worth converting to overdrive if there isn't already one fitted. Also think about raising the back axle ratio, for more relaxed cruising – although this will blunt the acceleration.

driven hard, so if you're thinking of power increases you'll almost certainly need to beef up the transmission too – especially if you're aiming to make use of that extra grunt.

The most useful upgrade you can make is to fit an overdrive gearbox if there isn't already one fitted; it makes for much more relaxed cruising, especially if you also opt for a taller back axle ratio at the same time. The separate panel guides you through which ratios were fitted to the various editions of the Spitfire and GT6; incidentally, 3.89:1 Spitfire diffs have an FH prefix, while those with a 3.63:1 ratio have FR in the serial number.

Before you start swapping diffs, you need to be aware of the fact that two sizes of flange were fitted throughout the years, to the various shafts within the transmission. Until the Spitfire Mk3 there were small flanges on everything; the propshaft, half-shafts and differential. However, part-way through Spitfire MkIV production a move was made to a bigger flange for the diff, propshaft and half-shafts. At least things are simpler for the GT6, as all editions of this featured the larger flanges, making swaps easier – although changing between sizes is easy enough should you need to.

As far as gearbox swaps are concerned, you're best sticking with a Triumph unit unless you've got deep pockets. Modern five-speed transmissions can be fitted, but they're usually big money for an entire kit – typically the same sort of price as a whole car in reasonable condition. However, while expensive, these gearboxes are stronger, lighter and

usually more durable and they're also often available in standard or close-ratio forms. If you're still tempted despite the guaranteed high cost, take a look at the Ford Type 9 conversion – it's a cracker.

Suspension

The front suspension is of classic racing car design: double wishbones with coil springs and telescopic dampers. So while the layout is pretty much perfect, the damper and spring rates can be fettled to personal taste. Koni and Spax offer various damper set-ups, with adjustability for stiffness all part of the package. While the Konis are arguably better built (and they can also be rebuilt if necessary), they also have to be taken off the car to be adjusted – whereas the Spax items don't.

The rear suspension is a different matter, as the swing-axle design was crude and led to the car jacking up during hard cornering. It's only the Spitfire MkI-3 and the GT6 MkI that are affected, along with the final GT6 Mk3s, as these were the only editions fitted with a basic swing-axle layout.

While it's not really on to convert to rotoflex couplings without fitting a GT6 chassis originally built to this design, it is possible to fit the later (MkIV and 1500) Spitfire's swing spring, as described already in Chapter Five. This tidies up the handling enormously, but it's possible to go further with the adoption of a negative camber spring which reduces the

When re-bushing a classic car you can opt for rubber or polyurethane. The latter is more durable but can firm the ride up a bit too much if you use polyurethane throughout.

ride height as well as the tendency for the wheels to tuck under during hard cornering. However, you need to be careful here because less suspension travel means more chance of bottoming out on badly surfaced roads.

It's also worth thinking about the suspension bushes, as it's possible to swap the standard rubber items for some made of polyurethane. Invariably more durable, polyurethane bushes can also make the ride uncompromising if you've already gone for stiffer springs and dampers. The jury is out on just much difference it makes, but if you're aiming to stiffen up the suspension a lot, make sure you're not going to find any further stiffness too uncomfortable to bear.

Brakes

While both the Spitfire and the GT6's brakes are adequate, for the committed driver they're not really up to the job. There's a multitude of solutions available to increase stopping power, the easiest being to fit later Spitfire brakes to an earlier car or GT6 brakes to any Spitfire. Doing so will reduce any tendency to fade, but if it's just more reassurance from the system that you're after, you could fit a servo if there isn't one already installed. Bear in mind though that a servo doesn't reduce a braking system's tendency to fade during hard driving – but it does take the effort out of being able to pull up in a hurry as long as the discs and pads aren't operating above normal temperatures.

If you're aiming to take your car onto a track your first step should always be to completely overhaul the braking system; whether you're upgrading your brakes for road or track use it's worth fitting Green Stuff pads. These have proved to be the best all-round pads available for fast road use, and if you also fit braided brake lines you'll also improve the pedal feel – although not by a massive amount, admittedly.

Converting to GT6 brakes means fitting the uprights and everything associated with them: the stub axles, hubs, discs and callipers. It's not that big a deal as the whole lot simply slots into the wishbones – which are interchangeable between the Spitfire and GT6. While you're at it, it makes sense to upgrade the discs to something at least grooved, if not cross-drilled too.

Of course you don't have to stick with a largely standard Triumph braking system on your Spitfire or GT6; there are numerous conversions available to increase stopping power. One of the most common has been the fitment of Capri

Swapping the standard front discs for grooved items can make some difference to stopping power and feel, but to make a big jump you need to fit a vented set-up.

2.8i ventilated discs with Princess four-pot callipers. While the discs are still easy to source (don't ever be tempted to fit used items), the callipers are now proving hard to find. An alternative to this system is the Caterham Seven setup, which needs minor modifications to fit, but it can provide phenomenal stopping power if done properly.

Other braking system modifications worth considering include switching to braided brake hoses and filling the hydraulic system with silicone brake fluid (DOT 5) instead of the standard mineral-based (DOT3/4/5.1) stuff. The braided hoses are claimed to improve braking feel by not expanding during hard braking; whether or not you can really tell the difference is debatable.

The swap to silicone brake fluid is something you don't undertake lightly because it can only be done as part of a complete overhaul of the braking system, where every component is replaced – or at least anything that contains a rubber seal. Silicone and mineral brake fluids don't mix; if they're combined in the same system, any rubber will end up disintegrating and all pressure will be lost.

If all this makes you wonder why it would be worth changing to silicone – especially with the fluid typically costing three or four times as much as the mineral-based alternative – it's because of the performance of the higher grade fluid.

There's a huge array of alloy wheels available; what you fit is down to personal taste. Minilites are very popular, but so too are wires.

Not only does silicone fluid not absorb water, but it's also less compressible than the conventional fluid. This first point is very important, because it means there's little danger of corrosion within the braking system, which prolongs the life of the various components. Perhaps more importantly, the fluid's boiling point isn't lowered during prolonged heavy braking so you're less likely to have problems with the system overheating. As an added bonus, because silicone fluid doesn't absorb water, you don't have to replace it every two or three years; conventional fluid absorbs water over time, which is why it has to be renewed periodically.

Wheels and Tyres

One of the easiest ways of improving a Spitfire or GT6's handling is to fit wider wheels and tyres, as the standard items were pretty skinny. All Spitfires and GT6s were fitted as standard with pressed steel wheels, although wires were a factory-fitted option on some models. Many cars have already had wheel and tyre transplants, with Minilite-style alloys proving especially popular. As long as the wheels fit correctly that's fine, but Triumphs have an unusual offset: zero at the rear but 1in (2.5cm) at the front and it's not unusual for owners to try to fit wheels that simply won't fit.

Nothing wider than a 6J rim should be fitted, and if the car has been lowered even this might be too wide, because of clearance problems as the wheel is rising and falling on

the move. To be safe you could always stick with pressed steel wheels but still upgrade; a Mk3 GT6 option was 5.5J wheels which will go straight on to any Spitfire or GT6. They look discreet, they're durable and best of all, you know there won't be any clearance issues unless major suspension changes have been made.

If you don't like pressed steel wheels and you're not a fan of alloys either, your only alternative is to go for wire wheels. They look period sure enough; both the Spitfire and GT6 were offered with them, but they need more effort to keep clean than alloys or pressed steel rims, and they're not as durable either.

Interior

The most common interior upgrades tend to focus on more supportive seats and extra instrumentation. More enthusiastic owners will build special consoles, start again with the dash and shoehorn the most amazing bucket seats imaginable into the cabin. While some of these changes are an acquired taste, they're generally reversible because decent used parts are normally available to return a car to standard spec. However, replacing a dashboard because it's been cut about to accommodate a modern radio or extra gauges is not something to undertake too lightly; it's easy enough, but generally very time consuming.

Electrics

The best thing you can do with any Spitfire or GT6 electrics is to keep them in good condition; deviating from standard isn't generally necessary. The addition of the odd fuse or relay in certain circuits might be worthwhile, but as long as the loom isn't allowed to chafe and the connectors are kept in good condition you should find the system reliable.

There are a few worthwhile upgrades you can make however. The first, in the case of earlier cars, is to replace the dynamo with an alternator, as the latter offers a far more efficient method of charging. You can buy a rebuilt alternator very cheaply (or just opt for a decent used unit) and fitting it is an easy DIY proposition.

The original sealed beam headlights fitted to these cars weren't that great when the cars were new; they're now woeful, especially when compared with modern cars. Standard 7in (17.7cm) units, you can buy halogen replacements

The fitment of an alternator will help keep the lights and wipers going when you're sitting in traffic. If the car is used all year round, an alternator is essential.

very cheaply and fit them yourself in a few minutes – as long as the retaining screws haven't rusted solid, which they may well have done. You don't need to worry about upgrading the loom because the replacement bulbs won't draw a significantly higher current – they're just a lot more efficient. However, when you've got everything apart you might want to replace the bowls in which the headlights sit. The originals are steel and tend to rust, but plastic replacements are available.

The other electrical upgrade that's worthwhile is the fitment of a high-torque starter motor, which is more compact and far more efficient than the original units. They're not especially cheap; buying one of these typically costs three or four times as much as simply buying a reconditioned conventional starter motor, but you'll get more reliable starting. And because these more modern units are significantly shorter than the originals, they don't sit as close to the exhaust manifold, so they're much less prone to overheating.

A high-torque starter motor draws less current from the battery and doesn't sit so close to the exhaust manifold, so it's less likely to overheat.

CHAPTER TWELVE

SPITFIRE AND GT6 IN MOTORSPORT

Triumph had first started competing as a works team in 1954, using TR2s under the guidance of Ken Richardson. When Triumph was absorbed by Leyland Motors in 1961, the new owners decreed that all racing must stop, in a bid to save money. However, competing in high-level motorsport gave Triumph the credibility that many rivals lacked, which is why Harry Webster decided to continue with factory-backed racing, albeit on a greatly reduced budget.

The new Competitions Department was set up in 1962, with Graham Robson as its manager. Initially the focus was to be on rallying the Vitesse and TR4, but the decision was also made to develop the Spitfire into a racing machine. The big news though, was that a modified car would be built for the Le Mans 24 Hours: a project that would require significantly more development.

However, before such work began in earnest, Triumph elected to compete in some lower-level racing with 412 VC, which had started out as one of the press demonstrators. The car didn't prove particularly successful – but it did give Triumph's engineers some valuable indicators as to where they needed to concentrate their efforts if the Spitfire was to become internationally successful.

The Le Mans Cars

It was in April 1964 that Triumph revealed its first attempts at creating a Spitfire for that year's Le Mans 24 Hours, to compete in the 1.3-litre Group 3 class. Entered as prototypes, on account of the fact that Triumph hadn't yet created the requisite 100 production examples, pretty much anything was possible in terms of deviating from the standard specification, up to a point. Of course, Triumph would never go on to offer a road-going edition of the

Le Mans cars as such: in effect, this was the car that would go on to become the GT6 due to its closed configuration.

For the Spitfire to be competitive at Le Mans, Triumph's engineers would need to hone the car's aerodynamics while also making it lighter, more powerful and faster through the bends – the braking would need to be beefed up significantly as well. The project began in October 1963, even though it wasn't signed off by Triumph's board until two months later! Testing would need to begin by spring 1964 in time for the race that June.

Visually, it was the adoption of a glass fibre hard top with a fastback profile that separated the Le Mans cars from their production counterparts. As Graham Robson goes to great pains to point out in his own book on the Spitfire and GT6, the Le Mans Spitfires were developed from the GT6 prototype, rather than the other way round – despite what Triumph's contemporary advertising might have led consumers to believe.

The racing Spitfire's bodyshell was also made of aluminium instead of steel, while all the windows, apart from the windscreen, were fabricated from Perspex. Both of these changes were to reduce weight as much as possible: the result was a car that tipped the scales at around 1631lb (740kg), fuelled and ready to go. Initially there were no faired-in headlights, but by the time of the race there was a much more aerodynamic nose in evidence. The bumpers were dispensed with, but the over-riders were retained, while the radiator grille was reduced in size for aerodynamic reasons.

Naturally there were also major mechanical changes, the key one being the Spitfire's motive power. While the block wasn't that different from the production car's, the head was completely new: this was where Triumph's engineers focused their efforts to achieve the greatest possible power increase. After all, it was reckoned the

SPITFIRE AND GT6 IN MOTORSPORT ■

**The Spitfire makes its Le Mans début: here the three works racers are
lined up for the traditional start of the 1964 24 Hours.**

Spitfire's engine would need to produce around 100bhp, so the car could average 100mph (160km/h) during the 24 Hour race, with a peak speed of around 130mph (209km/h).

The all-new cast-iron cylinder head was an eight-port affair, which featured reprofiled camshafts along with gas-flowed inlet and exhaust manifolds. There was also a raised compression ratio (now 11.75:1) and a stage two tuning package, while fuelling was courtesy of a pair of twin-choke Weber carburettors in place of the standard SUs. A free-flowing exhaust system was installed, with a four-branch manifold and twin silencers. The result of all this work was

an engine that could produce 98bhp at 6,750rpm. With a 3.89:1 differential fitted (a precursor to the one that would be seen in the production GT6), the Le Mans Spitfires were capable of 134mph (215km/h) all in.

The suspension wasn't changed very much: shorter, stiffer springs were fitted at the front and the camber of the transverse leaf spring at the back was adjusted: that was it – although there were adjustable dampers all round. More effort was put into upgrading the braking system with the fitment of 9.5in discs at the front, in place of the standard 9in items, while at the back the usual 7x1.25in drums were swapped for 9x1.75in items. To comply with the rules, there

Testing the Spitfire at Le Mans in April 1964.

with an oil cooler for the engine. An all-synchro four-speed gearbox was fitted, taken from the TR4 for greater reliability, while the differential was a limited-slip item, developed specially by Salisbury.

Four Le Mans Spitfires were built, registered ADU 1B through to ADU 4B. It's likely that these identities were switched between cars at various times; what is known is that ADU 1B and ADU 3B were comprehensively crashed in 1964, so they were replaced by new cars that carried the same identities. For the race weekend, ADU 4B was the back-up car, leaving the other three cars to compete. ADU 1B was driven by Mike Rothschild and Bob Tullius. ADU 2B's drivers were David Hobbs and Rob Slotemaker, while Jean-Louis Marnat and Jean-Francois Piot were responsible for ADU 3B.

Although just one of the Spitfires completed the race, the cars acquitted themselves admirably for a first outing, proving to be completely reliable. The car that managed to last the whole twenty-four hours was ADU 2B, which achieved a twenty-first placing, averaging 94.7mph (152.4km/h) over the twenty-four hours. This Spitfire also came third in its class. Sadly, the other two Spitfires didn't fare so well, both being involved in crashes, forcing them to retire.

Triumph returned to La Sarthe for the 1965 event, this time with all four cars entered. The assumption had been that there was no way all four cars would be accepted. When they were, it was clear that the costs would be on the high side and the mechanics would be stretched to keep all four cars running. In the event, this would prove to be the Spitfire's finest hour.

was also a tandem hydraulic system installed, while 5.00-13 Dunlop R6 rubber was fitted to lightweight alloy wheels.

In a bid to improve reliability and competitiveness, the Le Mans Spitfires incorporated a multitude of detail changes, such as a quick-action fuel filler, alloy long-range, 18.5gal (84.1ltr) fuel tank and a Bendix electric fuel pump, along

The Le Mans Spitfires were fitted with an 1147cc engine, seen here on the workshop floor and also *in situ*.

The Spitfire of Hobbs and Slotemaker in the 1964 Le Mans 24 Hours.

The cars were prepared to a similar specification as for the previous year's race, although there were now extra lights either side of the grille and the chassis was made of thinner steel, in a bid to reduce weight further. Triumph had also developed an alloy cylinder head (for further weight saving) while the gearbox was now taken from the Vitesse instead of the TR4. The result of the weight-saving measures was a car that tipped the scales at 1521lb (690kg), and when this was combined with a power hike to 109bhp (at 7,300rpm), the Spitfire was now capable of hitting 140mph (225km/h).

Despite Triumph's resources being stretched, the 1965 Le Mans race proved to be generally successful as it dem-

onstrated the car's inherent strength and durability. While ADU 1B crashed and ADU 2B had to retire because the oil cooler split, leading to the engine failing, ADU 3B finished fourteenth overall with ADU 4B one place ahead, averaging 95.1mph (153km/h) in the hands of Jean-Jacques Thuner and Simo Lampinen. While thirteenth and fourteenth overall doesn't sound too bad, it has to be said that only fourteen cars finished of the fifty-one that started – meaning Triumph's best result was still last and second-last. That may have been better than the other thirty-seven cars that didn't even finish, but it clearly wasn't a good enough result for Harry Webster, as Triumph would never return to Le Mans after 1965.

Le Mans 1965, and the Spitfire of Thuner and Lampinen, which finished thirteenth overall and first in the 1000-1300cc GT class.

Between the 1964 and 1965 events at La Sarthe, the Le Mans Spitfires also did a tour of duty in the 1965 Sebring 12-Hours. All four Spitfires were flown out there, with ADU 3B acting as the spare car this time. ADU 1B was rolled by Peter Bolton and it subsequently had to undergo an extensive rebuild in time for Le Mans. However, ADU 2B (Tullius/Gates) and ADU 4B (Barker/Feuerhelm) enjoyed rather more success, coming in third and second in class respectively, behind the special-bodied MG Midget of Andrew Hedges and Roger Mac.

The 6-cylinder Spitfire project, photographed in 1965 prior to it being dismantled.

Once Triumph had finished its exploits at Le Mans, the cars were lent to a group of privateers who campaigned them in the six-hour relay at Silverstone.

ADU 2B was then sold in 1966 to Bill Bradley, who had originally piloted it at Le Mans in 1965. He would race it throughout Europe. Ultimately that car would be wrecked, but it was rebuilt using redundant parts from Triumph's now-aborted Spitfire racing programme. ADU 2B was actually a replacement for ERW 512C, a factory-prepared Spitfire raced by Bradley at various tracks across Europe with great success.

It's worth adding a final post-script on the GT6R, an aborted project instigated to eke out the life of the Le Mans Spitfires. Knowing that the rule changes would render the cars uncompetitive, Harry Webster asked the Competitions Department to come up with a more powerful car. The solution was a 6-cylinder Spitfire, equipped with the forthcoming GT6's engine fitted with a trio of Weber carburettors – a move to Lucas fuel injection was envisaged. However, by February 1966 Triumph's racing programme was being scaled back and the car was never completed: instead it was dismantled.

The Rally Cars

As well as the Le Mans cars, in 1964 Triumph also built six Spitfires for rallying. The first four were registered ADU 5B through to ADU 8B, with a fifth car carrying the number AVC 654B. This latter example was a left-hand drive Spitfire built for the 1965 season; all previous racing editions were right-hand drive. It was created for new signing Simo Lampinen, who insisted on the steering wheel being on the left. As well as these five factory-backed racers, there was also another car developed at the same time as the ADU cars. It was constructed for the Stirling Moss Automobile Racing Team and registered ADU 467B.

All of these rally-spec Spitfires were based on standard road cars, each fitted with a factory hard top and painted powder blue – apart from the Stirling Moss car, which was finished in a lurid green, as were all his team cars.

Although the cars looked fairly standard apart from their bumpers being removed, there were many differences under the skin. Certain body panels were made of aluminium, while there was an alloy cylinder head for the Le Mans-spec 70X engine. Courier van 4.5in wheels were fitted, the gearbox featured Vitesse ratios, the limited-slip diff had a

The **Spitfire** rally car makes its début on the **1964 Alpine Rally** in the hands of **Terry Hunter.**

Simo Lampinen pilots the only left-hand drive works Spitfire on the 1965 Alpine Rally. The outing proved successful, with Lampinen bringing the car home first in the Prototype class.

Three of the works rally Spitfires on the 1964 Tour de France.

4.55:1 ratio, and the braking system was beefed up front and rear with Vitesse items. By the time extra lighting, special seats and other additions had been made, these cars really were substantially different from the standard road-going versions.

The cars made their début in the June 1964 Alpine Rally, with ADU 5B driven by Jean-Jacques Thuner and John Gretener. Roy Fidler and Don Grimshaw drove ADU 6B, while Terry Hunter and Patrick Lier were responsible for ADU 7B. Valerie Pirie and Yvonne Hilton drove the SMART car (ADU 467B). The rally didn't go well for the Spitfires, with only ADU 7B finishing – third in class.

Next came the Tour de France in September, for which the cars were fitted with fastback-style roofs, to give a profile similar to the Le Mans cars. They also gained Le Mans-style bonnets at the same time, along with an 18gal (81.8ltr) fuel tank and an all-synchro gearbox – a lack of synchromesh on first gear had made it hard going for the drivers when climbing twisty mountain passes. This second rally of the season also went badly for Triumph, and once again only ADU 7B made it to the finish at the hands of Rob Slotemaker and Terry Hunter who secured a class win.

The Geneva Rally in October saw just two factory-backed Spitfires taking part (ADU 6B and ADU 7B). The former came in fifth overall and second in class, while the latter managed to win its class, taking second place overall.

For 1965 there was a new signing to the team: Finnish driver Simo Lampinen who had shone in the 1,000 Lakes Rally at the wheel of a Saab 96. This season would also see further changes made to the Spitfires, with auxiliary lamps set into the bonnet to ensure the drivers could see where they were going – something which would prove to be useful!

Kicking off the season was the Monte Carlo Rally in January, in which ADU 6B, ADU 7B, ADU 467B and AVC 654B were entered – only the first would cross the line, however, with the Moss car retiring before it even started. Lampinen was the only starter for the next event, the Tulip Rally of May 1965, but clutch failure thwarted his attempts to finish.

Things started to pick up after this, however, with ADU 5B achieving a class win and fifth overall placing in June's Geneva Rally; second in class was ADU 467B. However, the party would soon be over, as rule changes for the 1966 season would render the Spitfires uncompetitive. There was still time for one last blast though, in the Alpine Rally of July 1965.

This would mark the last time that factory-backed Spitfires would take part in a competition in Europe, and for this finale all the ADU cars were fitted with prototype 1296cc engines that would make their production car début in the 1300 saloon soon after. This engine wouldn't appear in a Spitfire until the Mk3, a couple of years hence – but it would never produce the 117bhp (at 7,000rpm) of the racers. Only two of the Spitfires finished the Alpine Rally, but it was still quite a result for Triumph as Lampinen romped to victory in the prototype category with ADU 654B, while Thuner came next up in ADU 5B.

The Macau Racer

The Macau Spitfire was commissioned by Triumph's Hong Kong importer Walter Sulke, to race in the 1965 Macau Grand Prix. This race was the only Grand Prix in the world in which amateur enthusiasts could take part, rather than the experienced works drivers who were eligible for all the other Grands Prix.

Based on a Le Mans car, the Macau Spitfire featured a Le Mans stage two powerplant, with a peak power output of 108bhp at 7,200rpm. A 4.11:1 differential ratio was specified

as being the most appropriate for Macau's hilly Guia circuit, while the suspension was to the same specification as the Le Mans cars. However, unlike those earlier competition Spitfires, Sulke's car was fitted with 5.5in wide wheels, shod with Dunlop R7 tyres. There was also a long-range 22.5gal (102.2ltr) fuel tank fitted in the tail.

Bodywork changes were significant, with an aluminium tub and glass fibre rear deck complete with fairing behind the driver. The Le Mans bonnet with its faired-in headlamps improved the aerodynamics enormously: when the car was performance tested at MIRA before its despatch to Macau, it was clocked at around 130mph (209km/h).

The car made its race début on Saturday 27 November 1965, at the hands of Albert Poon, one of the leading drivers in the Far East. That first event was the Auto Club of Portugal's Trophy race, which took in thirty laps of the 3.8-mile

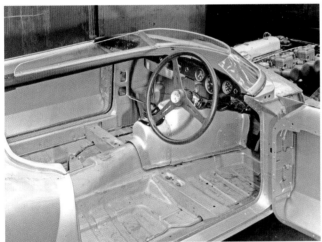

Photographed before being delivered to its Hong Kong-based owner in 1965, the Macau Spitfire raced only briefly in Asia before moving to America, where it continued to be developed.

THE MACAU REPLICA

If you've got a Triumph, there's a good chance that you've already come across Bernard Robinson, as he's been the Editor of the Triumph Sports Six Club's magazine, *The Courier*, for many years now. He's also the owner and builder of a superb recreation of the Macau Spitfire.

The original car's return to Britain proved very useful for Robinson, who referred to it frequently to ensure his replica was as accurate as possible. The replica is based on a 1969 Mk2 Spitfire, so it's quite a bit later than the original car. Robinson spent fifteen years researching and creating his replica, so it's as accurate as possible; many of the parts had to be hand-made specially.

Robinson's aim was to recreate the car as it would have been delivered to Sulke in 1965 but, as already related, the car was the subject of a lot of bodywork modifications subsequent to its racing début. As a result, Robinson had to refer to original photographs and work out dimensions and proportions from those. Mark Fields at Jigsaw Racing conveniently recreated the Le Mans wheels and glass fibre bonnet, which saved Robinson a huge amount of hassle. The mechanicals are also much the same as the genuine car would originally have been. While there's little prospect of the car making its way to Macau, Robinson did get it onto the track during the 2008 Le Mans Classic weekend.

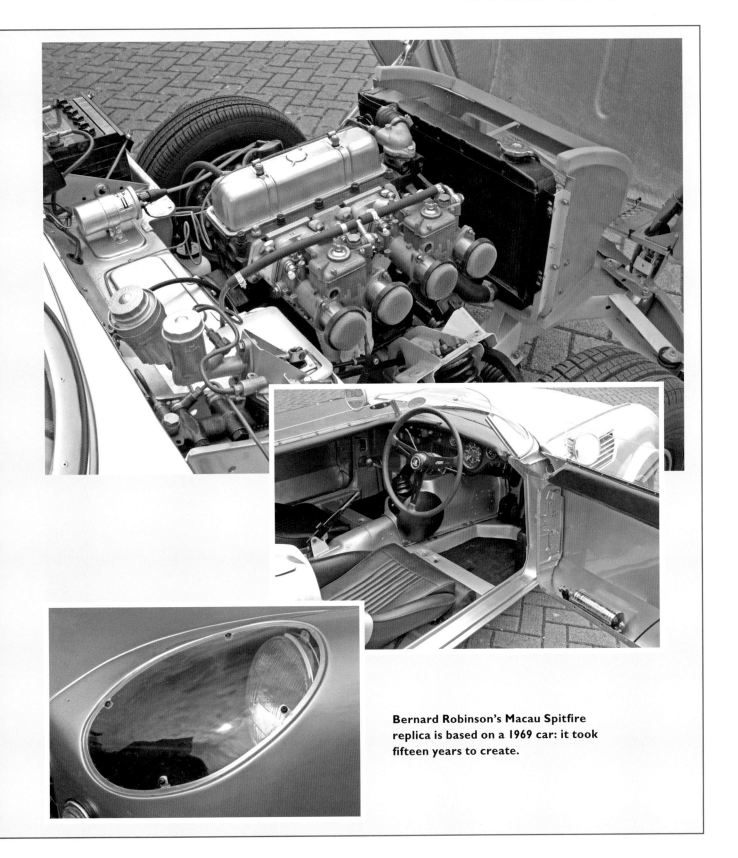

Bernard Robinson's Macau Spitfire replica is based on a 1969 car: it took fifteen years to create.

(6.1km) long circuit. Next day came the big one, though: the sixty-lap Macau Grand Prix, in which the Spitfire acquitted itself admirably, coming third against some stiff competition.

By 1966 the car was racing in the US under the ownership of Kas Kastner, who swapped the car's 1147cc for a 2-litre six-cylinder unit. It then passed through a succession of hands during the 1970s, 1980s and 1990s; the car was even registered for road use at one point. In 2001 the car was bought from a Swiss collector by Dave Pearson of Triumph specialist Canley Classics. Pearson has since recommissioned it, to add to his collection of significant Triumphs.

Racing in the US

Triumph had started its American racing programme in 1962 by preparing TR4s for privateers: the work was done by ex-racer Kas Kastner. The following year marked the arrival of the Spitfire. Almost immediately there was a factory racer competing in road races along with a series of privately-campaigned examples. The factory offered a stage two tuning kit along with suspension upgrades to help tame the wayward chassis, and it wasn't long before the Spitfire carved itself a decent reputation in SCCA (Sports Car Club of America) events, thanks to its reliability.

By 1967 Kas Kastner was working on the Spitfire Mk3 as well as the newly introduced GT6. Later editions of the latter were developing an astonishing 218bhp, thanks to the fitment of a 2.5-litre cylinder head and triple Webers. The cars enjoyed some success over the next few years but, by 1970, Kastner was running the works cars on an outsourced basis, which he did until the end of 1972 when Triumph killed off its official US racing programme.

Kas Kastner prepared Spitfires and GT6s for circuit racing in the US. Shown here are John Kelly's 1973 Spitfire and Mike Downs' 1968 GT6.

ENGINE DEVELOPMENT AND DATA, VINs

Take a look at the Spitfire engine's origins, and you'll see they're hardly the stuff of legend, as the powerplant could trace its roots back to the Standard Eight of 1953. However, despite these humble origins, the four-pot engine was tough and dependable, which at this end of the market was more important than cutting-edge engineering or ultimate power.

When it was first unveiled, this power unit displaced just 803cc and could generate all of 26bhp at 4,500rpm, but within a year there had been a capacity increase to 948cc. It was in this form that the engine was fitted to the Eight's bigger brother, the Ten. The two engines continued to be produced alongside each other; then in 1956 the larger of the two received a compression ratio increase from 7:1 to 7.5:1. Within a year this was increased again to 8:1 so the

unit could run on premium fuel. With the aid of a modified camshaft and larger carburettor, power output was boosted to 36bhp at 5,000rpm; in the meantime the maximum power from the 803cc unit had also been increased to 30.5bhp.

When the Herald arrived in 1959, it didn't take long for Triumph's engineers to work out that another capacity increase would be needed if the car was to remain competitive. To that end, the bore was increased from 63mm to 69.3mm, taking the capacity to 1147cc and boosting peak power to 41bhp at 4,600rpm in the process – although this unit wouldn't be offered until the launch of the Herald 1200 in 1961.

As has already been discussed in previous chapters, even when the Herald was at the development stage, the think-

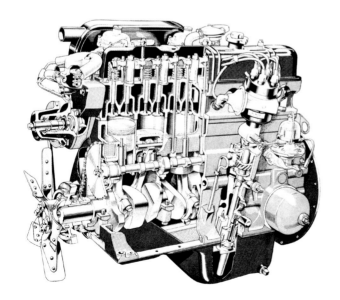 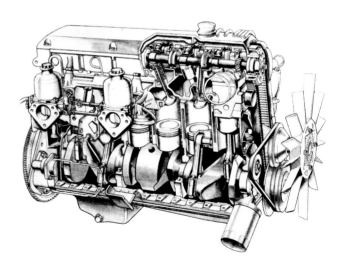

All GT6s were fitted with a 2.0-litre straight-six engine, seen here from either side in cutaway form.

ing was that there would be further spin-offs on the same chassis, including a two-seater sports car. For this reason, before the Herald had even been built, it was assumed that at some point there would be a requirement for a more powerful edition of the 1147cc unit – which is why it was quickly developed still further.

To coax a few more horses out of the 1147cc engine, a revised inlet manifold was produced, complete with twin 1¼in (3.17cm) SUs. Also revised was the cast-iron inlet manifold, while the compression ratio was increased to 9:1 – these, combined with valve timing adjustments, enabled the unit to produce a healthy 63bhp at 5,800rpm. It was in this form that the 4-cylinder engine made its début in the Spitfire 4 of 1962; the rest of the engine development is charted in the individual Spitfire chapters.

The GT6 engine is also directly descended from the 803cc unit originally seen in the Standard Eight. Soon after Harry Webster was made director of engineering in 1957, Triumph's engineers were instructed to come up with a 6-cylinder version of the engine, which they duly did. The earliest prototypes displaced just 1422cc, but by the time

the powerplant made its début in the Vanguard of 1960, the displacement had grown to 1998cc, to give 85bhp and 113lb ft of torque.

Before the straight-six would be fitted to the GT6, Triumph would also install it in the Herald-derived Vitesse, in 1596cc form. This featured a bore of 66.7mm whereas the unit in the Vanguard had a 74.7mm bore; the consequent drop in power meant the early Vitesse could muster all of 85bhp and 92lb ft of torque – but it was the engine's deliciously smooth power delivery that made it so appealing.

By the time the GT6 was introduced in 1966, the displacement was once again 1998cc – the same as that found in Triumph's big 2000 saloon. All the way through GT6 production the displacement would remain at 1998cc, even though a 2498cc edition of the powerplant was developed for use in the TR5 and TR6 plus the 2500 Saloons and Estates. In most cases the engine was also fuel injected, using a Lucas mechanical system, but Triumph didn't ever offer anything other than carburettors in the GT6. That's not to say it can't be done though – as many owners have proved since the GT6's demise in 1973.

Triumph Engine Numbers

Engine prefix	Displacement	Fitted to:	Engine prefix	Displacement	Fitted to:
BE	948cc	Standard 10	FE	1296cc	Spitfire MkIII
CC	2498cc	TR250 & TR6 (carb)	FH	1296cc	Spitfire MkIV
CF	2498cc	TR6 (carb)	FK	1296cc	Spitfire MkIV USA
CG	1998cc	TR7 (Europe) 1976-78	FM	1492cc	Spitfire 1500 (1973-80)
CL	1998cc	TR7 USA/Can 75-76	FL	1492cc	Spitfire MKIV/1500 Sweden
CP, CR	2498cc	TR5PI & TR6 (injection)	FP	1492cc	1500 MG Midget (1975-79)
CT	2138cc	TR4			
DG	1296cc	1300 Toledo	G	948cc	Herald 948 Saloon
DH	1296cc	1300 Dolomite	GA	1147cc	1200 Herald, Courier
DM	1492cc	1500 reconditioned engine if ESS suffix is used	GB	1147cc	1200 Herald Mk2 (Export)
DM	1492cc	1500 Toledo (Export)	GD	1147cc	1200, 12/50 Herald
DS	1492cc	1500 Toledo (Export)	GE	1296cc	Herald 13/60
FC	1147cc	Spitfire MkI	GK	1296cc	Herald 13/60
FC	1147cc	Spitfire MkII (starting at FC50001)	GY	948cc	Herald Twin-Carb Saloon
			HB	1596cc	Vitesse 6
FD	1296cc	Spitfire MkIII USA	HC	1998cc	Vitesse 2 litre MkI
			HC	1998cc	Vitesse 2 litre MkII (starting at HC50001)

Engine prefix	Displacement	Fitted to:
KC	1998cc	GT6 MkI, MkII (starting at KC50001)
KD	1998cc	GT6 MkI, MkII (anti-smog)
KE	1998cc	GT6 MkIII
KF	1998cc	GT6 MkIII USA
KG	1998cc	GT6 MkIII (Sweden)
MB	1998cc	2000 MkI
MG, MM, MN	2495cc	2500
ME or ML	1996cc	2000 MkII
RD or RF	1296cc	1300 FWD
TS	1991cc	TR2/3/3A
TSF	1991cc	TR3B
TT	1247cc	Mayflower
WB	1492cc	1500 FWD
WF	1850cc	Dolomite 1850
Y	948cc	Herald 948 Coupe/Convertible
YB	1492cc	1500 FWD
YC	1492cc	1500, Dolomite

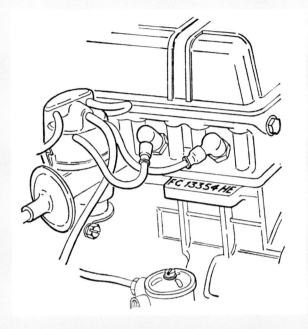

Spitfires and GT6 engine numbers are on the distributor side at the back of the engine, on a flat area between the head and block.

Notes:

GA, GB, GD engines are similar to Spitfire FC units.

GE, RD, RF engines are similar to Spitfire FD/FE units.

DG, DH, FL, GK engines are similar to Spitfire MkIV FH and FK units.

WB, VB, YC, DM, DS, FP engines are similar to Spitfire 1500 units.

RD, RF engines are similar to GE and FD units.

Engine Number Suffixes

H: High compression.

L: Low compression.

U: USA with pollution equipment.

C: California (catalyst fitted).

E: Engine (added to avoid confusion between engine and commission numbers).

SS: Factory-supplied replacement engine.

SK: Applied to the Herald only to denote a factory-supplied replacement engine.

FRE or FR: Factory Reconditioned Engine. These engines often had the original number overstamped with an 'X', with a plate riveted to the block to carry the original engine number.

ES: Engine Spare. Replacement engines supplied as warranty spares.

Identification numbers

Spitfire

Model	Date	Comm. N°	Body	Engine
4 (MKI)	10/62-12/64	FC	I FC	FC
MK2	12/64-1/67	FC 5000I	FC 5000I	FC 5000I
MK3	1/67-12/70	FD I	422 FD	FD
MK3 USA	1/67-12/70	FDU	FDU	FE
MKIV	11/70-12/74	FH	I FH	FH
MKIV 1300 US	1971-72	FK		FK
MkIV 1500 US	1973-74	FM	I FM	FM
MKIV 71 Sweden	1971	FL		FL
1500	12/74-10/79	FH 7500I	7500I FH	FM
1500 USA	1975-79	FM 2800I	2800I FM	FM 2800I UE
1500 RHD	10/79-08/80	TFADWIAT		FM
1500 RHD O/D	10/79-08/80	TFADW5AT		FM
1500 LHD	10/79-08/80	TFADW2AT		FM
1500 LHD O/D	10/79-08/80	TFADW6AT		FM
1500 USA	10/79-08/80	TFVDW2AT		FM 109890 UE
1500 USA O/D	10/79-08/80	TFVDW6AT		FM 109890 UE
1500 California	10/79-08/80	TFZDW2AT		FM 109890 UCE
1500 California O/D	10/79-08/80	TFZDW6AT		FM 109890 UCE
1500 Canada	10/79-08/80	TFLDW2AT		FM
1500 Canada O/D	10/79-08/80	TFLDW6AT		FM
1500 Canada	1981	TFLDW2BT		

GT6

Model	Date	Comm. N°	Body	Engine
GT6 (MKI)	10/66-9/68	KC	I KC	KC I E
GT6 (MKI) USA	10/66-9/68	KD		KD 500I E
GT6 MK2	10/68-12/70	KC 5000I	KC50001 E	KC50001
GT6+ (MK2 USA)		KD 5000I	KD50001 E	KC
GT6 MK3	10/70-12/73	KE	KE	KE
GT6 MK3 USA		KF	KF	KF

Gearbox	Diff	Diff. Ratio
FC	FC	4.11
FC	FC	4.11
FD	FC	4.11
FD	FC	4.11
FH	FH	3.89
FK	FK	4.11
FK	FH	3.89
FH	FH	3.89
FR	FR	3.63
FT	FH 50001	3.89
FR	FR	3.63
FR	FR	3.63
FR	FR	3.63
FR	FR	3.63
FT	FH	3.89
FT	FH	3.89
FT	FH	3.89
FT	FH	3.89
FR	FR	3.63
FR	FR	3.63

The Commission plate is on the right-hand side of the bulkhead, the gearbox number can be found stamped into the casing above the filler plug while the rear axle number is on the underside, near the drain plug.

Gearbox	Diff	Diff. Ratio
KC	KC	3.27
KC	KC	3.27
KC	KD	3.27 3.89 (O/D)
KC	KD	3.27 3.89 (O/D)
KC	KD	3.27 3.89 (O/D)
KC	KD	3.27 3.89 (O/D)

173

1979-80 Vehicle Identification Numbers (VINs)

In October 1979 commission numbers were replaced with 13-digit V.I.N. (Vehicle Identification Number) numbers, which featured eight-digit prefixes:

VIN Prefix	Class	Transmission	Steering
TFADW19T	United Kingdom	Manual	Right-hand drive
TRADW29T	Europe	Manual	Left-hand drive
TFADW59T	United Kingdom	Manual plus overdrive	Right-hand drive
TFADW69T	Europe	Manual plus overdrive	Left-hand drive
TFVDW29T	US	Manual	Left-hand drive
TFVDW69T	US	Manual plus overdrive	Left-hand drive
TFZDW29T	California	Manual	Left-hand drive
TFZDW69T	California	Manual plus overdrive	Left-hand drive
TFLDW29T	Canada	Manual	Left-hand drive
TFLDW69T	Canada	Manual plus overdrive	Left-hand drive

How to decipher the code:

First character
T: Triumph

Second character
F: Spitfire

Third character
A: European
V: US
Z: California
L: Canadian

Fourth character
D: two-seat convertible

Fifth character
W: Triumph 1500cc

Sixth character
1: Right-hand drive without overdrive
2: Left-hand drive without overdrive
5: Right-hand drive with overdrive
6: Left-hand drive with overdrive

Seventh character
9: 1979
A: 1980
B: 1981

Eighth character
T= Triumph plant, Canley, Coventry

Example: TFADW5AT 009898 (the final Spitfire off the assembly line)
Triumph Spitfire, European spec two-seater with 1500 engine, right-hand drive with overdrive transmission, and built in 1980 at the Coventry plant.

INDEX